BRITISH COLONIAL ADMINISTRATION
IN THE MID-NINETEENTH CENTURY:
THE POLICY-MAKING PROCESS

JOHN W. CELL

British Colonial Administration in the Mid-Nineteenth Century: The Policy-Making Process

NEW HAVEN AND LONDON
YALE UNIVERSITY PRESS
1970

Library of Congress catalog card number: 70-99822
Standard book number: 300-0-1191-1
Designed by Sally Sullivan,
set in Caledonia type,
and printed in the United States of America by Vail-Ballou Press, Inc., Binghamton, N.Y.
Distributed in Great Britain, Europe, Asia, and Africa by Yale University Press Ltd., London; in Canada by McGill University Press, Montreal; and in Latin America by Centro Interamericano de Libros Académicos, Mexico City.

For John Wesley Cell
(1907–1967)

Preface

For Great Britain the mid-nineteenth century was an age of expansion, not an interval of withdrawal sandwiched between two periods of aggressive overseas activity. Never, certainly, had the pace of commercial growth been more rapid than it was in the age of free trade, when British exports were increasing six times in the thirty years after 1840, while the volume of foreign investment was turning over at a comparable rate. As their shipping lines thrived, as their railroads began to bite into the interior of India and the Americas, as their overseas trade boomed as never before, Englishmen saw no good reason to suppose that favorable conditions would not continue almost indefinitely. Relatively secure behind their yet unchallenged naval and commercial supremacy the British sought primarily to enjoy the economic benefits of informal empire without unduly adding to the administrative and financial burdens of a formal one.

Despite the frequent wars and threats of broader conflict, despite occasional years of financial downswing, the middle decades of the nineteenth century were marked by an air of confidence. They were not a frantic time of "pegging out claims" against a grim and uncertain future when those markets of the world that were not controlled directly by Great Britain might be shut tight against her. To be sure much territory was formally annexed: areas suitable for European colonization in Australia and New Zealand; extensions of existing colonial boundaries in India, southern Africa, and the western region of British North America; commercial toeholds in China and West Africa. But despite these considerable acquisitions it remains true that the contemporary documents supply no evidence to support the contention that Great Britain was engaged in a concerted effort to extend her political dominance. There was certainly no widespread wish to repeat the experience in India. Missing too from those documents is the tone of strident racism common to the era of Rhodes, Milner, and Hobson. In these respects the age of free trade was an era of expansion but not of "imperialism," a word that was itself the invention of a later time. The debates surrounding empire in the 1860s and the 1890s both revolved around the common thread of continuous dynamism overseas, but they were conducted on rather different planes.

Expand Great Britain did in the mid-nineteenth century. More than the representatives of any other Western nation her settlers, merchants, construction engineers, missionaries, administrators, soldiers, and sailors carried on the central theme of modern history, the expansion of Europe. More continuous than the causes of successive annexations, more constant than the motives of administrators or the English climate of opinion with respect to empire, it is this larger fact of Britain's growing cultural influence in the world that must be stressed. The British Empire, that which was in process of becoming as well as that which was painted red upon the maps of the Colonial Office, was far more than an instrument of power and profit. It was a massive and complicated framework of cultural confrontation and interchange. It linked the diverse and previously fragmented peoples of six continents. It subjected relatively traditional peoples to a multitude of disturbing influences that emanated from a dynamic modern culture: the Protestant Ethic, the idea of nationalism, the freehold system of land tenure, the model of Western urban development. It served as well as a mechanism through which non-European peoples —Ashanti and Ibos under slavery in the West Indies; Indian coolies in the South Pacific, southern and eastern Africa, and the West Indies—were brought into contact with one another.

Within this imperial framework migrated a large number of primary products—the potato, the rubber tree, the cotton plant—many of which required high degrees of social reorganization in the areas where they penetrated. For the simultaneous interchange of cultural influences from a rich variety of societies the Empire was thus a network of communications, a direct agent, and a catalyst.

In the mid-nineteenth century Britain's worldwide cultural influence spread further and penetrated deeper than that of any other Western nation had ever done before, an impact that was primarily the result of such advances in technology as the railroad and the telegraph. And, although the phenomenon extended to areas in which the application of inventions was insignificant, it is perhaps not entirely coincidental that the middle decades of the nineteenth century witnessed a strong initiation of what was to grow into a general wave of anti-European reaction. In the Chinese opium wars, the Kandy rebellion in Ceylon, the Indian Mutiny, the Maori King movement and the subsequent wars of the 1860s in New Zealand, and the ever fiercer Kaffir wars and the strange and tragic Xhosa cattle-killing of 1857 in South Africa are present more than mere hints of the twentieth-century revolts of Asia and Africa.

None of these events can properly be regarded as a direct reaction against imperial policy or even against the policies of particular local administrators. More than policy it was the far larger and far more disturbing fact of European presence that provided the setting and the causation for retaliation. Nor can it be assumed that such overt, dramatic, and therefore comparatively well-documented events were by any means the whole story, for they were themselves parts of larger cultural responses. Whether intentionally or not the fact of British cultural presence undermined and corrupted the political and social fabric of native societies, dividing them into Westernized and conservative factions, and initiating the working of that process which social scientists have referred to as "modernization." Much and perhaps even most of the native response must have been more "normal," quieter and subtler and therefore harder to analyze than the hostile outburst that was only part of the larger spectrum.

Because colonial policy is so imperfect a prism through which to view the responses of non-European societies to the challenges of British cultural influence, and above all because such responses are properly studied only "from below," I have reluctantly decided not to include in the present work a discussion of what used to be called, without apology, "native policy." I say reluctantly because I have devoted perhaps more attention to this aspect of British colonial administration than to any other. Yet to attempt to analyze here the effects of British contact upon one or more native cultures would destroy what continuity this study of the making of colonial policy might possess. Moreover, in this age when the histories of various Commonwealth countries are being rewritten by sophisticated scholars acquainted with anthropology, sociology, and linguistics as well as with the sources contained in oral tradition and local archives, the kind of treatment of "native policy," with its ethnocentric emphasis upon British humanitarianism, that used to satisfy students of imperial history now seems inadequate and rather naïve.

The British Empire-Commonwealth stands as the most fully documented and most readily accessible case study of large-scale cultural interaction in the history of the world. Ultimately Great Britain's imperial history will need to be evaluated, not merely according to the criteria of political and constitutional evolution, but "by studying first the center . . . of prime disturbance, and then considering how the other peoples of the earth reacted to or against what they knew or experienced of the innovations that had occurred in . . . [this prime center] . . . of cultural creativity."[1]

1. W. McNeill, *A World History* (New York, Oxford University Press, 1967), p. vi.

All this is by way of attempting to establish the broader framework in which this study of colonial administration in the mid-nineteenth century must be set. In this book I have tried to deal with only part of it. I have sought to explore what political scientists have called the "decision-making process" in the making of British colonial policy between about 1840 and about 1870. This book is an essay. It makes no claim of comprehensive treatment of all the problems and subjects that might conceivably be grouped under "colonial policy." It is not primarily intended to provide a narrative of relations between Great Britain and her colonies or a detailed analysis of events in any particular colonies. It is not aimed at identifying dominant attitudes within the Colonial Office toward such questions as free trade, native affairs, or colonial self-government. Nor is its object merely the description of bureaucratic machinery that is assumed to be static. It seeks instead to arrive at some understanding of how the policy-making process worked.

By "policy" I mean something different from the dictionary definition of "a settled course adopted and followed," an attitude formed as a whole and then purposefully carried into action. Theoretically, at least, the structure of imperial government could operate that way, and I by no means discount the force of individual initiative. Yet I regard policy as being something rather less fixed, something rather more historical. A "settled course" is encountered often enough in analyses of the past or in predictions of the future. In the present such certainty tends to evaporate. At any given moment there is not so much policy as policy formation, an unsettled and changing set of responses by government to the continual interaction among men, forces, ideas, and institutions. Policy in the present is a thing in flux, and it is this sense of its uncertainty that I have tried to convey.

Policy making is a perpetual adjustment between ends and means, and it is the latter which the historian must ordinarily emphasize. The ends of government—peace, prosperity, imperial power, humanitarianism, conciliation—are often accepted by a broad consensus. It is at the level of concrete action that these ends are defined, and it is there that conflict and uncertainty are most likely to be found. When Churchill told the British people in June 1941 that his policy was to ally with Russia against Germany, that at least seemed clear enough. But what did it mean? A second front? A Russian sphere of influence in Eastern Europe as a protection against a resurgent Germany? Or merely those measures against Hitler that happened to be in Britain's own self-interest? It was such questions as these that would constitute the stuff of policy. Churchill's declaration of alliance was rather the beginning than the end of policy making. Such at least is my notion, my "model," of what policy is all about.

The plan of the book is comparatively simple. Part I (Chapters 1-2) isolates the simplest, most direct machinery of policy making, emphasizing the evolution of the Colonial Office and the centers of administrative authority in the colonies. Since administrative history must involve far more than the analysis of bureaucratic machinery in a vacuum, Part II (Chapters 3-6) concentrates upon the most crucial and most continuous question that colonial administrators had to resolve, the problem of self-government in colonies of European settlement. I have tried to provide here a general treatment of how responsible government came to the British Empire and how it spread, what its implications were, and what its effects were upon the working of colonial administration at the local level and upon the relationship of local authorities to those at the center. For the purposes of this book these chapters constitute one case study of bureaucracy at work, and of the evolution of policy as it unfolded against the pressures of colonial and British politicians, from the press, and from "public opinion" generally. Part III (Chapters 7 and 8) consists of two case studies of interdepartmental relations. Here the focus upon the Colonial Office that dominates most of Parts I and II is enlarged. I emphasize the collective nature of government decision making in imperial affairs, and attempt to illustrate within comparatively limited areas how the perpetual readjustment that is policy making actually happened. Thus the parts of the book constitute three related efforts to answer questions, some of which have been posed by Helen Taft Manning's recent thoughtful article [2]: Who ruled the British Empire? What machinery did they rule through? How did their policy evolve? How did they bring their disparate and often conflicting views together? How did the policy-making process work?

To provide definitive and comprehensive answers to all these questions would be an impossible task, and I have not attempted it. Instead, I have tried to write an essay that employs both general analysis and detailed case study. Some of the sources upon which the book is based have not been investigated before. And I hope that I have to some extent succeeded in the effort to look at some of the very familiar material—such as that surrounding responsible government—in the somewhat different perspective of administrative history.

The writer of such a book as this compiles a formidable list of obligations. The most important are those to scholars who have preceded me, such as Chester Martin, John Galbraith, John M. Ward, and James Rutherford. I have used their work heavily. In particular, I wish to single out the fine book of W. P. Morrell, *British Colonial Policy in the Age of Peel and Russell,* a classic to which I found myself continually referring even while attempting to take an independent line.

The U.S. Department of Health, Education, and Welfare (and ultimately the American taxpayer) financed my graduate education and my first year of research in Great Britain. The Committee on Commonwealth Studies and the Research Council at Duke University provided the money for additional

2. "Who Ran the British Empire—1830–1850?" *Journal of British Studies,* 5 (1965), 88–121.

work in Canada, Australia, and Britain. Needless to say, without their generous assistance the book could not have been written at all.

I wish to thank my dissertation director and continuing adviser, W. B. Hamilton, for his help, counsel, and encouragement. Conversations with Gerald Graham, Manning Clark, and John Ward gave me several valuable ideas. I must acknowledge the permission of the trustees of the estates of Lord Clarendon and Lord Palmerston to consult those collections. Among the archivists, I wish to thank particularly the staffs at the Public Record Office and the Public Archives of New South Wales, who helped me in several instances to plan my research. Robert Kubicek of the University of British Columbia read an earlier version of the manuscript and made many helpful suggestions. Much as I might like to do so, I am unable to share responsibility for the shortcomings of the book with any of these individuals.

I must thank the editors of *Historical Studies, Australia and New Zealand* for permitting me to revise an earlier version of Chapter 1 that appeared in that journal.

Finally, I wish to acknowledge the help of a historian and critic for whom I have considerable respect, my wife, and the long-time encouragement of my mother. I am dedicating the book to the memory of my father.

J.W.C.

Durham, North Carolina
October 28, 1968

List of Abbreviations

Unless otherwise indicated, the place of publication may be assumed to be London.

Add. MSS.	Additional Manuscripts, British Museum.
CHBE	E. A. Benians, et al., eds., *The Cambridge History of the British Empire* (9 vols. in 8, Cambridge, Cambridge University Press, 1929–59).
CO	Colonial Office Records, Public Record Office.
CSSB	Colonial Secretary, Special Bundles, Public Archives of New South Wales, Sydney.
FO	Foreign Office Records, Public Record Office.
3 *Hansard*	Great Britain, *Hansard's Parliamentary Debates,* 3d Series.
ML	Mitchell Library, New South Wales Public Library, Sydney.
PAC	Public Archives of Canada, Ottawa.
PP	Great Britain, *Parliamentary Papers,* House of Commons.
PRO	Public Record Office, Private Collections.
WO	War Office Records, Public Record Office.

Contents

PART I

The Machinery of Colonial Administration

Any Man may read the Correspondence and learn what has been done. But to know the motives of past measures, and the motives why particular measures were not taken, the Student must look further than to our Despatch and Entry Books.

Sir James Stephen

1: The Colonial Office

There are chronic evils of our system, which might seem almost to have been produced for the express purpose of producing them.
Sir James Stephen

The focus of the process of imperial decision making was a pair of venerable seventeenth-century houses at Numbers 13 and 14 Downing Street that formed the old Colonial Office. It was an unsuitable establishment, having like the neighboring Foreign Office already been declared inadequate, unsafe, and unworthy of substantial repair.[1] While ceilings were shored up against impending disaster, a building inspector speculated on the long-term effects of a medieval sewage ditch that had flowed nearby.[2] On the ground floor the librarian George Mayer shared the discomfort of a counterpart at the Foreign Office who complained of a room made so unpleasant by smells and draughts that "scarcely a Day passes, in which Persons do not express their astonishment that any one can inhabit it." [3]

When the Colonial Office had added the house at Number 14 in 1827, passageways had been opened between the buildings on the first and second floors. On these two levels were offices for the secretary of state, two of the undersecretaries, and their private secretaries, along with rooms for the senior clerks

1. Select Committee on Public Offices, PP, 1839 (466), *13*, 235.
2. Henry Seward, ibid., 241–42.
3. Lewis Hertslet to Lord John Russell, 14 Feb. 1853, Russell Papers, PRO 30/22/10.

of the four geographical departments as well as for most of their assistants. On the unconnected ground floors were the offices of the chief clerk and an undersecretary, the library, and the waiting room. Here disgruntled colonists, in Wakefield's famous caricature, nervously rehearsed tales for "Mr. Mothercountry." To the basements were relegated the bookbinders, living quarters for housekeeper and office-keepers, the copyists' room, and storage space for the library. In the attic were placed junior clerks and unheated rooms for servants.[4] That the office was cramped and unsuitable was generally recognized by about 1840. But not until 1876 would new quarters be secured.

Matching the defectiveness in accommodation was a lack of equipment, a condition that even a contemporary might judge "destitute and deplorable." Complained the youthful parliamentary undersecretary Lord Carnarvon:

> We have no maps that are fit to be consulted—none of the mechanical apparatus for carrying on the Govt. of fifty Colonies in various stages of civilization and in different parts of the world. We have no furniture—carpets, chairs, tables are all decrepit.[5]

As colonial secretary Sir Edward Lytton remarked, however, the term "mechanical apparatus" was not particularly applicable to the conduct of official business in the mid-nineteenth century. If the office was unaided by apparatus, "apart from what we carry on our shoulders," it was also unfettered. Without typewriters or female typists, telephones or dictaphones, the malfunctioning of which would bring a modern establishment to a halt, the Colonial Office carried on with a minimum of equipment. The chief clerk had only to make available a

4. Memorandum of Peter Smith (chief clerk), 24 Apr. 1856, CO 323/248. See London County Council, *Survey of London, 14, St. Margaret Westminster*, pt. 3 (1913), 154–64. (Unless otherwise indicated, the place of publication may be assumed to be London.)

5. Minutes on Office of Works to C.O., 25 Oct. 1858, CO 323/252.

few essentials: paper, pens, ink, coal, oil for the lamps, and pins, as well as the proverbial red tape. Here in this deteriorating edifice—which its occupants might perversely have compared with the state of the empire they administered—worked those whose job it was to make colonial policy.

Theoretically responsible to crown and parliament for the performance of that function was the Secretary of State for the Colonies.[6] And, to a larger extent than might be supposed from the degree of emphasis that has sometimes been attached to the role of subordinate officials,[7] the political heads of the Colonial Office worked at their jobs with diligence and care. The third Earl Grey was probably justified in complaining that official business left him neither time nor strength to attend to personal matters or political affairs.[8] Indeed, it was a rare piece of paper that did not cross the desk of the secretary of state. The difficulties of adjustment to life in London by a Ceylonese medical student, the number of blankets to be sent to a tribe of Australian aborigines—such trivia by no means escaped his attention.

Nevertheless, the amount of Colonial Office material was not so large as that which passed through the Treasury or the Foreign Office, whose responsible ministers also conducted

6. Secretary of State for War and the Colonies until 1854, when the duties were divided between two ministers. The two departments had long been separate in practice.

7. The recent tendency has been to be more critical of Stephen and other subordinate officials than was P. Knaplund, *James Stephen and the British Colonial System, 1813–1847* (Madison, 1953). See R. Pugh, "The Colonial Office, 1801–1925," *CHBE, 3,* 711–69; J. S. Galbraith, *Reluctant Empire: British Policy on the South African Frontier, 1834–1854* (Berkeley, 1963), pp. 14–23; H. Manning, "Who Ran the British Empire—1830–1850?" *Journal of British Studies, 5* (1965), 88–121. Other useful works on Stephen and the Colonial Office include D. Young, *The Colonial Office in the Early Nineteenth Century* (1961); J. Beaglehole, "The Colonial Office, 1782–1854," *Historical Studies, Australia and New Zealand, 1* (1941), and E. T. Williams, "The Colonial Office in the 'Thirties," ibid., 2 (1943), 141–60.

8. Select Committee on Official Salaries, PP, 1850 [611], *15,* 352.

personally a large proportion of business. The job was not impossible. A singularly able administrator—a Peel, a Gladstone, or a Palmerston—who was fortunate enough to obtain a sufficiently lengthy tenure might have waded through the details while maintaining somehow enough breadth of vision to frame a deliberate and fairly consistent series of decisions that could, in the usual sense, be called a policy. But no colonial secretary between 1840 and 1870, with the possible exception of Earl Grey, did so.

It is not that secretaries of state were generally incompetent. Only Sir Edward Lytton really deserves that description.[9] It is true enough that the devotion to duty of such capable men as the elder Stanley and Earl Granville was not always so single-minded as it might have been. And the generalization may be accepted that the prestige of the office was insufficient to attract a great man at the height of his powers. Yet a survey of the nineteen colonial secretaries who served in the three decades after 1840—including such conscientious administrators as Lord John Russell, Sir George Grey, and the younger Stanley—yields no good reason to suppose them more or less capable than ministers before or since.

Only a little about the relative absence of firm direction can be explained by the fact that periods in office were frequently short. The elder Stanley served for five years (1841–45), Lord Grey for six (1846–52), the Duke of Newcastle in his second appointment (1859–64) for five. No one else held the seals for more than two, and the year 1855 witnessed a procession of four secretaries of state and a pair of temporary administrators. Yet the political instability of the 1850s, though unusually severe, is easily overstressed. Nineteenth-century governments changed and colonial secretaries came and went with a good deal of frequency after the fall of Lord Liverpool. Long periods in office were the exception, not the rule.

9. Cf. J. Rutherford, *Sir George Grey, 1812–1898: A Study in Colonial Government* (1961), p. 423.

Probably more significant is the relatively obscure and miscellaneous nature of the Colonial Office's business. A politician might well have obtained a grasp of the essential principles of British policy toward France or Russia before he became foreign secretary. An entrant into the Colonial Office was unlikely to know anything about Labuan or the Bahamas, or even about Australia or the Cape. A newcomer had to learn afresh both principles and details. The Palmerstonian ideal that ministers were to make policy themselves out of their own knowledge and experience could not in practice be achieved. In fact, observed James Stephen,

> the Secretary of State has always been, and, I apprehend, must ever continue, dependent upon others for information and assistance in the discharge of his duties, to an extent scarcely known in other Departments, which are conversant with topics with which Statesmen are, from the nature of their ordinary pursuits, habitually familiar.[10]

The detailed basis of policy formation must usually have been provided, if at all, by the permanent staff. Such assistance the Colonial Office possessed in a core of knowledgeable, experienced, hard-working civil servants whose membership changed extraordinarily little during the mid-nineteenth century. If effectively used by colonial secretaries willing to follow their advice, they were fully capable of providing the continuity of a colonial policy.

At the top of this structure was the permanent undersecretary. His role in the policy-making process was crucial, and nothing in the correctional emphasis that is placed (either in these pages or in other recent interpretations) upon personal and procedural limitations ought to be regarded as being in any way a denigration either of the position or of the exceptional men who filled it. It was a difficult job—more strenuous,

10. Memorandum, 30 Mar. 1832, CO 537/22.

thought one who held both, than a similar position at the India Office.[11] It is the obvious fact that without Sir James Stephen, Herman Merivale, and Sir Frederic Rogers the Colonial Office could not have functioned as it did.

The permanent undersecretary was responsible for the smooth working of the office routine. His recommendations were usually decisive in determining how the work should be divided and performed: in such matters, for instance, as minuting procedures and the employment of extra copyists. Although he had no part in the distribution of patronage,[12] he advised on promotion and the placing of junior clerks on the permanent establishment after their year's probation. Two of the men, Stephen and Rogers, combined the undersecretaryship with the time-consuming position of legal adviser to the office.[13] Under their sharp eyes passed all the acts of the many colonial legislative bodies.

The real importance of the permanent undersecretary cannot, however, be explained by analyzing his duties. It grew out of his intimate contact, from day to day and from year to year, with the minutiae of the business of administering the British Empire. The undersecretary stayed, learned, and absorbed; the secretaries of state and parliamentary undersecretaries moved in and out above him. The personal feelings of responsible ministers toward their highest subordinate varied, of course, with personalities. But though some treasured his advice more than others, none ignored it or more than occasionally departed from it. For above all the crucial significance of the permanent undersecretary lay in his role as "the deposi-

11. Merivale to Sir George Clerk, 3 Jan. 1862, Clerk Papers, India Office, Eur. D. 538.

12. On one patronage letter that was addressed to him, Stephen commented that "the writer has formed a whimsical misconception of my duties and of the extent of my authority here." Minute on P. Jeremie to Stephen, 28 Jan. 1840, CO 323/226

13. See D. Swinfen, "Attitudes Within the Colonial Office Towards Imperial Control of Colonial Legislation, 1826–65" (unpublished D. Phil. diss., Oxford University, 1965).

tory of all that knowledge of which the Secretary of State must daily avail himself." [14]

So well known is the career of Sir James Stephen that, in the absence of enough material for the full biographical treatment he deserves, the discussion here will be limited to interpretations that are somewhat new or different. For with the generally favorable opinion that has been formed of him by scholars little quarrel can be found.[15] He was a meticulous, methodical, and overworked administrator; a sincere and lifelong humanitarian; a thinskinned individual deeply hurt by unjust attacks against himself and his department; a wise and liberal counselor able to view the problems of empire in the dimensions of ethical principle, the continuity of history, and the reality of detail. He is remembered as being responsible, along with Lord Elgin and Lord Grey, for the fact that the second empire was not destroyed by the attempts of its administrators to preserve it as it was.

More than anyone else Stephen created in the office a methodical and systematic routine. To the relatively efficient operation of that procedure the well-kept Colonial Office records from the mid-nineteenth century attest. His impact upon administrative techniques can best be measured by sampling those records for the three decades after 1820. The material for the 1820s gives the unmistakable impression of sloppiness. Incoming letters are often haphazardly arranged. Drafts of replies and the extremely valuable private minutes of the staff are available only infrequently. Often it is difficult to determine what action if any was taken in regard to any particular matter or by whom. The conscientious parliamentary undersecretary Howick (later Lord Grey) introduced greater order —as well as characteristically voluminous quantities of writing

14. Stephen memorandum, 30 Mar. 1832, CO 537/22.

15. See Knaplund, *Stephen*, a useful book written without the aid of Stephen's private papers. Some of these have recently become available, and are being used in the writing of several Ph. D. dissertations at the University of London under the direction of Gerald Graham.

—into the conduct of business in the early thirties. But the most noticeable dividing point occurs in 1836, the year that Stephen replaced R. W. Hay as permanent undersecretary. Much of his impact is apparent at once, some of it is felt more gradually. By the early 1840s the Colonial Office system—Stephen's system—has stabilized. And it alters almost not at all until the early 1870s.

The immediate change, indeed, is striking. A stamp is introduced on all papers. Containing the names of officials down to the rank of senior clerk, it permits at a glance the determination of who has seen a given document and when. Stephen himself minutes or initials every paper, and his example is contagious. Drafts of outgoing letters begin as a rule to be kept. Frequently it can be determined how they were revised and from whose opinions they were formed. Where channels of communication before were uncertain, they are now precise. Precedents are easier to find, verify, and use. The administrative procedure of the Colonial Office becomes, almost at once, more regular and more methodical. It becomes, in the sense Max Weber gave to that word, more rational.

Yet, for all the significance of Stephen's considerable contribution, the praise of this exceptional civil servant must be qualified. He had weaknesses as well as strengths, and the understanding of the Colonial Office's decision-making process and of Stephen's role in it requires acknowledgment of both.

If Stephen was overworked, he himself was partly responsible. A basically insecure man, quick to take offense and apprehensive of opposition that was sometimes of his own invention, he seems to have attempted to make himself the indispensable administrator. The fact that, as permanent undersecretary, he *was* indispensable, did not satisfy him. He consistently refused either to delegate part of his work load to colleagues or to have some of it lifted from his shoulders altogether.[16] In the early 1840s, for example, it was several times suggested

16. Cf. Pugh, *CHBE*, 3, 723–24.

that the responsibility for reviewing colonial legislation should be transferred to the Board of Trade. Though Stephen frequently complained of this work as pure drudgery—"such a mass of uninteresting details it would be difficult to bring together from any other quarter"[17]—he always found something wrong with the proposals, not the least of the difficulty being that he was unsure of qualifying for a pension if he were to relinquish the task.[18] Moreover, the truth of the matter would seem to be that Setphen relentlessly tortured himself, somewhat masochistically delighting in the physical and mental anguish brought about by the mountain of detail in which he deliberately immersed himself. The reason for such behavior—whether an escape from private unhappiness, or perhaps a lack of confidence in his own abilities—may be unclear, but the pattern seems evident.

The seminal impact of Stephen upon administrative procedure has already been analyzed. Here too, however, there must be qualification. The substantial improvements that can be traced to him had to do with techniques, and mostly with his own techniques at that, rather than with people. Years later Stephen would give a low opinion of most of the clerks who had served under him. But his own working relations with them had never been close,[19] and there is no evidence that he seriously attempted to improve either their working habits or the methods of selecting them.[20] The efforts for reform came almost entirely from outside the office, and after he had left it.

His influence, moreover, did not extend to the critical area

17. Stephen memorandum, 17 Oct. 1840, CO 318/148.

18. Stephen minutes on Treasury to C.O., 26 Mar. 1842, CO 323/228; on Board of Trade to C.O., 13 Feb. 1845, CO 323/230; and on Treasury to C.O., 28 Mar. 1845, ibid.

19. Sir Henry Taylor told Grey "that Stephen was a much more difficult person for those under him to get on with than I had any notion of." Grey's Journal, 2 Aug. 1847, Grey of Howick Papers.

20. Cf. Pugh, *CHBE*, 3, 724.

of improving interdepartmental relations. Always quick to shift responsibility for delay to other departments, he was ineffectual in smoothing and expediting the conduct of business. Relations with the Treasury were of course the worst example. Stephen compiled lists of arrears and complained to his superiors, estimating average lengths of time required to obtain answers. To behave in this fashion, as he once admitted, accomplished nothing: the Treasury's

> duties are so vast, and many of them are so much more urgent and momentous than their correspondence with us, that it is hardly possible that they should give to this Office the degree of attention we require except at the sacrifice of other objects which are justly entitled to take preference.[21]

The remedy would appear to have been the simple expedient of a friendly working relationship with a department a few doors away. Stephen did not really attempt to establish one. And it was his successor, the less sensitive and more matter-of-fact Merivale, who reminded his colleagues "how essential it is, whenever there is any reason for desiring an answer with any speed, to mention this to the Treasury in the letter of reference."[22] Stephen was at his best when dealing, by himself, with abstractions, with situations from which he was separated by broad expanses of salt water. He was less effective in his relations with people or in solving problems close at hand.

Finally, though the wisdom of his advice is a generalization that must be accepted, Stephen was not always right. His opinions were not always in advance of the attitudes of his contemporaries, a point which is best illustrated by a reference to his position on the most crucial question that faced the Colonial Office during his undersecretaryship: Canada. In the year

21. Memorandum of Jan. 1840, CO 323/226.
22. Minute on Treasury to C.O., 13 Dec. 1850, CO 201/435.

of the rebellions Stephen was shocked at the demonstration of British weakness in Lower Canada:

> A resolute stand made by a resolute man a few weeks ago would have subdued this violence. I cherish the hope that even yet there is time to stem the torrent by opposing a stern & uncompromising front to the Agitators. To see such a game lost merely from the want of one vigorous effort made in due time, would indeed be enough to put to flight the patience of Job himself.[23]

Thereafter Stephen adopted a generally conciliatory attitude. But so did most of his contemporaries. The crucial question of the early 1840s (as will be argued in a later chapter) was not *whether* to conciliate, but *how*. And the fact is that the Colonial Office documents do not reveal that he played a very forceful part in the making of policy on the issue of responsible government for Canada.

Indeed, his attitude from day to day is obscure. It is quite possible that Stephen's reticence can be explained by a civil servant's natural reluctance to give advice on a subject which he knew full well was being constantly agitated and decided in cabinet above him. It is clear that he felt uncomfortable and insecure in his personal relations with the elder Lord Stanley.[24] In any case, although he read incoming public dispatches (much of the important material was contained in private letters to the secretary of state) he rarely commented on

23. Stephen to Sir George Arthur, 22 Nov. 1837, Arthur Papers, ML–A2164.

24. Stephen identified himself very closely with the Whigs, and particularly with Lord Howick, in large part because his rival Hay had been appointed by the Conservatives. No evidence has come to light to indicate that Stanley ever treated him unfairly, and Stephen's frequently expressed fears about a plot to remove him seem to have been wholly unfounded. See Stephen to Howick, 9 July 1835 and 7 Jan. 1836, Grey Papers. In the late 1840s, ironically enough, it was a Whig, Lord John Russell, who refused to permit him to return.

them. And in 1844 he wrote what may well have been his true attitude:

> Canada is what you told me Canada must become—a mere theatre for selfish conflicts veiled under them the specious pretext of Public Spirit—the French and Radicals united against the English and Loyalists, and endeavouring to make the Governor a mere Kingdog who might just well be in bed and asleep as not. But Sir Chas. Metcalfe has no notion of wearing the Nightcap, and fights splendidly against a Body of assailants the like of whom no Governor, and few Gentlemen, in my time, have had to deal with. I think he will beat them for he is a man of large soul and understanding: but, in the long-run (if the run should be long) more democracy must triumph there: and all those things must float to the surface of Society which one would wish to have kept out of sight. The ultimate catastrophe it is not difficult to foretell.

Stephen did not in the early 1840s realize responsible government to be the panacea that it would become within the decade. He was not really far in advance of Lord John Russell or even of Lord Stanley. And his undeniable leaning toward conciliation was an attitude of resignation to what he regarded as an unpalatable inevitability. It was not the optimistic faith of a Grey or an Elgin.

Stephen indisputably created, however, much of the character and quality of the old Colonial Office. He more than any other deserves to be remembered as its founding father. And, it must be reemphasized, the attention that has been given here to weaknesses must be understood in the context of his better-known strengths. He is an attractive man, combining with his sensitiveness a whimsical view of himself and his place in Britain's imperial history. As he wrote to Sir George Arthur: "What a land this is; with its subject Continents and Islands, hardly able to maintain the Peace in Ireland, and yet conquering Nations on the Indus, and the Emperor of the third part of the human race at Amoy and Chusan."[25]

The touching story of Stephen's departure from the Colonial Office has already been told in detail.[26] He left in 1847 and then resigned the following year, somewhat under a cloud. His resignation stemmed partly from ill health (he would appear, in fact, to have suffered a nervous breakdown), partly from the opposition of prime minister Lord John Russell to any of Lord Grey's schemes to keep him on in an advisory capacity. Off went Stephen, instead, to fill the Regius professorship of modern history at Oxford. The reasons for the premier's intransigent attitude are obscure. His claim that Stephen was an important political liability could not have been justified by an accurate appraisal of voting blocs in the House of Commons. Perhaps nearer the truth is the supposition that the rather pathetic civil servant, constantly complaining of his health and his plight while strongly pressing his claims, tried too severely the patience of a politician for whom the image of Job would never have been particularly appropriate. Much to the discomfort of Lord Grey, left to face his Australian and South African troubles with only an occasional letter of advice from his wise counselor, Stephen was out.

Three men replaced him: Merivale as permanent undersecretary; T. F. Elliot, an old hand who occupied the new position of assistant undersecretary; and Frederic Rogers who, in addition to his duties at the Colonial Land and Emigration Commission, took over the function of legal adviser on colonial legislation.[27] In one way, at least, Stephen's departure marked the end of an era. Never again would the work of one man encompass so large a portion of the business. Yet there was substantial continuity. Save for his unstinting devotion to

25. Stephen to Arthur, 6 Feb. 1844, Arthur Papers, ML–A2164.

26. J. Ward, "Retirement of a Titan: James Stephen, 1847–50," *Journal of Modern History, 31* (1959), 189–205.

27. Office circular of Grey (in Merivale's hand), 20 Dec. 1847, C.O. Minutes, no. 41 (Colonial Office Library).

the humanitarian cause, most of Stephen's attitudes were shared by his successors, and his administrative procedures remained in force. The office continued in Stephen's image.

The son of an academic, and himself a former professor of political economy at Oxford, Merivale came to the office primarily on the strength of his classic *Lectures on Colonization and Colonies* (1841), the best contemporary analysis of the popular subject of emigration. He had been a precocious child, reading Latin at the age of four, and had taken a first at Oxford in the classics. Like Stephen he was a prolific contributor to the best literary journals of the day,[28] his articles exhibiting a good prose style and a wide range of interests that for gentlemen who read for pleasure may have compensated for the superficiality of much of his writing. He was a newcomer to the civil service, and how he came to be considered for the position of undersecretary is not clear. Rogers had been installed in the office by Gladstone in 1846 on the understanding that it would be he who should eventually succeed Stephen. But Grey for some reason—perhaps because he vented on the appointee his dislike of the patron—formed a low opinion of Rogers' abilities and determined to ease him out.[29] Sir Henry Taylor of the West Indian department was considered first

28. C. Merivale, *Herman Merivale* (1884), lists 66 articles in the *Edinburgh Review,* 9 in the *Quarterly Review,* and 5 in the *Foreign Quarterly Review,* in the areas of classical and modern literature, geography and travel, and modern history. Merivale also edited with Henry Davison, *Reports of Cases Argued and Determined in the Court of Queen's Bench* (1844); with Joseph Parkes, *Memoirs of Sir Philip Francis* (2 vols., 1867), in which he speculated that Francis was Junius; with Sir H. Edwards, *Life of Sir Henry Lawrence* (2 vols., 1872). He also wrote *Historical Studies* (1865), a collection of his articles; and the prize essay at Oxford, *The Character of Socrates, as Drawn from Xenophon and Plato* (Oxford, 1930).

29. "I had a long conversation with Mr. Stephen & Hawes about the state of the office the result of which is that I have determined that Mr. Rogers shd. if possible be induced to leave it, & I have with that view written to offer him the situatn. of Secy. to the Govt. of Malta, pretty plainly intimating to him what is my object." Journal entry, 1 Dec. 1846, Grey Papers.

and then, on his advice, James Spedding (a former office clerk and the biographer of Bacon) was made an offer. Finally Grey decided on Merivale, though he was personally unknown to him: "I hope he will answer & I like what little I have seen of him." [30]

Compared with the men who followed and preceded him as permanent undersecretary, Merivale cannot be termed a great administrator. No more brilliant than he, those two superior civil servants possessed more forcefulness and personal strength. Stephen's administrative system contained certain weaknesses. Merivale did little to correct them, and made no effort to make the office routine his own. Though the possessor of a legal background he did not, like Stephen and Rogers, combine the undersecretaryship with the function of legal adviser. It would be a mistake, however, to take the man or his influence too lightly. In one respect he was a distinct improvement over Stephen: he established a much more effective working relationship with members of other departments, most notably the Treasury. Under him the office became considerably more popular.

Merivale was a capable undersecretary whose advice was sought and valued by every secretary of state until 1860, when he left for a similar position at the India Office which he held until his death in 1874. His minutes are perceptive and pragmatic, displaying a wide knowledge of comparative colonial history and the contemporary United States. He was a free trader, and he continued Stephen's predilection for letting colonies look after themselves as much as possible. It was probably he who persuaded Sir John Pakington in 1852 to concede to the Australian colonies the control over their gold and land.

It is therefore only in comparison with Stephen and, perhaps to a lesser degree, with Rogers that Merivale suffers. Efficient and valuable while he served, he made relatively little lasting impact. In the 1860s he was not missed as Stephen

30. Journal entry, 3 Nov. 1847, ibid.

had been. The difference was that Stephen had taken the job and, infecting the Colonial Office with an influence that lasted for decades, had lived it. Merivale merely did it well.

One of the reasons why Merivale's departure created so little disruption was the efficiency of the third of the mid-nineteenth-century undersecretaries, Sir Frederic Rogers.[31] The possessor of a double first at Oxford in classics and mathematics, as well as being one of the founders of the *Manchester Guardian,* he had expected with Gladstone's sponsorship to advance rapidly. But, although naturally offended by Lord Grey's peremptory rejection, as well as by his own failure to secure a position that had been promised him, Rogers had applied himself manfully to make the best of a consolation prize, commissioner for Land and Emigration. There he underwent a valuable apprenticeship. His work on emigration and land questions took him to the very heart of the colonizing process. Moreover, the task of reporting on colonial legislation, which he carried with him, gave him an excellent practical course in the subject of comparative colonial institutions and societies. Like Stephen, Rogers dwelt not upon legal niceties, but upon the utility of law as a function and expression of society. His legal opinions, which are usually shorter and sometimes clearer than Stephen's, yield the impression of a brilliant mind at work.[32]

If Lord Grey had been correct in his assessment of the capacity and staying power of the bright, well-educated, but somewhat cocky young man he had found installed as Stephen's heir apparent, then the fourteen years of preparation made all the difference. Particularly did Rogers distinguish himself in the late 1850s in the delicate and important negotia-

31. See W. Tyler, "Sir Frederic Rogers, Permanent Under-Secretary at the Colonial Office, 1860–1871" (unpublished Ph. D. diss., Duke University, 1962).

32. On Stephen as legal adviser see Swinfen, "Attitudes Towards Colonial Legislation."

tions on the Coolie Convention with France.[33] Then he proved himself master of the art of diplomacy as well as of the immensely complicated details of the subject. Confident of his own knowledge and demonstrated ability, the man selected in 1860 by the Duke of Newcastle to be undersecretary had made himself a superior administrator.

The love of Rogers' life was not his work but his religion. Indeed, his private correspondence with his friend and patron Gladstone pertains to little else. He had, however, well-formed opinions on imperial questions. Utterly resigned to the inevitability of the eventual independence of colonial societies and to the attendant disintegration of imperial ties, he understood his role to be one of smoothing the way for friendly relations thereafter. Like his two predecessors he opposed the annexation of further territory.

It was during his tenure that the office faced up fully to the implications of responsible government. Reluctantly Rogers brought himself round to the view that self-governing colonies must be conceded control over native affairs. Much less reluctantly he used his influence and his sometimes acid pen to help throw upon such colonies the responsibility and cost of their own defense. It would be easy to overestimate the importance of his expectation of ultimate colonial independence. His attitude did not greatly differ in most respects from those of Stephen and Merivale (though the latter did envision some kind of continuing imperial relationship). And it is difficult to detect any impact his philosophy may have had upon his conduct of day-to-day administration.[34]

Rogers was an impressive administrator, from that standpoint probably the best of the three undersecretaries. He worked nearly as hard as Stephen, and much harder than Merivale. Unlike Stephen he knew how to delegate work to others, and established cordial relations with members of the office

33. See below (chap. 8) for a detailed discussion of this treaty.
34. Tyler, "Rogers," passim.

and with other departments. Under him the office routine ran smoothly. Probably the 1860s saw the Stephen system at its highest point of efficiency.

But it was still Stephen's system, which Rogers did comparatively little to change. His administrative alterations had almost entirely to do with redistribution, devoted to the improvement of details of the system, not to its substantial reform. But the circumstances to which that system had been geared were not standing still. Communications were becoming dramatically swifter. A new conception was beginning to form of Britain's role in her dependent, nonwhite empire. The people who had grown up with Stephen's system were aging, and they all were growing old together. Although Rogers began in 1868, at Granville's direction, to analyze the defects of the routine and the distribution of work, he opposed such fundamental changes as unrestricted competition for entrance. Seen in retrospect Rogers looms as a conservative. Substantial reform had to wait until his departure, and then it came with a rush.[35]

Thus three able men, at least two of whom were truly superior administrators, served as permanent undersecretary. Their contribution was considerable. Though all of them remembered their subordinate status, and though all were on occasion overruled, their influence transcended their specific advice. For it was they who shaped the character of the Colonial Office, the focus of the imperial decision-making process. It is in this sense, rather than in the way it was intended, that they deserved the title "Mr. Mothercountry."

A handful of senior officials—the assistant undersecretary, précis writer, and senior clerks—made up the balance of the effective office working force. The rest of the staff—the junior clerks, who provided almost purely mechanical assistance; the

35. See B. Blakely, "The Colonial Office: 1870–1890" (unpublished Ph.D. diss., Duke University, 1966). See also D. Farr, *The Colonial Office and Canada, 1867–1887* (Toronto, 1955), chap. 1.

service personnel, such as the librarian and bookbinder—lay well outside this inner core. At their best the senior officials complemented by their backgrounds and their specialized expertise the qualifications and overall direction provided by the permanent undersecretary. Like the undersecretaries they were drawn from the upper or upper middle class, from the ruling class but not necessarily from the aristocracy. Unlike the undersecretaries (and unlike the pattern that would be prevalent a generation later) they had entered the public service as boys from school. The undersecretary had graduated with high honors from university; his subordinates had received only the vocational training provided by the office itself. Perhaps most important was their length of service. Even more than the undersecretaries they provided continuity of personnel.

Assistant undersecretary T. F. Elliot had entered the service through his family connections and he rose on the basis of ability. Son of a governor of Madras and cousin of the Earl of Minto, he was educated at Harrow, but not at university, receiving his Colonial Office appointment at seventeen.[36] In his early years he demonstrated "powers & aptitudes of such a nature as would in any profession in which competition had free scope ensure . . . success & even eminence."[37] Made précis writer in 1827 and senior clerk of the North American department in 1833, he earned his reputation as assistant to a commission of enquiry in Canada from 1835 to 1837. Becoming agent general of the Land and Emigration Commission in 1837, he was promoted in 1847 to the position of assistant undersecretary which he held until his retirement in 1868. Under Lord Grey's scheme of reorganization following the loss of Stephen,[38] Elliot dealt primarily with special subjects—land and

36. Biographical information from the obituary in *The Times*, 24 Feb. 1880.
37. Stephen to Howick, 10 Feb. 1832, Grey Papers.
38. Grey memorandum, 20 Dec. 1847, C.O. Minutes, no. 41.

emigration, transportation of convicts, military expenditure in the colonies—leaving the more general correspondence to Merivale. When Rogers replaced Merivale, bringing with him the legal adviser's job, Elliot added supervision of the North American, African, and Mediterranean colonies.[39]

Elliot's minutes reveal him to have been the most outspoken of the permanent officials, particularly on such favorite subjects as British government guarantees for Australian railway loans. He was a painstaking, able, and imaginative, if somewhat impulsive man who served the office well.[40] Lacking, however, the education of the undersecretaries, he also lacked their brilliance and their savoir faire. The Duke of Newcastle was wise to resist his claims in 1860,[41] for Rogers was much the better man.

The senior clerks in charge of the general and the four geographical departments had backgrounds similar to Elliot's, possessing specialized vocational experience rather than general education. With Elliot they formed a distinct generational grouping that lasted roughly from the mid-1820s to the period 1867–72. Peter Smith, chief clerk until his retirement in 1860, fell outside the dominant generation, having been appointed in 1810. Arthur Blackwood, Sir Henry Taylor, Sir George Barrow, and Gordon Gairdner had all joined the office in the great shake-up of 1824–25,[42] Charles Cox only a few years later. When Smith retired Gairdner replaced him as chief clerk, combining the general department with the Australian until Cox added that business in 1863 to his eastern department. Taylor led the West Indian division from 1825, Black-

39. Tyler, "Rogers," p. 46.

40. I do not share the disparaging opinion of Elliot professed by G. Serle, *The Golden Age, A History of the Colony of Victoria, 1851–1861* (Melbourne, 1963), p. 195.

41. The process of selection is explained in George Arbuthnot to Gladstone, 4 Apr. 1861, Gladstone Papers, Add. MS. 44,096.

42. Young, *The Colonial Office in the Early Nineteenth Century,* pp. 47–84, 271.

wood the North American, and Barrow the African from the late thirties.

They had, of course, considerable individual variation. Smith lacked imagination and the ability to go to the heart of a question, and filled his tedious memoranda with vast quantities of precedents. The barely competent son of a distinguished and influential civil servant, Barrow merely summarized incoming dispatches. Contrary to standard office practice he rarely gave advice.[43] Gairdner, Blackwood, and Cox had a good deal of initiative, as well as very detailed knowledge of local colonial politics and intimate connections with colonists in England and abroad. And the fabled Taylor, known in his own day for his poetic drama and in ours for his classic work *The Statesman* (1836), was more like an undersecretary or, as he put it, a "statesman" than a clerk, so forceful were his directions, so independent were his working habits, and so great was the respect of his superiors for his advice.

Along with William Strachey, Lytton's eccentric uncle who had served in the Indian Civil Service and who was appointed précis writer in 1848,[44] the senior officials formed an impressive core of assistants. Taken as a group they were knowledgeable, industrious, and extraordinarily continuous. As a committee of investigators concluded in 1849, they blended nicely with the permanent and assistant undersecretaries. The latter, usually selected from outside the office, contributed "the legal and general knowledge . . . [not] . . . easily acquired" within, while the senior clerks added "the long experience and the practical ability which are the foundations of the regular and successful transaction of public business." [45]

43. Cf. Galbraith, *Reluctant Empire*, p. 16.

44. See C. Sanders, *The Strachey Family, 1588–1932* (Durham, N.C., 1953), pp. 211–12. The précis writer was a sort of troubleshooter, dealing with such laborious special subjects as the Newfoundland fisheries and the finances of Ceylon and Hong Kong. An odd recluse, he was the least valuable member of the upper echelon.

45. Report of Commission on Public Offices, PP, 1854 [1715], 27, 80.

Continuity and purpose need not, therefore, have been precluded by even so rapid a turnover of secretaries of state as the one that occurred in the 1850s. The upper echelons of the permanent staff were fully capable of providing the knowledge and the intellectual capacity for the formation of a purposeful and fairly consistent colonial policy, directed from this office that was the focus of imperial decision making. Their role in that process, moreover, was meant and understood to be a large one.

> Mr. Merivale and Mr. Elliot should both take care [directed Lord Grey] that before Papers are forwarded by them, all information required for deciding upon them is collected, and that when it is possible (as it generally is) they shd. be minuted with such full suggestions upon them, as to require no more than the initials of Mr. Hawes and myself as assenting to what is suggested.[46]

Outside Barrow's poorly conducted African department this standard—Stephen's standard—was generally fulfilled.

Yet the fact is that the Colonial Office did not control the flow of events. It drifted with them. No one "ran" the British empire.[47] It may well be, of course, that the intimate study of imperial policy making in any period would reveal a similar situation. Perhaps the model of the forceful administrator who manipulates events—the Palmerstonian or Bismarckian ideal—bears so little relation to reality that it ought to be abandoned. The mid-nineteenth-century Colonial Office, at any rate, did not fulfill it. But since it was apparently the goal of such colonial secretaries as Lord Grey, it is perhaps useful to attempt to discover wherein the office failed.

First there were physical obstacles. As noted already the condition of the building was crowded and uncomfortable. The arrangement of offices made difficult the access of the sec-

46. Memorandum of 20 Dec. 1847, C.O. Minutes, no. 41.
47. This is essentially the conclusion of Manning, "Who Ran the British Empire?"

retary of state to the undersecretaries.[48] Frequent interruptions at the office made standard the practice for senior officials of doing most of their work at home in the evenings. This procedure increased the difficulties of communication between interior divisions. Complained Gairdner: "Each department is as distinct in its working as if each was an independent Office of the Government." [49] Contact was especially difficult with Taylor who, afflicted as he was by asthma, appeared only occasionally, dispatch boxes being sent down to him in Bournemouth as though he were a member of the cabinet. Granted that the government in general managed to function in similar surroundings, there is little doubt that the core of top officials would have functioned better in more suitable circumstances.

More important was the maldistribution of work, the inefficient use the office made of the subordinate members of its staff. The number of theoretically potential participants (including all the clerks but not the service personnel) was only about thirty in 1855, a figure that remained virtually constant throughout the mid-nineteenth century. The amount of work increased little until the early seventies, after which it sharply expanded. Thereafter the size of the staff lagged behind its sharply rising productivity.[50] By 1890 the "establishment" carried sixty-five persons, an increase of only three from 1870, while the work had nearly doubled, from 25,000 pieces of correspondence to 46,000.[51] The conclusion seems obvious: the office of Stephen and Rogers had laxer standards. As early as 1832 Stephen had remarked that "we have no good division of labour intellectual & mechanical." [52]

It was a common observation that the most fundamental weakness of the Colonial Office system lay in the selection and

48. Memorandum of Peter Smith, 24 Apr. 1856, CO 323/248.
49. Minute on Gov. Barkly (Victoria) to C.O., 11 Apr. 1859, CO 309/48.
50. See Blakely, "Colonial Office," especially chaps. 1, 2, and 8.
51. Tyler, "Rogers," p. 40.
52. Stephen to Howick, 10 Feb. 1832, Grey Papers.

training of the clerks. "Drawn from a rank in society to which a liberal education & a cultivated address belong as a matter of course," the clerk entered the service still a boy. After the formality of a year's probation he had a secure career for life. He might be dull or bright, lazy or industrious, but the office had to train him in business habits and for life itself. And the office was "a bad school."

Even if the lad were promising the obstacles were formidable. His first ten to fifteen years, no matter what his abilities, were spent in tedious labor that any could perform as well as the rest, but none with real distinction. He copied, sorted papers, looked up precedents, ran errands. He might be allowed to draft a dispatch now and then, but only of the most unimportant kind, amounting in fact to copying the minutes of higher officials. Never—and this applied even to the second-class clerks of twenty years' service—did he make a decision. Small wonder that there were frequent disciplinary problems, general unruliness and noisiness, and shoddy performance of the small amount of work that was discharged. Said Stephen: "One Man writing at ld. per folio would do more work, and do it better, than twelve Young Gentlemen copying Papers in the interval between their Morning Rides and their Afternoon Dinner Parties." [53]

Nor did the office provide much incentive. The fourth-class clerk began at £100 a year—less, thought Taylor, than the "income on which a young man *can* live as a gentleman in London" [54]—with an annual increment of £10 up to a maximum of £150. Movement to the top three ranks, with the first class carrying the comfortable maximum salary of £1,000, was supposedly based on merit. Actually promotion rested almost entirely on seniority, since the functions of the juniors provided neither a test of ability nor a reason for penalization.

Chances for advancement fluctuated, the channels being

53. Stephen memorandum, 30 Mar. 1832, CO 537/22.
54. Memorandum of 25 Apr. 1857, CO 323/249.

clogged by the tendency toward generational turnover. The situation was fairly open in the period before 1840: Taylor became senior clerk within a year; Gairdner, Blackwood, and Barrow had to wait between twelve and eighteen years. But once their generation settled into the top positions those below them stagnated. One clerk appointed in 1832 had reached only the third division by 1855. Not until the late sixties did the condition change, and then only for a few years before the dampers were put on again.

The clerk who rose above such obstacles to become a useful civil servant must have possessed unusual qualities indeed. Even then the years of tedium must have left their mark. The investigating committee of 1849 concluded that the clerks

> generally receive their original appointments to the Establishment before their education is finished or their characters are developed; and the early age at which they become their own masters, the dry and distasteful nature of their duties, and the various attractions of a London life, are very unfavourable to the formation of those habits which make good public servants. . . . If after ten or fifteen years spent in incessant copying and other routine work, the spirit, mental activity, and the wide extent of acquired knowledge necessary for vigorous intellectual exertion in the transaction of business like that of the Colonial Office, are wanting, it is the fault of the system, and not of the individuals who have been placed in circumstances so unfavourable to them.[55]

The readily apparent solution was to reduce the number of clerks to those who could be effectively employed in something more than purely mechanical work. The more menial side of the office routine could be performed by men of a different social class, selected entirely for that purpose and paid

55. Report by W. Craig, C. Trevelyan, and Merivale, 15 Dec. 1849, PP, 1854 [1715], 27, 81–82.

on a piecework basis. But, although the remedy was proposed as early as 1832 by Stephen, it required more than a generation to implement, and only then as the result of outside pressure. As Stephen admitted it was "a great [though] perhaps not a practicable improvement."[56] The office was filled with young men who were well-connected and who had been promised secure employment, and who could not easily be dismissed. No scheme could hope to apply to more than new appointees. And there was also considerable opposition from politicians and conservative civil servants alike, the latter notably represented in the office by Sir Frederic Rogers.

Stephen's recommendation was elevated into the famous Northcote-Trevelyan report of 1853, from which the modern British civil service is usually dated. The authors, who were permanent officials at the Treasury, made a forceful indictment against the whole system of contemporary administration, basing their attack on studies such as one that had been made of the Colonial Office in 1849. They concluded that the civil service was largely composed of incompetents who were unable to succeed in business or in competitive professions, and who were further handicapped by maldistribution of work and by lack of incentive. They considered the root of the problem to be that traditional scapegoat the patronage system. For it they proposed to substitute the open competitive examinations already employed by the Indian Civil Service. To secure uniformity, examinations would be administered by a central agency. Once appointed, clerical personnel would be separated into "intellectual" and "mechanical" divisions, reducing to a minimum the amount of stupefying copying to be done by potential thinkers. Finally, promotion should be made solely on the basis of merit and the incentive further increased by throwing open to officials within the ranks the top positions hitherto usually filled by outsiders.[57]

56. Stephen to Howick, 10 Feb. 1832, Grey Papers.
57. The report is reprinted in *Public Administration, 31* (1954), 1–16.

The Northcote-Trevelyan report was supported by such Utilitarians as John Stuart Mill at the India Office, who hailed it as the opening of a new "era in history," and Edwin Chadwick at the Board of Health, as well as by Gladstone.[58] But it was stiffly resisted. Writing from his elevated professorial perspective Stephen agreed that most civil servants were indeed incompetent. He opposed the remedy, however, dryly wondering if a place in the world ought not to be reserved for mediocrity.[59] The Aberdeen coalition split, with the Peelites in favor and the Whigs opposed,[60] and Lord John Russell effectively stated the case for the opposition. What was wanted, he said, was not brilliance so much as "unquestionable loyalty & . . . industry." The issue involved the whole system of party government: "No Man changes his politicks on account of this patronage. But an adherent of the Ministry attends more constantly, and is less flighty in his votes when his interest in his county or borough may be promoted by the Minister." [61]

In the event a compromise was adopted. By Order in Council of May 1855 the Palmerston government established the Civil Service Commission, decreeing that all junior appointments would thereafter be made by examination. Details of the test and the procedure of selection were left, however, to the individual departments. The Foreign Office chose not to

58. For Mill's views see Papers re reorganization of the Civil Service, PP, 1854–55 [1870], *20,* 92–98. See also the documents from the Gladstone and Trevelyan papers edited by E. Hughes, "Sir Charles Trevelyan and Civil Service Reform, 1853–5," *English Historical Review, 64* (1949), 53–88, 206–34.

59. Pugh (*CHBE, 3,* 722) has called Stephen's view too severe. Yet nearly all of the able men he lists were also praised by Stephen. It would be hard to rank such capable clerks as Gairdner and Blackwood much above the level of "meritorious public servants." And it would be still more difficult to fault his strictures against the general run of junior clerks

60. Hughes, *E.H.R., 64,* 62.

61. Russell to Gladstone, 20 Jan. 1854, Gladstone Papers, Add. MS. 44,291.

participate. Several departments, including the Colonial Office in 1856, adopted a limited scheme in which patronage and competition were combined. The secretary of state submitted a list of candidates who were tested in an examination worked out by the office itself. The examination lasted three days, stressing classics, modern history and literature, and précis writing. It does not seem to have been particularly rigorous, but Merivale judged in 1860 that it had kept out inefficient men.

It is not likely that the change imposed a hardship on colonial secretaries. Patronage had long been something of a nuisance, especially in the upper levels of the home service where there were too many applicants for the available positions. The secretary of state may, indeed, have been thankful for a mechanical means of selection that eliminated the necessity of making inevitably unpopular decisions himself.

Moreover, the immediate impact of the reforms was small. Clerks already on the establishment were not affected. The character of the candidates submitted for examination did not markedly change. And the separation of intellectual and mechanical labor, which in fact had been tentatively begun under Lord Grey, could be taken only so far. For as Merivale observed there was not enough "intellectual" work to occupy any but the seniors.[62]

Further progress in implementing the Northcote-Trevelyan report depended on the individual departments, and in the Colonial Office of the 1860s it was slow. The reason was primarily a generational problem: senior officials who had served under the old regime for thirty to forty years were reluctant to change. Pressure for the move to open competition began in earnest when the Gladstone government came to power in 1868, and was centered in the Treasury under Robert Lowe. Members of the office resisted. To Sir Frederic Rogers the es-

62. Evidence before Select Committee on Civil Service Appointments, PP, 1860 (440), 9, 310, 311.

sential issue was one of social status, which he thought "some guarantee for certain moral qualities . . . , integrity & honourable *esprit de corps,* [that] are as really valuable for our purposes as intellect & its appendages."

But the mid-Victorian generation's day was over. Between 1867 and 1872 retired Blackwood, Gairdner, Strachey, Rogers himself, Barrow, and Taylor. They were replaced by men who were not so respectful of old ways. "The new Colonial Office would not necessarily be a better office, but it would be different."[63] In 1870 Granville bowed to the Treasury, agreeing to open competition. Two years later, Kimberley having replaced Granville and Robert Herbert having taken Rogers' position as undersecretary, a comprehensive scheme of reorganization was drawn up and implemented. Two divisions of clerks were established, the upper division supposedly being devoted entirely to "intellectual" work. The number of upper-division clerks was reduced from twenty-six to eighteen, and the office was reorganized into two large geographical departments and a general one.

The effects were considerable. Open competition made the office more attractive to university graduates. The transition to better-educated men, begun slowly in the 1860s under the limited scheme, became nearly complete among the entrants of the seventies. And, although it would be wrong to disparage the abilities of such men as Taylor, Blackwood, and Gairdner, there can be little doubt that the quality of the members of the office as a whole greatly improved.

The mode of selection and training of the clerks was, however, only part of the problem. Patronage could not of course be eliminated entirely, and no really satisfactory criteria have ever been established for determining that administrator's nightmare, "merit." The Northcote-Trevelyan report was perhaps characteristically liberal in its readiness to blame the "system" rather than the limitations of the people. And it at-

63. Blakely, "Colonial Office," pp. 50, 30.

tacked only the most obvious administrative weaknesses. Left unnoticed were others that lay deeply embedded in the milieu of the office's pace and routine.

The habits belonged to an era less complicated and less demanding than our own. The permanent staff normally worked a five-day week, six hours a day, eleven to five. Such, at least, was the "prevalent understanding" until Stephen made the rule explicit in 1843.[64] It was still the normal pace three decades later, when Herbert directed that clerks must arrive no later than twelve, "as the time of the Principal Clerks and Under Secretaries is wasted if the despatch of business is not commenced . . . early in the day." [65] From this total must be subtracted time off for lunch—prepared in the kitchen and carried up to the gentlemen between two and three—and for tea. Liberal annual vacations were also extended.

Such a portrait of laxity is not, of course, quite accurate. The office did not turn out its work by the day, but instead was geared to the periodic "crises" of the arrival and departure of the mails.[66] On these occasions clerks were kept till late at night. The pace also quickened when parliament was in session. Nor did the relaxed routine govern the habits of the seniors, most of whose effective work was done away from the office. Their jobs, however, were made more difficult by the lack of participation of the juniors, who gave them less than five hours of assistance a day. Stephen was not alone in feeling the strain.

Yet the fact is that, given the office's routine, there was not much reason for junior clerks to work longer. There was little enough for them to do when they were there. For under Stephen's administrative system they were left out of the decision-making process entirely.

64. Memorandum of 27 Jan. 1843, C.O. Minutes, no. 17.

65. Memorandum of 8 Oct. 1872, CO 878/5.

66. See the amusing account of Henry Taylor to his mother, 19 Mar. 1831, E. Dowden, ed., *Correspondence of Henry Taylor* (1888), pp. 33–35.

From the time of its stabilization in the late thirties the routine did not change until the seventies. An incoming letter was registered and sent to the senior clerk of the appropriate geographical department. He minuted it, usually proposed the answer, prepared a précis in some cases, and sent it (depending on the subject) to the undersecretary or assistant undersecretary. Favored with undersecretarial observations, the document went next to the parliamentary undersecretary and then to the secretary of state, "who records his decision," sometimes calling for further information. The paper returned through the same channels to the originating department, it being the senior clerk's responsibility to study the decision to ensure its consistency with facts, regulations, and precedents unknown to his superiors. He or his assistants, or in important cases the undersecretaries or even the secretary of state, prepared a draft which was sent up again for approval and back down for copying.

Like Stephen himself, this procedure had the virtues of being systematic and methodical. It was simple. It clearly defined the channels of communication. It was virtually all-embracing, encompassing all official and semiofficial correspondence with other departments, with colonial governors, and with subordinate officials and other individuals throughout the empire. The only important exception was private correspondence, notably that between secretaries of state and governors (important and extensive in the cases of Grey, Newcastle, and Carnarvon), which usually went directly to the man concerned. The routine brought the best minds of the office automatically to bear on every important question. It helped to insure, though of course there were lapses, that no subject could long be ignored. On the whole it was a successful solution to the problem of achieving smoothness and "rationality" in bureaucratic operation.

There were, however, weaknesses. The most crucial was the lack of any filtering mechanism. There were no means of determining what was an important question worthy of the attention of the secretary of state. Once registered, every paper traversed the same course. Neither senior clerks nor undersecretaries stopped the flow. They might remark that papers were insignificant, but sent them up in any case. The system lacked discrimination. It lacked a mode of delegation of authority.

The major fault of the Stephen system was that it did not fully exploit the resources of the office. Its effect was to focus the decision-making process sharply at the top. Senior clerks summarized, gathered information, and frequently made recommendations. Undersecretaries sifted details and gave advice that was usually taken. But in all cases the decision no matter how perfunctory was the secretary of state's.

Left out were all but the top officials: the secretary of state, the three undersecretaries, the précis writer, the chief clerk, and the four senior clerks in charge of departments. The effective work of the Colonial Office was done by ten individuals. The rest merely enabled them to function. And these ten were themselves immersed in the operation of a routine that served almost as an end in itself. As a contemporary analysis of another department (the Treasury) concluded:

> The most experienced officers of a department ought not to be so completely engrossed in disposing of the current business, as to have neither time nor strength to attend to general objects connected with their respective duties, which are often of more importance to the public interests than the every-day transactions of official routine.[67]

The defect of the Colonial Office system was not merely, as Northcote and Trevelyan assumed, the manner in which the clerical staff was selected and trained. The junior members were not effectively used, and too heavy a burden of detail

67. Reports of Commission on Public Offices, PP, 1854 [1715], 27, 79–80, 36.

was thrown in consequence upon the overworked seniors. Clearly this is part of the reason—and there would be other reasons in other ages, for it was ever thus—why the office operated largely on an ad hoc basis.

The weaknesses in routine and "personnel management" were interrelated. Stephen's procedure, in which the lack of delegation of authority decreased the efficiency of the secretary of state, could not have included much more devolution than it did. Such ministers as the elder Stanley and Russell simply would not have accepted it. Stephen would have thought the junior clerks too unreliable to be trusted. So no doubt they were. Yet untrustworthiness is partly the result of not being trusted. The procedure of the office weakened the effectiveness of the staff, whose unreliability undermined the efficiency of the routine. The Stephen system contained a self-depressing cycle.

Substantial change did not begin until about 1870. Its inception was partly the result of an increasing work load accompanying the Ashanti wars, the addition of the Straits settlements to the office's responsibilities, and the successful completion of cables to colonies both west and east. But to some extent the change anticipated the necessity, being partly traceable to the personality and experience of Granville. The pleasant and rather carefree Granville was unwilling to work too hard, but was intelligent enough to compensate for his dilatory habits in a constructive way. What he did was to implement methods he had observed at the Foreign Office, where the significant quickening that affected the Colonial Office in the seventies had long been evident.

Under Granville responsibility first began to be systematically delegated. Undersecretaries he authorized

> to sign on my behalf Despatches which merely convey acknowledgements, or transmit documents, or request formal information, or signify the acquiescence of the Secre-

> tary of State in arrangements of detail, on which it is not usual to interfere with the discretion of the Governor.

His successor Kimberley approved and the practice was thereafter extended. At Granville's direction Rogers analyzed the flow of paper through the office, concluding that it moved too slowly. The same document came around too many times in different form to the same officials. The routine could be streamlined. Subordinates could more frequently anticipate the decisions of their superiors. In most cases letters could be sent up for signature at once. Shortcuts could be found. Drafts could pass directly from the undersecretaries to the copyists without going through the originating department.[68]

The working of these recommendations into an institutionalized pattern of bureaucratic behavior lies outside the province of this book. But the outlines of the change from Stephen's office to the one that served Chamberlain seem clear.[69] Authority was delegated. Senior clerks and assistant undersecretaries came to deal routinely with matters which would earlier have been decided personally by the secretary of state. A far larger segment of the office participated in the process of decision making. The clerks, in short, were put to work.

The Colonial Office certainly changed over the course of the nineteenth century. How is such an alteration in bureaucracy to be evaluated? Can it be related to something larger and more significant?

According to the famous seminal model of Max Weber,[70]

68. Granville circular to colonial governors, 30 June 1869; Rogers memorandum, 8 Apr. 1870; CO 878/5.

69. See Blakely, "Colonial Office," C. Parkinson, *The Colonial Office from Within, 1909–1945* (1947), and R. Kubicek, "Joseph Chamberlain and the Colonial Office: A Study in Imperial Administration" (unpublished Ph. D. diss., Duke University, 1964), which will soon be published by the Duke University Press.

70. The following discussion is taken from his *Theory of Social and Economic Organization*, T. Parsons, ed. (New York, 1947), pp. 329–41. Useful introductions to the subject and the literature are R. Merton et al.,

the Colonial Office and the British government as a whole might be expected to have been undergoing a transition from rule by notables to administration by a modern bureaucracy. That this is broadly what happened (though of course it began long before the nineteenth century) is not terribly surprising in view of the fact that Weber constructed his model in part on the basis of British experience. In further refining his "ideal type," Weber went on to define administrative modernization. His discussion has a good deal of relevance to what a number of writers have recently referred to as a nineteenth-century "revolution" in government.[71]

A modern bureaucratic department is staffed by appointed officials responsible only for the discharge of their duties; organized in offices whose spheres of competence and hierarchy of responsibility are clearly defined; remunerated entirely by fixed salaries usually determined by seniority; occupied at least primarily by official duties which constitute for them a "career"; and subject to discipline and control. Moreover, administration is carried on in a "rational" way (i.e., purposefully directed toward a given end) and in an orderly manner. Its progress at every stage is recorded in writing, even when oral communication is also involved. As much as possible it operates impersonally on the basis of written and ascertainable rules and precedents.

At the time of Stephen's appointment as undersecretary in 1836 the Colonial Office had already acquired many of these

---

eds., *Reader in Bureaucracy* (New York, 1952); J. LaPalombara, ed., *Bureaucracy and Political Development* (Princeton, 1963); and R. Braibanti, ed., *Asian Bureaucratic Systems Emergent from the British Imperial Tradition* (Durham, N.C., 1966).

71. See O. MacDonagh, "The Nineteenth-Century Revolution in Government: A Reappraisal," *Historical Journal, 1* (1958), 52–67; H. Parris, "The Nineteenth-Century Revolution in Government: A Reappraisal Reappraised," ibid., *3* (1960), 17–37; J. Hart, "Nineteenth-Century Social Reform: A Tory Interpretation of History," *Past and Present, 31* (1965), 39–61; and V. Cromwell, "Interpretations of Nineteenth-Century Administration: An Analysis," *Victorian Studies, 9* (1966), 245–55.

"modern" characteristics, albeit some of them only quite recently. Only the secretary of state and parliamentary undersecretary were subject to external accountability or were responsible for more than the discharge of their official duties; but Weber excepted the top position in an administrative hierarchy. Other officials were appointed and, though controlled by the Treasury and ultimately by parliament, made the office their secure career. They were entirely remunerated by fixed salaries, although only in the 1830s had the fee system been abolished for the colonial agencies that had been held until that time by senior clerks.

Much was to come, particularly in the civil service reforms of the 1850s and the 1870s. In 1836 the permanent undersecretary alone was appointed to the office on the basis of proven qualifications, the rest of the permanent officials having entered on the basis of patronage. A partial step toward modernity in selection occurred in 1856 with the adoption of the limited competition scheme, a more pronounced one being implemented in 1870 in the move to open examination. The results were better-educated and more efficient entrants, added prestige, and a higher esprit de corps, all of which are incorporated in the Weberian model.

The sphere of competence of the Colonial Office had been defined only in 1812, the American colonies having been administered previously by the secretary for the Home department. Thereafter, the office's preserve was fairly well understood. It administered territories held formally by the crown, as distinguished from such informally dominated territory as protectorates, which belonged administratively to the Foreign Office. And, with the exceptions of Ceylon and Hong Kong, it did not administer extensions of the Indian empire until the latter part of the century. Yet the precise delineation of responsibility is probably the least applicable of Weber's criteria. Most of the departments in the government had in some way or other to do with aspects of colonial administration.

Disputes over which offices held primary jurisdiction were frequent, and it seems unlikely that a satisfactory solution could have been devised.

Also progressively delineated were the duties of the colonial secretary, although it continued to be true that if need be any secretary of state could perform the functions of any other. In the eighteenth century, when there had been two secretaries of state, the secretary for the Home department had combined the administration of overseas possessions with numerous other duties. In 1801 the position of secretary for war and colonies had been created. In 1854 those functions were further separated, the colonial secretary becoming for the first time responsible for the colonies alone. The bureaucratic department beneath him, however, had already acquired a clearly defined competence, and the effects of the change of 1854 on the Colonial Office were therefore minimal.

Yet perhaps the most significant characteristic that was acquired was the methodical routine created by Stephen. Before its stabilization the office had of course followed precedents and rules, but not apparently according to any fixed and rational system. Business was sometimes done in writing, sometimes not. Nor do patterns of administrative behavior appear to have been either continuous or institutionalized. It was Stephen, primarily, who changed these things. It was he who made the Colonial Office a "combination of written documents and a continuous organization of official functions." [72]

After Stephen the system jelled further under Merivale and Rogers, who preserved and improved it slightly. In the 1870s it was modified but not replaced. Officials continued to preserve their primary loyalty, as Stephen had done, not for the empire they administered but for the prestige of the office of which they were members. In the Weberian sense their office did not necessarily get "better." But it did become more modern.

The question is why. Why did the office change at all? Why

72. Weber, *Theory of Organization,* p. 332.

did it change in certain directions? Why was the rate of change faster at some times than at others? It is at this level that Weber's model rapidly loses its effectiveness as an "operational" tool. The "ideal type" helps to identify changes that were taking place, and to fit them together into a pattern that may or may not be valid, but not to explain why they happened. Weber's model helps to define what a "modern bureaucracy" is, but not how one works. In order to do that, one needs to return to the analysis of process, and of cause and effect.

In evaluating the changes that took place in the Colonial Office, the term "revolution in government" seems inappropriate. The word "revolution" must pertain to rapid changes *in kind,* what social scientists call "systemic change." In the Colonial Office there were primarily changes in degree. Even the imposition of the Stephen system, innovative though it was, can hardly be classed as revolutionary, for it was mostly a rationalization of existing procedures and machinery. Instead, the pattern in the Colonial Office, and probably in the other established departments like the Treasury and the Foreign Office as well, is of a grudging and in most cases a belated adaptation of outmoded machinery and procedures to new functions demanded by changing circumstances.

What were these changes in circumstances? MacDonagh mentions several:

> The Northcote-Trevelyan inquiries and recommendations; the Crimean scandals; the doctrine of utilitarianism; the sentiment of humanitarianism; the new economic relationships and the living and working conditions of urbanization and industrialized environments; and the implications for executive government of the process of political change initiated by 'economical reform' or 1832 or what one will.[73]

73. "Nineteenth-Century Revolution," p. 53.

None of these factors can be rejected. Yet while they serve to explain much about the milieu from which emerged the impulse for social reform and the creation of new machinery to implement it, they do not touch the problem of change in an existing organization, a "complex pattern of communications and other relations in a group of human beings." [74] The list does not include the single most important factor that promoted change in the nineteenth-century Colonial Office, which was a rapid and indeed a revolutionary alteration of the base of communications itself.

The Colonial Office system at any point in time can be usefully analyzed as a function of the evolving base of communications that so largely established the preconditions within which the department could operate. By such a standard the Stephen routine can be regarded as a singularly effective mode of adapting to the advantages and disadvantages of the age of sail. It would not have served so effectively the Foreign Office, much of whose correspondence was carried by rail and ferry, or the Treasury, who corresponded largely with other departments on the same street. But it served the Colonial Office well. As the base of communications altered in the course of the nineteenth century, and particularly in the latter part of it, so too the Colonial Office system came to feel the strain of inflexibility and the need for adaptation in the face of changed conditions.

In essentials the base of communications on which the Colonial Office operated in the early nineteenth century had not changed since the first establishment of colonies nearly three centuries before. Its fundamental ingredient was the monthly mail. At more or less regular and predictable intervals a group of related abstractions from the ongoing temporal reality—i.e. a bag of governor's dispatches—was detached from its context

74. H. Simon, *Administrative Behavior: A Study of Decision-Making Processes in Administrative Organization* (2d ed. New York, 1957), p. xvii.

in time and place and deposited after an ocean voyage of varying duration in the Colonial Office. There it was sorted, methodically scrutinized, and processed. The misplacing of one document out of the several that arrived together might well be insignificant. So long as the correspondence was carried out on this one-to-one basis between the office and the governor, the Stephen system was faultless: it was when responses from other departments had to be obtained (which were often neither regular nor predictable) that it broke down, much to Stephen's consternation. Still, there was no particular hurry, for the remote governor would have to act in any case; and the more urgent the matter the more likelihood that he would have to act before the office's instructions could possibly arrive. At length, usually spurred on by the approach of the regular and predictable departure of the outward mail, the office would formulate a response. It too was an abstraction from the reality of time and place, and by the time the governor received it, it was perhaps as irrelevant as his own had been at the time of its consideration in London. In time he too would have to answer. And thus, abstraction eliciting abstraction, the process of imperial decision making ground on. Crises, wars, disputes, governors, colonial secretaries came and went: for nearly three hundred years the basis and the pattern of communications continued much the same. Yet in the Colonial Office the administrative potentialities of the age of sail were effectively rationalized only as that era was drawing toward its close.

Man is a creature of habit, and those who worked the Stephen system maintained it as long as they could. Much of it still exists. Parts of it lingered on long after innovations in communications had made them anachronisms. There was superimposition as well as displacement.

The advent of the oceangoing steamship caused little strain in the system: in the twenty years after it was introduced in the 1840s the routine of the office altered hardly at all. The exchange of abstractions from reality became somewhat more frequent and somewhat more predictable, but they continued to arrive in interrelated bunches.

The great dividing point was the telegraph. By this medium information was transmitted piecemeal; abstractions from reality arrived and departed quickly, irregularly, and unpredictably. A clerk had to stay at the office through the night in case an emergency arose. The length of temporal removal from the source of information was progressively reduced from a week, to a few days, to a few hours. Responses had to be made quickly, and officials at either end tended to build a mosaic from isolated bits of information rather than from interrelated clusters of it. There was no longer the time for the methodical flow of the Stephen system. Not regularity but jerkiness came to characterize the process of imperial decision making.

Yet there was superimposition of one medium upon another, not displacement. The monthly mails continued to arrive and depart. Their volume was increased rather than diminished, since every cable had of course to be repeated and amplified in writing to keep the record straight. The bags of dispatches were now used, when read at all, to add another dimension to the impressions that had been derived from the piecemeal accumulation of information by telegraph.

In the altered circumstances there was no choice. The telegraph bred a state of continual "crisis"—it was as nothing in comparison to the constant state of emergency that would one day accompany the intrusion of the jet airplane, television, and the communications satellite into the process of decision making—and the office had to cope with it. Its productivity and therefore the role and efficiency of its junior members had to be increased.

There was not of course the dramatic suddenness that the preceding analysis would perhaps imply. There was a substantial time lag between the introduction of a technological innovation and its working into the institutionalized pattern of bureaucratic behavior. There was no sudden shift, but rather a process of continual adaptation, a blending and merging of the old and the new, changes in degree that in time accumulated into changes in kind. The administrative effects of the telegraph cannot be traced here with any precision. It was employed as a toy in the 1860s, long after the Foreign Office had come to depend on it in the conduct of European diplomacy. But it is unclear when the Colonial Office came to rely on it: perhaps in the Ashanti or Zulu wars, perhaps the Jameson raid, perhaps even as late as the Boer War.

The alteration in the base of communications is a necessary but not a wholly sufficient explanation of the changes that took place in the Colonial Office system. The Northcote-Trevelyan report can hardly be attributed to the introduction of the steamship or to an anticipation of the telegraph. The entrance of better-educated men into the civil service was to some extent inevitable: for one thing there were more of them around. To some extent their better preparation necessitated their more effective employment. And the spread of administrative techniques from the Foreign to the Colonial Office predated the full acceptance of the telegraph. Yet to analyze the performance of an office against the capabilities permitted by its base of communications seems a useful standard of comparison, as well as allowing some understanding of how and why it changed.

2: The View From Government House

In my eyes the almost sole business of the Colonial Office should be to breed up a supply of Good Colonial Governors: & then leave them & you to manage your own affairs.
Charles Buller

In the days before the telegraph had altered the base of imperial communications the inability to run the British Empire from Downing Street was patently obvious—to the governors if not always to Downing Street. "My instructions were drawn up from the latest information received," mused Sir William Denison shortly after his arrival in Van Diemen's Land, "and they contemplated a state of things exactly the reverse of what I found to prevail." [1] "It would undoubtedly be in the highest degree absurd," echoed Lord Grey, the man who had been responsible for those instructions, "to attempt to govern from Downing-street." [2] Although "some kind of authority must be exercised from home" if an empire were to be maintained at all, the secretary of state could lay down only the most general principles, hoping to assert his control primarily by means of salutary reviews of actions long since taken. The details of policy as well as its application, both of which did so much to define it, had to be left to the local authorities.

1. Opening quotation from Buller to Joseph Howe, 10 Sept. 1846, in C. Martin, ed., "The Correspondence Between Joseph Howe and Charles Buller, 1845–1848," *Canadian Historical Review, 6* (1925), 316. W. Denison, *Varieties of Vice–regal Life* (2 vols., 1870), *1*, 18.
2. H. Grey, *The Colonial Policy of Lord John Russell's Administration* (2 vols., 1853), *1*, 19.

It was a long-standing precept that the man on the spot, when confronted with a situation not covered by his instructions, should ordinarily be supported. "He says he was left (in one paragraph he names 6 Months) without instructions. If that is so, it is the best defence he has set up,"[3] declared the Duke of Newcastle of Sir George Grey at the end of a famous feud between a governor and the Colonial Office. And the office often found its remoteness to be an advantage, as in the case of the crises on the Victorian goldfields in the 1850s:

> It is perhaps fortunate that the distance between us & Melbourne is so great, for I doubt if the means in the hand of government in this country could be of much service in such a case, & the long interval which must elapse before instructions can be received will force the executive of the Colony to rely on themselves.[4]

Of necessity, then, if not always from choice, the government of colonies was primarily the responsibility of the governor.

The rules of the game were well understood by the players. Had they been capable of being completely realized in practice they would have made for a dull affair, hardly worth the playing. None of the great feuds, such as continually marked the stormy careers of a Grey, a Gordon, or a Lugard, could have taken place. Fortunately there was plenty of room for maneuver. Disagreement could occur over the demarcation between what was "detail" and what was "principle." Had changing conditions in the area really made a set of instructions inapplicable? Did the novelty of the latest crisis really excuse the governor's flying in their face? Or, conversely, should the governor have waited so timidly for new instructions in an emergency that had cried out for the exercise of his initiative? Thus did differences of interpretation, misunderstandings, and

3. Minute on Grey to S. of S., 31 July 1859, CO 48/397.
4. Merivale minute on Latrobe to S. of S., 3 Dec. 1851, CO 309/2.

general lack of clarity happily intervene to prevent the players from putting on a wholly apathetic performance.

The governors and their staffs were essential to the formation and execution of a successful colonial policy. In the age of sail, particularly, they were crucial. Without effective government at the local level the Colonial Office itself might improve or decline, might process its papers quickly or slowly: but the imperial administrative network would simply fail to function.

From an administrative standpoint, as distinguished from analysis of the roles and personalities of particular governors, the "other end" of the process of imperial decision making has received comparatively little attention. What happened to a dispatch from Downing Street? Was it followed to the letter, modified, or ignored? Through what channels did it pass? More important, how did the local government function as a system of administrative communications in regard to the colonial society itself? How did it change and evolve? With a few significant exceptions we know very little about such things. Accounts of the transition to responsible government, for example, have dwelt almost entirely upon problems of principle and personality, neglecting the dimension of the changing bureaucratic system that lay beneath. Many specialized studies of the rich veins of material in various local archives need to be undertaken and published before we can begin to be at all confident of generalizations about how the government of colonies really worked.

The first step must be to find out something about the people. Who were they? What were their origins, their social classes, their levels of education, their connections, their previous occupations? How were they selected? Did they use their colonial appointments as interim stages on the way to something else, or did they regard them as their "careers"? How much interchange was there between the two main segments—the Indian and the colonial—of the imperial service?

The biographical data to be presented here must unfortunately be restricted to governors. To attempt a systematic survey of the subordinate officials—the colonial secretaries, treasurers, auditors, chief justices, etc.—would be an ambitious and an extraordinarily difficult research project in itself. The *Colonial Office Lists* did not begin publication until 1862, and not until the latter part of the century—when the colonial service gained more prestige and began to take itself more seriously—did they begin to contain much biographical information. Only comparatively rarely did lesser imperial servants find their way into the standard biographical sources, while the governors at least are readily accessible.

The lists that were published for parliament from time to time of governors and lieutenant governors (or in some cases administrators or presidents) of colonies and Indian presidencies between 1830 and 1880 contain about 300 names, 262 of whom could be traced in the *Dictionary of National Biography* and other standard biographical sources. Of these exactly half were active or retired military or naval officers, although 28 served but one essentially military appointment in such stations as Malta and Bermuda. The martial flavor of the service was therefore rich, but perhaps not so overwhelming as might have been expected.

In the mid-nineteenth century there was already what seems a surprisingly high degree of professionalism. Only 91 men, including administrators of military stations and governors-general of India, served in just one assignment; whereas 168 could be identified as having risen out of the lower ranks of the service. There was remarkably little interchange between India and the colonies, no more than 50 either moving like Bartle Frere or Charles Metcalfe from the Indian service to a colonial governorship or achieving, like Lord Elgin or William Denison, the colonial governor's dream of an Indian presidency or the governor-generalship. Fifty-nine of them had been involved in politics, the domestic civil service, or the diplomatic corps, while 24 had received legal training. Of those who could be positively identified, 139 were English, 34 were Scottish, and 33 were Irish. They were largely from families of the gentry or the upper middle class, only 21 of them being nobility, while 54 were recorded as having gone to university.[5]

More revealing is a selected list of 37 governors who might be called "hard-core" professionals, the men who, averaging slightly less than 27 years of duty, dominated the mid-nineteenth-century colonial service. Usually presiding, according to the Colonial Office's rule, for no more than six years in any particular location, they moved about over the empire—from palm to pine, from settlement colony to plantation. Sir Henry Barkly, a fairly typical example, came from a West Indian merchant and planter family, was a Conservative M.P. in the early 1840s, and went from British Guiana to Jamaica, Victoria, Mauritius, and the Cape. Sir Hercules Robinson served in seven colonies, his brother William in as many as twelve. The lives of these governors reveal much of the character of imperial administration which they did so much to shape. Only six of them, however—Lord Elgin, Sir Arthur Gordon, Sir George Grey, Sir Edmund Head, Sir Charles Metcalfe, and Sir John Pope-Hennessy—can be said to have received adequate biographical treatment.[6]

5. I have not included lieutenant governors of Canadian provinces after 1867 since they were essentially Canadian rather than British appointments. I shall include here two statistics in which I have little confidence: 137 came from families which I thought could probably be classed as gentry; and 57 were recorded as having gone to public schools. I wish to acknowledge with gratitude the assistance of a Duke graduate student, Wesley Turner, who did much of the work on this tedious project.

6. See J. Morison, *The Eighth Earl of Elgin* (1928); J. Chapman, *The Career of Arthur Hamilton Gordon, First Baron Stanmore, 1829–1912* (Toronto, 1964); J. Rutherford, *Sir George Grey, 1812–1898: A Study in Colonial Government* (1961); D. Kerr, *Sir Edmund Head, A Scholarly Governor* (Toronto, 1954); E. Thompson, *The Life of Charles, Lord Metcalfe* (1937); and J. Pope-Hennessy, *Verandah: Some Episodes in the Crown Colonies, 1867–1889* (New York, 1964).

They were a richly diverse group of individual personalities. Sir Edmund Head and Sir George Bowen were respected classical scholars, Sir William Robinson a musical composer, Sir William Denison an avid collector of seashells, Sir George Grey a pioneer of Polynesian and Bantu anthropology. Pope-Hennessy took to the wilds of Ireland to escape his creditors. Denison worked out a sort of Malthusian population equation, starting with two and allowing for war, disease, and natural disaster, to show that *Genesis* contained a more reliable date for the creation of the earth and the human race than the theories of Lyall and Darwin. Barkly became president of the Royal Geographical Society, Rawson W. Rawson a noted collector of statistics.

Of the 37, thirteen had military backgrounds, and a similar number had begun their careers in subordinate positions in the colonial service. Ten had some legal training, while eleven had been in the domestic civil service, politics, or the diplomatic corps. Only Sir George Anderson, Sir Bartle Frere, and Lord Metcalfe served in India before receiving colonial appointments; whereas seven—Anderson, Sir George Arthur, Elgin, Denison, Sir Henry Pottinger, Sir Gaspard Le Marchant, and Sir Philip Wodehouse—were given the distinction of a high Indian position on the basis of their colonial service. Two—Elgin and the Marquis of Normanby—became governors after they had been raised to the peerage; 28 could be identified as gentry, seven as middle-class. Nineteen had been to university, ten to public schools, six to military academies, and only Frere to Haileybury.

Taken as a whole they were competent and in some cases brilliant administrators. The careers of some—Grey, Gordon, and Pope-Hennessy, for example—amounted to one long conflict with London and with local interests. Others—such as Elgin, Barkly, and Denison—were tactful men who went about their work smoothly and quietly. The personalities and working habits of Elgin and Barkly made them valuable in the delicate transition to responsible government, a situation in which Lord Aberdeen's vain son Arthur Gordon was a misfit. Some of these governors, including a few who have never been closely studied, are of sufficient importance and intrinsic interest to deserve full biographies. All of them need to be examined for what their lives reveal about colonial government in the nineteenth century.

So much for the biographical data. On the matter of selection and reappointment—that is, of patronage—one can be much less precise. A systematic survey would be virtually impossible, for there are no reliable records to speak of. The files of the Colonial office bulge with large numbers of applications, mostly for subordinate positions. Overwhelmingly unsolicited, they were overwhelmingly rejected: a letter to the Colonial Office was simply not the way one went about the business of getting appointed. There is better hunting in the private papers of the secretaries of state, but the evidence there is fragmentary and often inconclusive.

Yet the impression to be derived from a large sampling of this kind of material is that the colonial service was much less a "job," much less "corrupt" than might be supposed from the contemporary novels of a Thackeray or a Trollope. In the absence of examination procedures—which save for some of the eastern colonies the colonial service never adopted [7]—it was of course necessary for a candidate to be brought favorably to the attention of the secretary of state, either through personal acquaintance or through some other personal connection. Appointments were sometimes made for purely political or personal reasons: to find a place for a defeated parliamentary candidate or for "the elder brother of my daughter's fiancé." [8] Such governors, on the other hand, as Sir George Grey, Sir

7. See R. Heussler, *Yesterday's Rulers: The Making of the British Colonial Service* (Syracuse, 1963).

8. Sir Stafford Northcote to Carnarvon, Apr. 1877, quoted in B. Blakely, "The Colonial Office: 1870–1890" (unpublished Ph. D diss., Duke University, 1966), p. 213.

William Denison, and Sir Henry Barkly were personally unknown to the secretaries of state who appointed them, and were attractive more because of ability already demonstrated than because of their connections.

The number of positions actually at the disposal of the secretary of state was far more limited than might be expected. Much of the patronage in individual colonies belonged to the governors: a trend that increased in the mid-nineteenth century as departments in the British government such as the Treasury and the Post Office relaxed their hold and as the Colonial Office itself consciously enlarged the governor's appointments in an attempt to strengthen his local base of power.[9] In the case of appointments requiring technical skill, such as judicial and land-surveying positions, it was difficult to find qualified applicants whether they were well connected or not. Wrote Stephen: "Lawyers who have distinguished themselves here will not go. Those who have been long and unsuccessfully aiming at distinction are seldom fit to send."[10] Moreover, the fact that "Colonial Governorship has become a Profession" severely restricted the number of openings. A glance at the list of selected governors (in the Appendix, pp. 289–300) will show to what extent a few individuals monopolized the best positions. A man might well be selected at the outset of his career for political purposes or for personal reasons. He was retained and promoted, often by an opposing administration, because he had been at least tolerably successful. The Duke of Newcastle apologized to Sidney Herbert, who had requested an appointment for a friend:

> The only chances I am likely to have for *new* men are in the wretchedly paid or unhealthy small places, and in

9. See H. Manning, *British Colonial Government After the American Revolution* (New Haven, 1933), pp. 100–26; and J. Butler, "The Origins of Lord John Russell's Despatch of 1839 on the Tenure of Crown Offices in the Colonies," *Cambridge Historical Journal*, 2 (1928), 248–51.

10. Stephen to Sir George Arthur, 24 Apr. 1829, Arthur Papers, ML–A2164.

> such important Colonies as the Cape—where if I have nobody on my own List good enough to promote I must look in India or elsewhere for someone who has shewn a *spécialité* for the government of mankind.[11]

The importance of the top positions, in which an ineffectual man could cause trouble for a ministry far outweighing any political advantage arising from his appointment; the paucity of qualified applicants; and the great and growing degree of professionalism within the service combined, concluded Lord Grey, "to reduce the number of appointments really at the disposal of Ministers, within limits so narrow as to render the [colonial] patronage an object of no importance as a means of obtaining political support for an Administration." [12]

A colonial governor was more than the queen's representative overseas. There was far more to his job than his correspondence with the Colonial Office, his balancing of the revenue, and his supervision of the local administration. He, and more particularly his wife, had to serve as the leader of colonial society. What, if any, initiative and inspiration were applied to the improvement of public works or standards of living among the aborigines usually came from him. Several biographies—notably James Rutherford's study of Grey, J. K. Chapman's of Gordon, and the thoroughly delightful recent account of Pope-Hennessy by his grandson—permit a rather intimate understanding of the varied activities that made up their subjects' lives. The balls, dinners, and charity bazaars at Government House; the polo and the racing; the interminable personal clashes and frequent scandals that roused such disproportionate amounts of interest in small and isolated societies, were as much a part of the government of colonies as official business.

One governor, Sir William Denison, bears detailed examina-

11. 18 Nov. 1859, Newcastle Papers, NeC 10,889.
12. *Colonial Policy, 1,* 40–41.

tion here if only because he and his wife kept an extensive journal of their experiences in Van Diemen's Land, New South Wales, and Madras. The third son of a Nottinghamshire country gentleman, Sir William had gone to Eton and then to the Royal Military Academy at Woolwich, receiving a commission as an engineer when he was twenty-two. For the next two decades he worked on the Rideau canal in Canada and then at a variety of jobs in England. His first colonial appointment came in 1846 as a result of a routine request by Gladstone to Sir John Burgoyne, inspector-general of fortifications, for a suitable candidate for governor of Van Diemen's Land. Denison's politics did not enter the process at all, and it was actually Gladstone's successor, Lord Grey, who signified the appointment and issued the instructions.

Denison got no allowance beyond his traveling expenses, and had to go into debt for a great many necessities that would be prohibitively expensive in Australia. It was a long and uncomfortable trip around the Cape—Lady Denison would be pleased at the improvement in traveling conditions on her return to England in 1861 via the overland route in Peninsular and Oriental steamers—so that not until January 1847 did they arrive in Hobart Town.

Hobart had then a population of some 66,000, most of whom had been transported and 29,000 of whom were still classed as convicts. The circle of respectable society was therefore small and select. The Denisons set to work to establish themselves in what Sir William found a surprisingly quiet and peaceful environment: people locked their doors and windows in England against thieves, but left them open in Van Diemen's Land. Lady Denison fretted over her social obligations. At her first large dinner party she settled the delicate question of precedence by conferring that honor on the eldest female present, only to discover next day that the lady's reputation was such that she had never been received at Government House before: in Australia one couldn't be too careful; but then one didn't like to ask. The neglect of the builders to provide a ballroom meant that a temporary floor had to be put down every year for that "great leviathan," the celebration of the Queen's birthday, while the shabby state of the house caused her agony on the occasion of the visit of the great man of the Antipodes, and at least formally her husband's superior, Sir Charles FitzRoy from Sydney.

Active and enterprising, the Denisons introduced the "tableau vivant," using some of their large collection of prints as models. Sir William presided over the Australian version of the fox hunt, with kangaroos serving as the prey. His wife visited orphan schools, inspired the establishment of a kindergarten and a "house of refuge" for abandoned women, officiated at bazaars (where she was amused at the universal anxiety that she sit down), and gave a Christmas party for a mixed group of farmers and aborigines. Sir William founded a scientific society, asked friends to send objects of interest for the local museum, and worked hard to present a respectable exhibit from the colony at the Crystal Palace. Later at Sydney he encouraged the introduction of oranges on Pitcairn's Island, and advised the Macarthurs on the quality of their wines. He made available his considerable engineering experience, giving valuable advice on the construction of railroads, canals, docks, and racecourses, and on the improvement and defense of harbors. He conducted expeditions in search of profitable varieties of fish. Both the Denisons liked children—the governor went into ecstasy over a "Punch" he encountered in North Sydney—and entertained large numbers of them frequently.

Denison disapproved of the concession of responsible government to the Australian colonies, rather enjoying the discomfort of the politicians when they were at last confronted with the tedious realities of administration. But, with a minimum of ruffled feelings, he was skillful in conducting smooth relations with responsible ministers. He was happy and comfortable in Hobart and Sydney, generally popular and effective in European settlement colonies. He was never so much at ease in India.

He greeted with mixed emotions his promotion in 1861 to the Madras presidency. It was of course an honor and the salary would be considerably higher, but the unhealthy environment would mean a separation from at least part of his family. On the whole he was pleased that Secretary of State for India Sir Charles Wood had anticipated a favorable response, removing the necessity for a painful decision. He would do as he was bid. Like most governors he thought he would enjoy the degree of freedom that came with a crown colony or an Indian presidency: "I look forward with great pleasure to the idea of having something to do. In these responsible governments one sees much going on which is most objectionable, yet one is powerless either to do good or to prevent evil."

From the egalitarian plainness of Sydney the Denisons suddenly found themselves in oriental luxury. It was all so strange and exciting. The engineer's eye of Sir William examined approvingly their large and magnificent houses, one in Madras and a country home outside the city, and was impressed with the measures that had been taken against the heat. The city house was occupied by no less than two hundred servants: "the house is full of them" he reported; "you have nothing to do but call 'Peon,' and a man is at your elbow at once." As with other Western visitors in India, so much attention made him uncomfortable: "I cannot venture out into the garden or park but a man is sure to see me and rush after me with an umbrella. All this is to me rather a bore; but I suppose I shall get used to it." They soon settled into the usual routine of the British in India:

> We get up in the dark, about five; throw on some clothes, and sally out for a walk or a ride, as the case may be; come in, not later than half-past seven, have a bath, wash and dress; sit at home, working under a punkah, till half-

> past four, when the sun is low enough to allow us to go out without risk; ride or drive till seven; dine at eight; leave the drawing room about ten or half-past.

But they never really adjusted to it.

The Denisons had gone to Van Diemen's Land when Sir William was in his early forties. His Canadian experience had prepared him well for service in another colony of Europeans overseas. Ambitious and eager for novelty, the couple had thrown themselves into the challenge with enthusiasm. Now, fifteen years later, they were no longer so energetic or so amenable to change. Their children had grown up. They gave up dancing. Lady Denison returned to England for a year, leaving her devoted husband miserable. Denison still took an interest in engineering problems, his shell collection, the Darwin controversy, and his library of more than two thousand volumes. His administrative ability may not have suffered from his lack of personal involvement, though the history of his governorship of Madras has not been written.

The government of colonies was not for Denison a good preparation for Indian administration: the problems and the process were different, and the atmosphere of India was uncongenial to him. Aside from south Indian architecture, which he admired, he had no appreciation for its culture. He formed no bond of sympathy or understanding with either the leaders or the masses of the Indian people. His wife made some effort to learn Tamil; the only link with his subjects Sir William himself recorded was through his English-speaking barber. Not until more than a month after his arrival did he take much notice of the appalling conditions in "a portion of the town just in rear of Government House." [13] He traveled extensively, and did far

13. *Varieties of Vice-regal Life, 1,* 497; 2, 29–30, 52. When he did, however, his characteristic reaction was not simply to throw up his hands in horror but to conceive a project for cleansing and draining the gutters.

more on his excursions than hunt tigers. But his years in Madras were not enjoyable.

His posture in post-Mutiny India was conservative, his attitude realistic and frankly pessimistic. England had conquered India by the sword, and by the sword alone could she retain it. It was fanciful to think that Indians felt any affection for their alien rulers. Unlike Bartle Frere, he opposed the idea of gradually bringing educated Indians into the government, confessing that his opinion of them would be lowered still further if they should continue to submit after having once been given a share of power. "I cannot trust the Indian," he told his sister. "I cannot get the truth out of him; and by leaning on him I should come to grief, for not only would the staff break, but the splinters would run into my hand."

Fearful of concessions or change, he yet was cynically critical of the effects of British rule. Little positive impact could be detected. He could write, indeed, that the destruction of local manufactures and the closing of doors to Indian talent were largely responsible for a deterioration in the condition of the people: "I would willingly raise and stimulate the native to exertion [and] give his mental power better scope for action . . . but I confess I do not see my way to this." What little sympathy he had felt at the beginning receded as his years in India went by. Weary and disillusioned, he eagerly awaited his retirement and return to England after nearly twenty years abroad. As he confided to a friend: "To tell you the honest truth, I am tired of the people: they are a hopeless race, hanging upon our hands like a dead weight, which we strive in vain to lift. . . . All talk of educating them, of fitting them for liberty, of teaching them to govern themselves, is the veriest twaddle."[14] He had been a good if not a great governor, practical, conscientious, and resourceful. He came home to publish his journals and his memoirs, to write caustically

14. Ibid., 2, 248, 276–77, 394.

about responsible government in Australia and the colonists' part in the Maori wars in New Zealand, and shortly afterwards to die.

Denison's career illustrates some of the characteristics, some of the strengths as well as some of the weaknesses, of the pattern of British colonial government in the mid-nineteenth century and beyond. Governors were, and were expected to be, "generalists," and it was purely fortuitous that Sir William's engineering training so well qualified him for the technical side of service in young colonial societies that were attempting to develop economically. The contribution which the social leadership exercised by the governor and his wife could make to the success of his political role, an aspect which the Denisons' private letters and journals enable us to perceive so intimately, was certainly typical of any assignment. If anything, however, it was particularly crucial in responsibly governed colonies, where the governor's power was almost entirely a function of his personal influence.[15] Finally, Denison's unhappy experience in India, the result in part of having spent his earlier career in the entirely different setting of European settlement colonies, is by no means an isolated example. The Colonial Office faced a dilemma: if the governor should move too quickly from colony to colony his knowledge of local affairs and his local contacts suffered; if he remained too long he might become a local despot, or he might make so many enemies that the colony would become ungovernable. The six-year rotation was a conscious attempt to find a reasonable compromise between the two extremes.

Assisting or, as so often happened, conflicting with the governors were local bureaucracies that were at least superficially alike in structural form and in functional operation. The governments of British dependencies were supposedly ordered

15. See below (chap. 5) for further discussion of the role of the governor under responsible government.

more or less uniformly according to a set of rules and regulations published by the Colonial Office for the guidance of all branches of the colonial service, spelling out such things as conditions of leave and the forms of due process in the case of removal from office. Each colony had evolved a set of customary procedures of its own, some of which were formally recognized to the extent that they were included in the royal instructions received by the governor at the beginning of his term.[16] In their broader outlines, however, there was enough real or imagined similarity among local administrations to enable reasonably coherent books to be written on the subject of the forms and processes of colonial government.

The governor ruled with the advice of his executive council, an institution whose membership included the chief justice (who ranked next to the governor in precedence) and such other officials as the colonial secretary, treasurer, and attorney general. An advisory body that could be overruled by the governor, whose responsibility and authority were supreme, the council was supposed to consider all questions of importance. Its members were free to entertain whatever opinions they liked, but they were expected to uphold the governor's decisions and (a matter that was hotly disputed in several cases) to support them in the legislative council. If the governor's relations with his subordinates were smooth the council could be expected to lend weight to his measures and to act as a sounding board for his opinions.[17] If not, they could cause him a great deal of trouble, even after the Russell decision of 1839 that colonial officers held their positions at pleasure. And, of course, the relative power of the governor and his council varied greatly from place to place, as well as from time to time.[18]

Although the chief justice outranked him in precedence the

16. See J. Beaglehole, "The Royal Instructions to Colonial Governors, 1783–1854: A Study in British Colonial Policy," *Bulletin of the Institute of Historical Research*, 7 (1930), 184–87.

17. A. Bertram, *The Colonial Service* (Cambridge, 1930), pp. 22–25.

18. Manning, *British Colonial Government*, pp. 418 ff.

colonial secretary (sometimes called the chief or civil secretary) was in practice the leading official after the governor. He was the real head of the bureaucracy, and normally assumed the government in the absence of the governor. John Montagu, for example, ran the civil government in Cape Town for long stretches during Kaffir wars when governors were conducting military operations hundreds of miles from the capital.[19] The colonial secretary was the leader of the legislative council, responsible for presenting and defending the measures of the government there. He was normally the effective link between the governor and the colonists: petitioners were supposed to go through him to the governor, and only from thence to the secretary of state, while proclamations published in the colonial gazette usually carried his signature. As the leading administrative officer he was responsible for the efficient operation of the various subordinate departments; recommendations for promotion or disciplinary action of the clerical staff went through him.

No systematic biographical survey can be attempted here, but it is probably correct to say that colonial secretaries came from much the same origins and moved in much the same social circles as the governors. From Van Diemen's Land Sir William Denison carried on a lively private correspondence with Sir Edward Deas Thomson, the colonial secretary of New South Wales—which is more than he did with Sir Charles FitzRoy, the governor of that colony and his nominal superior. Clearly regarding each other as equals, Denison and Deas Thomson frankly discussed the demise of the convict system and the approach of responsible government, and exchanged potatoes for oranges and lemons.[20] Indeed, the colonial secretary normally

19. See W. Newman, *Biographical Memoir of John Montagu* (1855), and A. Fryer, "The Government of the Cape of Good Hope, 1825–1854: The Age of Imperial Reform," *Archives Year Book for South African History*, pt. 1 (1964), pp. 55–69.

20. Denison to Deas Thomson, 21 Mar. 1853, Deas Thomson Papers, ML–A1531.

bore much the same relationship to the governor that the permanent undersecretary in the Colonial Office bore to the secretary of state. Usually serving a maximum of six years in any one colony before moving on, governors came and went; colonial secretaries stayed. Permanent holders of office unless they were removed by the secretary of state, to whom they owed their initial appointment, colonial secretaries helped to provide continuity and the local knowledge not possessed at least at first by their superiors.

Alongside or beneath the colonial secretary in the local establishment were a number of other permanent appointees: the treasurer and auditor, the clerk of the executive and legislative councils, the chief justice and attorney general (and possibly a solicitor general as well), and probably a surveyor. The same sorts of comments apply to them as to the colonial secretary: which is to say that nearly everything depended on their personalities. Such a man as William Porter, attorney general at the Cape Colony, could build an exceedingly high reputation not only with successive governors but in London as well.[21] Finally, the local "establishment" included bishops of the established church, who often served (as Samuel Marsden did in New South Wales) as magistrates in addition to their more strictly clerical duties.

Although the practice varied with custom and usage from colony to colony, the Colonial Office's regulations with respect to the division of patronage were fairly precise. In the case of offices carrying salaries up to £100 a year the governor made the appointments, having only to report the names to the secretary of state. For positions up to £200 he was to report the existence of a vacancy and the qualifications of the man he had chosen provisionally to fill it, his recommendations being "almost uniformly followed." The same course was to be pursued for offices above £200, "but it must be distinctly understood

21. Fryer, "Cape Government," pp. 70–82.

that the Secretary of State has the power of recommending another instead."[22]

Because the governor was a transient placed atop a corps of permanent officials, because he not they normally served as the most convenient focal point of local discontent,[23] and because in a small and claustrophobic community there was so little else to do by way of amusement, the governor was usually at odds with one or more of his subordinates. The Colonial Office's files are brimming with whole volumes of evidence of disputes that lasted in some cases for several decades. So frequent, indeed, were the charges and countercharges that the Colonial Office had perforce evolved an explicit procedure for them. The governor had to communicate in writing to the offending official the charge and the grounds for it, the officer's reply having to be in writing as well. If the reply were unsatisfactory the governor might require the officer to defend himself both orally and in writing before the executive council. Should the decision there be for suspension the governor might then appoint a provisional holder of the office, but the whole affair along with the usually voluminous supporting documents had to be submitted to the secretary of state. And in the Colonial Office the papers were read with what might seem to be a surprising degree of care with regard both to legality and expediency.

Important as the local bureaucracy undoubtedly was, it would be an easy mistake to estimate its role too highly, especially in the period before the attainment of responsible government. Much of the business was transacted at Government House by the governor and his private secretary alone, with little or no reference to any other administrative agency. Thus

22. Colonial Office, *Rules and Regulations for Her Majesty's Colonial Service* (1856), pp. 20–21.

23. One reason why Montagu was so popular with successive governors of the Cape was that he allowed himself to bear much of the brunt of local opinion, leaving the governors relatively unscathed. Fryer, "Cape Government," pp. 62–63.

the student who has the opportunity to work in local archives may be surprised at the degree to which he must continue to consult the series of governors' dispatches, which are often the most complete and continuous record of the most routine transactions. In some instances this is to be explained by the failure to preserve certain kinds of departmental correspondence, but in others such material simply never existed outside Government House.

To go much beneath the comparison of the more obvious differences and similarities, to make that crucial step from the description of machinery to the analysis of how colonial bureaucracies worked, is a difficult task that has rarely been attempted. For of course what uniformity existed in the governments of colonies was only superficial. Each was a system of individuals and communications that had a life and a dynamic of its own.

The study of colonial institutions must deal not only with their transfer but with their transformation.[24] The basic administrative structures of the nineteenth-century empire had been evolved over the course of the experience of government in the preceding century and a half in the American colonies, and they were exported from the center as dependencies were added one by one. In such "new societies" as Australia, though it did not take place all at once, the process of transfer was at first a comparatively simple one. Where governments already existed, as at the Cape or in such traditional societies as Ceylon (or even in West Africa, for every society no matter how primitive has a "government" in the functional sense [25]) there was a blend of institutions from the beginning. After the initial period there was additional borrowing—new law, for example—from the center, which was itself an evolving mecha-

24. D. Lerner, "The Transformation of Institutions," in W. Hamilton, ed., *The Transfer of Institutions* (Durham, N.C., 1964), pp. 3–58.

25. See G. Almond, "A Functional Approach to Comparative Politics," in Almond and J. Coleman, eds., *The Politics of Developing Areas* (Princeton, 1960), pp. 3–64.

nism and therefore a source of new structures and practices. But the focus shifted to the interaction between the imported institutions and the local environment in which they seeded, grew, and changed.

How is such a complicated problem to be approached? How is the process of transfer and transformation of colonial government to be systematically studied? Two practical strategies suggest themselves, both of which employ the case method.

One is to isolate a single subject that must be a fundamental concern to any government—land, education, finance, defense—and trace its evolution over a relatively long period in one colony or preferably, since comparison is useful, in more than one. Since the subject is a "touchstone," institutions will eventually evolve to deal with it even if they do not exist formally in the early stages. As the government progresses and enlarges, as its functional center moves from Government House in much the same way as it moved from the household of the medieval English kings, the various administrative agencies that related in some way to the chosen problem can be perceived and analyzed in a substantive context.[26] Bureaucratic machinery need not be merely described, as it were, in a vacuum, for it is always seen at work. This method has the further advantage of enabling the student to observe one aspect of the imperial policy-making process in all its dimensions, both in London and in the colony. He can therefore trace the interaction of individuals and communications over time and space that is the essence of the process of decision making.

Two recent studies of colonial land policy, one centered in Australia and the other in the Cape Colony,[27] have followed

26. For a recent example of how this method can be fruitfully employed as a basis for the systematic study of administrative change, see O. MacDonagh, *A Pattern of Government Growth, 1800–1860: The Passenger Acts and their Enforcement* (1961).

27. See P. Burroughs, *Britain and Australia, 1831–1855: A Study in Imperial Relations and Crown Lands Administration* (Oxford, 1967), and L. Duly, *British Land Policy at the Cape, 1795–1844: A Study of Administrative Procedure in the Empire* (Durham, N.C., 1968).

this strategy with considerable success, arriving at very similar conclusions. Focusing on the problem of how the ideas on land settlement of Edward Gibbon Wakefield and the Colonial Reformers worked into the formation and execution of imperial policy, these two writers have detected a fundamental lack of effective communication between local and imperial authorities. In the first place local conditions quite as much as the pressure of ideology made the revision of land regulations a necessity, though ideology played the larger share in shaping the policy that was at first adopted. Yet, because Wakefield's theories were in fact inapplicable where intensive agriculture on the British model was unsuitable, the Ripon land regulations of 1831 were never really put into effect. In Australia the squatters, who held powerful positions in colonial society and politics, remained in possession of the land they already occupied; unpaid quitrents mounted and turned into uncollectable debts that were eventually written off. The regulations may have retarded the rate of settlement to some extent, and this was one of the objects Wakefield had in mind, but they had none of the expected long-term benefits he anticipated. At the Cape too there was a breakdown of machinery: land surveys in arrears, orders from London ignored or "put by," required reports left unsubmitted. In short, the Ripon regulations failed in both cases for want of implementation.

The conclusion to be drawn from these two studies is that effective imperial policy making required a high degree of communication between local and imperial authorities, and that on this extremely fundamental issue—for what could be more central in a colonial society than the land question?—such harmonious interaction simply did not exist. One wonders, of course, whether this pattern of faulty communication is not in fact the norm: whether the hypothesis of smoothly working imperial bureaucracy would ever be fully sustained under the skeptical scrutiny of systematic investigation. The conclusions of these two writers, at any rate, are essentially negative. They explain, and very satisfactorily, how something did not work: but that is still a stride away from explaining how something *did*.

For our own purposes it seemed better to adopt an alternative strategy: that of attempting to analyze the changing character of a colonial bureaucracy as a whole within a fairly limited period. For this case study the government of New South Wales was selected in the period roughly spanning 1820–60. This project resolved itself in turn into two focal points: the formative governorship of Sir Ralph Darling, 1825–31, and the transition to responsible government under Sir William Denison, 1855–61. The first of these two segments will be presented here, as an illustration of the working of a colonial bureaucracy, the second in a later chapter on the working of responsible government.[28]

When the administrative history of the colony of New South Wales comes to be written its primary theme will be the evolution of the rudimentary government of a comparatively uncomplicated community of convicts and their keepers into the more sophisticated bureaucratic machinery required to serve the more diverse and demanding needs of a society of free citizens. There will of course be other themes. One will concern the continuing process of borrowing and transfer, as civilian institutions became progressively more applicable than the essentially military structure with which the colonial government began. Another will be the establishment and eventual breakdown of the lines of communication of an Australian empire within an empire, this one being directed from Sydney, and the growth within it of increasingly independent centers of administrative authority at Hobart, Adelaide, Melbourne, and Brisbane. But the administrative changes that attended the transition from convict to representative to responsible government will command most of the attention.

28. See below, chap. 5.

Although the establishment of the institutions of Australian government began even before the landing of the first convict ships at Botany Bay, a logical and convenient starting point for this brief enquiry is the publication in 1822–23 of the famous report of Commissioner Bigge.[29] For that investigator, thoughtful and meticulous as he was, compiled an analysis so thorough that it is still being mined for its insight into the early history of Australia. He subjected to critical scrutiny most of what mattered: the conditions in the prisons and the convict ships, the assignment system, the nature and functioning of the judicial establishment, and the state and prospects of agriculture and trade. That he had little to say about the mode of operation of the government is not particularly surprising. For so long as Australian society was small and virtually single-directional, so long as it remained devoted almost entirely to the maintenance and discipline of convicts, not much governing was needed.

The colony that was investigated by Commissioner Bigge had, indeed, but 24,000 inhabitants, of whom less than 10 per cent were free immigrants or their children. Most of these, again, were linked to the convict establishment in some way. Small and simple, the society remained backward: cows still grazed in the main street of Sydney, and the treasurer kept the public money in his bedroom with his own.[30]

The structure and functions of the government corresponded closely to the state of the society it served. The governor himself, assisted by a private secretary and two clerks, carried on much of the routine business in addition to conducting virtually unaided the correspondence with the Colonial Office and other departments in London. His dispatches contain large quantities of information that can be found nowhere else in the government archives. The only administrative agencies

29. PP. 1822 (448), XX; 1823 (33, 136), X.

30. Report of the Board to consider the Treasury, 14 June 1826, N.S.W., Gov's Minutes and Memoranda, 4/990.

of any size were the colonial secretary's department, which contained fourteen clerks, and that of the surveyor general, whose strength was about equal. There was also a judicial establishment containing two judges, an attorney general (the solicitor general's position having been vacant for a number of years), and a dozen clerical and legal assistants. The other departments—including those of the treasurer, auditor, naval officer, surveyor of distilleries, post office, collector of revenue, office of roads and bridges, and so forth—were all a good deal smaller, carrying on with two or three clerks apiece.[31] This small government was overwhelmingly oriented toward the convicts. In the colonial secretary's department, for example, most of the clerks were habitually employed in the preparation of "indents" from lists of convicts as they arrived, in keeping track of their later movements and their changes in status, and in answering requests about them, usually from relatives at home concerning the disposal of property. The public works departments existed quite as much to keep convicts suitably occupied as to further the objects of their labor. Early New South Wales was an outdoor prison, and its government had been consciously built to keep it going.

What happened socially, economically, and politically in the three decades after Bigge's report has been ably described by Australian historians. Continued transportation, that went on until the early forties, and the growing stream of free immigration swelled the population of New South Wales to nearly 190,000 by 1850: within another decade the convict element had been swamped by immigration and the generational turnover. What in the early twenties had been an infant pastoral industry boomed into a thriving export trade, able to support the development of a sizable service sector and the rude beginnings of manufacturing. The society began to take on the urban character which it has ever since maintained. Political

31. Schedule of Fixed Civil Establishment, 1 Apr. 1827, N.S.W., Col. Sec. Special Bundles, 4/6305–06. (Hereafter cited as CSSB.)

development occurred, the base of advancing democracy being the city, featuring the growth of a colonial opposition to government that centered its agitation on such issues as the acquisition of the jury system and of representative institutions, the exercise of a free press, and most of all on the abolition of the system of transportation of convicts which had been the very raison d'être of the colony's existence. By the time of the gold rushes of the early fifties, the society of New South Wales and of Australia generally had survived the formative period of its history.[32]

One of the principal focal points of this period of development and growth has frequently been seen in the governorship of Sir Ralph Darling, 1825–31, primarily because it was he who first confronted the sustained agitation and opposition that rose under the dynamic leadership of W. C. Wentworth. In the far-flung reverberations of the celebrated Sudds-Thompson case (an incident involving two soldiers who died in irons while undergoing punishment) historians have detected a significant quickening of the tempo of politics. It was never quite the same again. There had been friction and opposition before, but not of such sustained and well-organized intensity.

The Darling-Wentworth feud has usually been written about, and the emphasis has by no means been misplaced, in terms of personalities. But it has also been perceived as the overt and dramatic reflection of a more profound transition that was going on underneath. Darling and Wentworth represented, as it were, opposing forces that were conflicting for control of the Australian society's future. There is, however, a dimension of this period of change to which but little attention has been given: the beginnings under Darling of

32. See particularly F. Crowley, "The Foundation Years, 1788–1821," in G. Greenwood, ed., *Australia, A Social and Political History* (Sydney, 1955); C. Clark, *A History of Australia,* vol. 1 (Melbourne, 1962); A. Shaw, *Convicts and the Colonies* (1966); and M. Roe, *Quest for Authority in Eastern Australia, 1835–1851* (Melbourne, 1965).

the development of a government bureaucracy equipped to deal with the increasingly complicated and sophisticated society that was emerging so rapidly, a development to which the rise of Wentworth bore testimony.

Trouble was freely predicted for Darling. The son of a sergeant major, he had joined an infantry regiment in the West Indies, becoming aide-de-camp to a general and participating in the Peninsular campaign. From 1811 until 1823 he had commanded the troops in Mauritius, where he had also administered the government for eighteen months. His wife was a colonel's daughter. His background, then, was thoroughly military, while his fairly humble origins may have given him a feeling of inferiority as he made his way up the ladder of an officer corps composed so largely of his social betters. He was, at any rate, stiffly formal. Wrote James Stephen: "I believe him to be a very honourable man possessing a sound & just understanding but with little reach of thought or variety of knowledge, inexorably stiff in his manners & I suspect a great formalist in business & a perfect martinet in military discipline." [33] From Lincoln's Inn, John Macarthur's son provided a similar analysis:

> His manners are so cold and repulsive that it would be difficult to become intimate with him. He evidently mistakes formality for dignity. . . . The manner, for I believe it is little else, is not, however, to be shaken off, whatever be his inclinations . . . and I foresee that whether he be so or not, he will, at least, be considered extremely proud & haughty. . . . He will be rigid in requiring the despatch of all official business, and strict attention on the part of the Govt. officers to their particular duties.[34]

33. Stephen to Arthur, n.d. [1825], Arthur Papers, ML–A2164.
34. John Macarthur, Jr. to John Macarthur, London, 12 June 1835, Macarthur Papers, ML–A2911.

Appointed to assist Darling as colonial secretary was Alexander MacLeay, a retired former secretary to the transport board. Together they were being sent out—Stephen called it a revolution in Australian politics—to replace Sir Thomas Brisbane and Major Frederick Goulburn, who by all accounts contemporary and recent had done singularly little to distinguish themselves.

The consequences of the insinuation of Sir Ralph Darling's coldly formal personality, with its emphasis on rigid military discipline, into the political atmosphere of New South Wales, is a matter of fairly notorious record. What is not so generally recognized is his role as a generator of administrative change. Administration was a subject that interested the governor and, particularly in the comparatively calm early years of his regime, the attempt to improve it occupied him quite as much as did political controversy.

Darling's campaign for reform began at once, for he was truly shocked by what he found. "Every department," he told the secretary of state, "appeared to act for itself, without Check or Control: and indeed without any apparent responsibility." Money was being drawn and spent without authority or vouchers. Contracts were being agreed upon without ever being put into writing. "In short the common routine and forms of Office were totally neglected." [35]

He set to work. He attacked what had apparently become an habitual laxity in regard to the observance of regulations. He reminded civil officers that only members of the executive council were authorized to wear uniform. From an Indian newspaper it appeared that the principal surgeon was engaged in private trade: let him be directed to report on this breach of regulations.[36] He ordered that proper requisitions must be submitted for office supplies of fuel, oil, and candles, along

35. Secret and Conf., 2 Feb. 1826, CO 201/171.

36. Minutes of 28 Jan. and 8 Feb. 1826, Minutes and Memoranda, 4/990.

with detailed accounts of the number of rooms to be lighted and heated. Heads of departments were told to communicate with each other in writing, instead of arranging business orally: "Their communications are to be concise and no unnecessary matter [is to] be introduced" into them.[37] Reflecting his military background he formed numerous investigating boards: to inquire, for example, into the state of the Bank of New South Wales. A board for general purposes prepared reports on the advisability of conferring the exclusive rights to government printing on one establishment and on the expense of starting a semiofficial government gazette; on the treasurer's claim for compensation for the use of his private residence as an office; on the salaries and qualifications of clerks. The civil engineer was directed to make a careful survey of the state of repair of all public buildings. It was a general and thorough shake-up.

Setting his sights on the more regular and efficient operation of government departments, the governor attempted to raise the prestige of the service by gradually bringing to an end the employment of convicts and emancipists as clerks, a practice which though necessary in the past had "degraded the offices by placing individuals in them who had forfeited every claim to character."[38] (This particular measure, however, was for some time difficult to put into effect: the ablest clerk in the colonial secretary's department, for example, was an emancipist.) To the same end he approved a general increase in salaries and a system of examinations (chiefly in regard to handwriting), and ordered probationary periods for clerks entering the service. He made every department head conduct a survey of the duties and productivity of members of his staff, and after careful study he "fixed" and in some cases reduced the various establishments.

The most important of his measures, however, was his effort

37. Memorandum of 8 Mar. 1827, ibid., 4/983.
38. Darling to S. of S., 20 July 1826, CO 201/172.

to streamline the government and particularly the department of the colonial secretary. As he explained in a lengthy minute, the circumstances of the society had been altering rapidly and the government must perforce change with it:

> When New South Wales was merely a Penal Settlement, the details connected with the management of the Prisoners were the objects which principally claimed the attention of the Government. But the character of the Colony has undergone a Material Change, and the attention of the Colonial Secretary may be advantageously directed to other matters, without his relinquishing that control which it is so important should be vested in his office, over the conduct of the Prisoners.

In Darling's view the time and energies of members of the colonial secretary's department were too much wasted by routine busywork: preparing indents and muster rolls, investigating the applications in regard to land and the employment of convicts, approving convict marriages, compiling the annual "blue book," and so forth. Such duties could be better handled by the departments to which they properly belonged. The superintendent of convicts, for example, should answer all requests for information about them, and should prepare the indents, sending copies to be filed in the colonial secretary's office. He could also approve convict marriages. The surveyor general was the proper authority to settle land claims. The blue book should be a cooperative effort, compiled by the pertinent departments.

Thus, instead of being a mere catchall for routine work, the colonial secretary's department would become the chief executive department of the government. It would exercise a role rather analogous to the Gladstonian conception of the place of the Treasury's place in the British system. It would devote itself to matters of general concern to the government of the whole colony, directing, checking, and controlling the carrying out of details by the subordinate departments:

> It is not enough that Orders are issued, or regulations made. There must be an immediate controlling power somewhere; and, under the Governor, it is the special and indispensable duty of the Colonial Secretary to see that all orders and regulations are properly followed up and carried into effect—and that they are not, by the supineness of others, allowed to remain a dead letter.[39]

Darling's devotion to administrative reform maintained this high degree of intensity for about two years, after which his zeal somewhat declined. As he confessed as early as November 1827 the exertion of trying to fashion anew the whole government, necessitating as it did an extraordinary amount of personal attention to detail, was a strain on his health.[40] He put himself on a rigid time schedule, making himself available to subordinate officials only at strictly specified times.[41] He probably grew weary of the constant struggle against bureaucratic inertia. And the feuds with Wentworth, Judge John Stephen (cousin of the permanent undersecretary), and others, as they gathered momentum, sapped his energy and his spirit still further. The governor's administrative minutes appeared less frequently, and then dwindled almost to the vanishing point. The burst of creative enthusiasm was over.

The immediate effects of Darling's efforts were neither so rapid nor so profound as he had hoped. For the government was not in fact purged of laxity and inefficiency, and it continued to be heavily oriented toward the management of convicts. It lagged behind the pace of development of the society

39. Minute of 10 Oct. 1827, Minutes and Memoranda, 4/991.
40. Darling to R. W. Hay, pvt., 1 Nov. 1827, CO 201/184.
41. Memorandum of 7 Feb. 1829, Minutes and Memoranda, 4/985.

as a whole. It was simply not equipped, for example, to implement the Ripon land regulations (an observation that would apply to the Cape with equal force).[42] A survey made in 1831 of the colonial secretary's department revealed that routine work, much of which had already supposedly been transferred to other offices, was badly in arrears. Darling, by this time having all but given up on reform, merely tried to force the clerks to work harder.[43]

The reshaping of the government of New South Wales from the inefficient, heavily convict-oriented administration of the 1820s to the relatively sophisticated administration that existed when the colony adopted responsible government in the late 1850s was the work not of a few years but of several decades. Most of the credit for that substantial transformation properly belongs to Sir Edward Deas Thomson, the extremely masterful colonial secretary who replaced MacLeay in 1836. It was he who in practice made the government the effective instrument of the altered society that Darling had envisioned. Much of Darling's reform remained for his own time at least a "dead letter." His primary achievement was to establish in New South Wales the ideal of a hierarchically arranged colonial government that was controlled and directed by an executive department at its center. As James Macarthur was later to remember,[44] this centralized bureaucratic structure was primarily the creation of Darling, institutionalized after him with but little basic addition by Deas Thomson. No decisive change occurred until the transition to responsible government: in the meantime it merely got better.

Sir Ralph Darling presided over a crucially formative period in the administrative history of New South Wales. His nega-

42. See Burroughs, *Britain and Australia,* and Duly, *Cape Land Policy.*

43. Memoranda of MacLeay, 21 May 1831, CSSB 2/1844, and Darling, 18 June 1831, Minutes and Memoranda, 4/1005.

44. James Macarthur to Stuart Donaldson, 5 July 1856, Macarthur Papers, ML–A2923. It should be noted that Macarthur was not speaking favorably of the system.

tive role in the struggle against Wentworth needs to be somewhat balanced. For he created, in his own mind and in his minute books if not immediately or fully in practice, what might well be regarded as a prototype of the structure and operation of the government of colonies.

PART II

The "Revolution" in the Second Empire

The normal current of colonial history is
the perpetual assertion of the
right of self-government.
C. B. Adderley

3: The Coming of Responsible Government

It needs no change in the principles of government, no invention of a new constitutional theory, to supply the remedy which would, in my opinion, completely remove the existing political disorders.
Lord Durham

In the three decades after 1840, as in other eras, a fairly sizable minority of Englishmen engaged in speculative argument about the character of their overseas empire and the future of their country's relations with it. The participants in this debate expessed themselves in books, pamphlets, reviews in periodicals, parliamentary speeches, and correspondence. Some of them were pessimistic, thinking that imperial ties must inevitably disintegrate. Others believed or hoped that somehow those bonds would endure or even grow stronger. There were other questions: the growing fads of racism and "survival of the fittest" lent themselves readily to the multiracial imperial setting; and a persistent argument revolved around the subject of land distribution in new societies. But the most vexing problem of all was that of colonial self-government.

Colonies, in the famous metaphor of Turgot and Josiah Tucker, became in time like ripe fruit, and in nature they dropped off the vine. Children grew up to manhood and left the household of their parents. Such metaphors on closer examination revealed other difficulties: What made some colonies ripen more rapidly than others? How could the quality of ripeness be detected? How was one supposed to treat a colony that was ripening but not yet mature? And if separation from the imperial vine was, indeed, inevitable, how could it be caused to happen so as not to harm the vine in the rending or the fruit in the falling?

The mid-nineteenth-century debate on colonial questions has already been subjected to a good deal of scholarly investigation. Enough has been written, in fact, to permit it to be divided into two schools. There is a traditional interpretation, closely following in many instances the analyses that were made by contemporaries. And there has recently been a general upsetting and, in some aspects, a replacement by a revisionist body of opinion.

Until the last few years the period between 1830 and 1870 was commonly characterized as one of pessimism and lack of interest in the empire, sharply differing from the climates of optimistic imperialism that came before and after. Why so many scholars should have concerned themselves so much about so little was never made entirely clear. Labels were applied: it was an age of "Little Englandism," or an age of "anti-imperialism." The British appetite for territory had been satiated, and the nation rested for a while. Instead of trying to join her colonies together in some sort of imperial unity, Britain treated her overseas possessions as a collection of encumbrances of which the proprietors merely wished to rid themselves as speedily as possible. No more was wanted and, except in India, very little was taken; little concern was felt about keeping the jewels already in the crown. The imperial ties endured only because the colonies chose to retain them after the mother country had given up on them. Not until the 1870s—Disraeli's Crystal Palace speech usually being singled out as the foremost landmark—and after the colonies had made their unexpected choice, did this attitude of withdrawal change. When the transformation of the pessimistic climate of opinion came it did so quickly, providing the energy which thrust Great Britain outward in a great wave of expansion called the "new imperialism."

Modern historians distrust such neatly drawn divisions between one period and another, and a number of scholars have strongly attacked this traditional interpretation. India and her dependencies had always been regarded as an exception—the traditional historians were merely following the usage of contemporaries. Now it was argued not that India was "the exception which proved the rule," but that any theory of imperial history that left out India must simply be inadequate and incomplete. It has been asserted that "Little Englandism" was a term of derision to be employed against one's opponents, not one to be warmly embraced as a rallying cry. It has been demonstrated that far too much of the traditional interpretation rested upon such flimsy evidence as one quotation drawn from one personal letter of one irate Chancellor of the Exchequer.[1] Palmerston, an aggressive foreign secretary and popular prime minister, has been stressed as the foremost spokesman of the age, replacing Cobden and Bright who never held responsible positions of administrative power. Indeed, the "myth of Little Englandism," as John S. Galbraith has called it, has been rather effectively demolished. And in the brilliant account of Robinson and Gallagher the mid-nineteenth century has become not the nadir of imperial activity but the finest hour.[2]

The traditional interpretation contained other implausible assumptions and contradictions. Contemporaries often complained that there was little interest in colonial matters. The traditional school took this contention at face value, although their own amply documented footnotes listing contemporary publications flew in its face. A politician who frequently ex-

1. S. Stembridge, "Disraeli and the Millstones," *Journal of British Studies*, 5 (1965), 122–39

2. J. S. Galbraith, "Myths of the Little England Era," *American Historical Review*, 67 (1961), 34–48; R. Robinson and J. Gallagher, *Africa and the Victorians: The Official Mind of Imperialism* (1961).

pressed "separatist" or "pessimistic" opinions—to adopt Carl A. Bodelsen's terminology[3]—cannot be accurately described as uninterested. Cobden was not unconcerned about colonies: they were a bread-and-butter issue. The traditional school, again following the statements of contemporaries, emphasized that colonial debates were usually poorly attended, instead of asking why such esoteric subjects as a new constitution for a handful of settlers halfway round the world from their own constituents should have been discussed at length by members of the British parliament at all.

A minority, then, but a relatively substantial and very articulate minority, concerned itself with colonial questions in general, and with the most perplexing problem of colonial self-government in particular. Within this minority, what broad groupings can be identified? What currents of thought were drawn upon? How were arguments usually couched? What analogies were commonly employed? What was really being argued about? Most important, what assumptions did the participants hold in common? Enough has been written to make unnecessary the kind of detailed examination that would easily make a book in itself. Some sort of discursive analysis must, however, precede an account of how responsible self-government was introduced into the British Empire of the mid-nineteenth century and how it worked.

In a sense, of course, much of the debate had been predetermined or at least strongly influenced by the events of the pre-

3. C. Bodelsen, *Studies in Mid-Victorian Imperialism* (reprinted 1960). See also K. Knorr, *British Colonial Theories, 1570–1850* (Toronto, 1944), and R. Schuyler, *The Fall of the Old Colonial System: A Study in British Free Trade, 1770–1870* (New York, 1945). It must be added that not all earlier writers adopted this interpretation. W. Morrell, *British Colonial Policy in the Age of Peel and Russell* (Oxford, 1930), argued instead that a "new imperialism" began with the wave of emigration in the second quarter of the nineteenth century, an interpretation which therefore stressed the continuity of imperial development.

vious century. The American Revolution stood out as the great "formative" period in the history of the empire. The issue of colonial self-government had already been fought out—not exactly for all time, as later events in South Africa, India, and even Rhodesia were to reveal—but with enough of an impact so that no Englishman could ever again confront a nation struggling to be free in quite the same way. The struggling nation might, indeed, be resisted, but the Englishman who did it had to shake himself free of the parallel, convincing himself that the case in question was somehow different from the American analogy.

It is quite true that the British did not "learn the lessons" of the American Revolution. They did not learn that colonies were valueless. Even the increase in trade with the former colonies after the revolutionary war, a trend which strongly reinforced the anti-mercantilist arguments of Adam Smith, did not diminish the pace of imperial activity and territorial accumulation throughout the world. And it is also true that the immediate policy toward the remaining possessions was to increase, not to relax, the degree of imperial control.[4] It would even be correct to assert that, if the analogy of the American Revolution was a powerful influence upon the minds of British statesmen and administrators in the mid-nineteenth century, it was acknowledged with surprising infrequency.

It might be plausibly argued, in fact, that little or nothing was learned from history, and that so far as later imperial history is concerned the American war might as well not have happened. Repeatedly, throughout the nineteenth and twentieth centuries, the British were caught unprepared by what seemed to be a sudden emergence of colonial nationalism. When a policy of conciliation was adopted at all, it was often

4. The thesis of H. Manning, *British Colonial Government after the American Revolution* (New Haven, 1933). See also V. Harlow, *The Founding of the Second British Empire, 1763–1793* (2 vols., 1952–56).

done grudgingly and on an ad hoc basis. When history was invoked, it was Lord Durham and not Franklin or Jefferson to whom appeals were usually made.

This interpretation would certainly accord with the evidence a good deal better than the view that the American Revolution directly transformed the mother country and, when the time was right, her later empire.[5] But it would seem to be greatly oversimplified and overstated. An analogy may not be expressed in a conversation for the good reason that it is not in the minds of those who are talking. But historians as well as psychoanalysts have long realized that the unstated is often more essential to an argument than the stated, that the implicit is the foundation of the explicit.

The Durham Report may well have provided the most powerful analogy for later recommendations of concession. It did not of course do so in the case of the Durham Report itself. What served as *its* precedent? A detailed analysis of the intellectual origins of that document—and despite several editions a study along the lines of Carl Becker's of the Declaration of Independence has not yet been written—would probably reveal that several explicitly identifiable currents of thought had been drawn upon. The lessons of the American Revolution are not among them. But, again, the absence in their writing of any careful comparison of the American situation in, say, the 1760s with the Canadian one in the 1830s may or may not stand as evidence that the parallel did not occur to Durham, Wakefield, and Buller.

The analogy certainly occurred to Stephen. In the 1820s he wrote, rather whimsically, to his friend Governor Arthur in Van Diemen's Land: "Be good children & dutiful & quarrel with us as little as you can help & we will be very tender & considerate parents. Young folks like you will grow big & un-

5. A Burt, *The Evolution of the British Empire and Commonwealth, From the American Revolution* (Boston, 1956), pp. 3 ff. See also R. Coupland, *The American Revolution and the British Empire* (1930).

ruly & we have at least learnt that it is to no purpose to use the rod . . . after our children have grown to men's estate."[6] By 1835, however, he was not so sure. For he complained to Lord Howick of the conduct in Upper Canada of Sir Francis Bond Head, who seemed to him "as stout as ever Mr. Grenville or Lord North were of old."[7]

Parallels with American colonial history were frequently, though not altogether accurately, invoked by members of the Mills committee of 1861 on colonial military expenditure to show that British colonies had not always been so dependent on the mother country as were New Zealand and the Cape Colony. From the rhetoric of such politicians as Sir William Molesworth and Lord John Russell can be pieced together most of the general thesis of such American historians as Bancroft.[8] But perhaps Gladstone put it best:

> They should recollect what might be cast on them by the events of the American Revolution [sic]. They should look to the time which might arise when these colonies should assert, he hoped with every regard to the mother country, that they were then suited by Providence for the management of their own affairs. Difficulties might attend the crisis, and modern history did not furnish them with instances of a mother country allowing her colonies to declare themselves independent. He was not very sanguine for the future; but when these new States came to be launched into the world, it was of the greatest importance that they should have amongst themselves the elements of good constitutions. In the United States, foolish and wicked as in other respects the conduct of this country might have been, we founded good institutions, and the people were now rewarded with the results.[9]

6. [1824?], Arthur Papers, ML–A2164.
7. 26 Oct. 1835, Grey of Howick Papers.
8. See, for example, speeches of Molesworth, 26 June, 1849, and Russell, 8 Feb. 1850; 3 *Hansard, 106,* 938; *108,* 545.
9. 22 Mar. 1850, ibid., *109,* 1340.

It was not only colonial America that provided material for comparison. The contemporary United States was cited far more often. The reasons for this are not difficult to discover. America was the most advanced example of what seemed, even to opponents, to be the universal trend toward democracy, and the American political system had been injected into the British political debate primarily by the Radicals.[10] It was also the most profitable field for British investment, the most crucial supplier of raw materials, and a potent rival both commercially and politically. One could become an "expert" rather easily—without for example going there—by reading newspapers, as well as the numerous travel books and the reviews of them in periodicals. Most of all, however, it was the extremely popular best seller of Alexis de Tocqueville, *Democracy in America* (1835), that created the prevailing British image of the contemporary United States.

Now it is not usually a very easy thing to trace the "influence" of a writer upon administrative action, even when we know the impact was considerable.[11] In 1835 the future third Earl Grey thought it appropriate, for reasons that are not altogether clear, to read the work aloud in French to his ailing wife.[12] Years later when he was colonial secretary, he never wrote down anywhere that his emphasis in the 1846 New Zealand constitution upon municipal government was an attempt to duplicate the development of "that germ of free institutions" of which Tocqueville had written. Nor did he ever attribute his campaign for a federal system in Australia to Tocqueville's argument that federalism had rendered democracy comparatively harmless in the United States. He did not say so, but then he may not have known. One cannot be

10. See D. Crook, *American Democracy in English Politics, 1815–1850* (Oxford, 1965).

11. See S. Drescher, *Tocqueville and England* (Cambridge, Mass., 1964), which is a systematic analysis of the English reception and its effect on Tocqueville.

12. Journal entry, 3 Nov. 1835, Grey of Howick Papers. Grey occasionally made notes of his reading, but not of this book.

sure.[13] But in 1858 Grey published a pamphlet, *Parliamentary Government Considered with Reference to a Reform of Parliament.* A frank comparison of English institutions with American, it posed the question of whether the English political fabric could successfully absorb the pressures of democracy. That pamphlet is extensively footnoted with references to *Democracy in America,* the only source the author thought it important to acknowledge.

Lord Grey was not alone in his attention to America. The minutes of Herman Merivale are full of comparisons. Major William Hogge, who was sent out as a special commissioner to southern Africa, observed erroneously that "the history of the Cape is already written in that of America, and the gradual increase of the white man must eventually though slowly ensure the disappearance of the Black."[14] Gladstone called the United States "the great source of experimental instruction, so far as Colonial institutions are concerned."[15] Edward Gibbon Wakefield buttressed his arguments for systematic colonization with an analysis of American land policy: in the United States they may have sold land too cheaply to permit the creation of a balanced society with an aristocracy at the top, but at least they did not give it away.[16] J. A. Roebuck used the Northwest Ordinance to support a plan for the evolution of settlements into provinces and of provinces into federations, the rate of transition to be determined automatically by the growth of population.[17] Of the American statehood system he observed

13. See C. Clark, *A Short History of Australia* (New York, 1963), p. 107, who makes the assertion about Tocqueville's influence a good deal more positively than I have been able to do here, though in the main I agree with him.

14. Letter to Lord Grey, 19 Dec. 1851, quoted by J. S. Galbraith, *Reluctant Empire: British Policy on the South African Frontier, 1834–1854* (Berkeley, 1963), pp. 257–58.

15. 21 May 1852, 3 *Hansard, 142,* 965.

16. *England and America: A Comparison of the Social and Political State of Both Nations* (New York, 1834).

17. *The Colonies of England, A Plan for the Government of some of our Colonial Possessions* (1849), pp. 212 ff. See C. Carter, "Colonialism

admiringly: "The whole thing was like a well-made watch—it went from that moment and never ceased to go."[18] Sir William Molesworth voiced the common complaint against the empire's lack of coherence: "The United States is a system of States clustered round a central republic. Our colonial empire ought to be a system of colonies clustered round the hereditary monarchy of England."[19]

The participants in the mid-nineteenth-century colonial debate used America frequently, and indeed they could not easily have avoided doing so. The question is whether it made any difference. Did colonial and contemporary America merely provide a body of material, such for example as classical studies or the Bible, to which one could look for support for one's own preconceived ideas? Or did it help to shape the contours and the conclusions of the debate itself?

America, certainly, had a history that was long enough and rich enough in its variety to lend itself to either side of almost any argument. It could also be used to justify the expedient or the inevitable. Lord Grey might have been influenced by Tocqueville, but what in any case was he to do in New Zealand's mountainous terrain and treacherous waters except to build up municipal government? Is it possible that a thing so obvious (that is to everybody except the colonists themselves) as federation in Australia would not have been encouraged even without the American precedent?

Moreover, the American Revolution did not contain a ready solution to Great Britain's problem of colonial self-government. It showed that angry ripe colonies might break away—that at least was clear enough. And it could be inferred, though not necessarily correctly, that British mistakes had

in Continental United States," *South Atlantic Quarterly, 47* (1948), 17–28, and W. Hamilton, "The Transfer of Power in Historical Perspective," in Hamilton et al., eds., *A Decade of the Commonwealth, 1955–1964* (Durham, N.C., 1964), p. 27.

18. 24 May 1849, 3 *Hansard, 105,* 937.

19. 6 May 1850, ibid., *110,* 1182.

been responsible for the rise of that anger and for the drive toward independence. (One would not want to become involved in the question of whether separation was inevitable, but, as Adderley wrote, "the normal current of colonial history is the perpetual assertion of the right of self-government." [20] But aside from the policy of imperial taxation (which had been settled in the Declaratory Act of 1778) it was not easy to draw up a catalog of measures that must be avoided. The American Revolution taught only the negative lesson of what would happen as the result of a failure of colonial policy; it did not reveal how to make policy successful. Nor did the American experience aid in the detection of when colonies were becoming "ripe." After all, few if any of the European settlement colonies in the mid-nineteenth century were really mature when compared to the American standard. Then, as later, "political maturity" came to mean in practice the ability to manufacture a respectably troublesome agitation, rather than a comparison with some more positive model of development. The American experience had to be invoked if only because it was there. But in facing the specific problems of colonial administration it did not necessarily help things very much to do so.

If the Englishman of the mid-nineteenth century had been less careless about his investigation of colonial and contemporary America, the story might have been different. But none until Sir George Trevelyan took the trouble to study American history with any thoroughness. Thus the model of a loose connection of wholly sovereign states, which was developed in the writings of several American leaders just before the outbreak of the revolt and which bears a striking resemblance to the modern Commonwealth of Nations, was missed. If, as a Canadian historian has written, the Commonwealth, "like so many other practical gadgets for making life on this planet

20. C. Adderley [Baron Norton], *Review of* "The Colonial Policy of Lord John Russell's Administration," *by Earl Grey, 1853; and of Subsequent Colonial History* (1869), p. 3.

more efficient and more comfortable . . . was invented in America,"[21] then unfortunately the British were unaware of it.

Did the American experience, then, add anything more than nonessential support for parliamentary rhetoric? The answer would seem to be yes. And the evidence would seem to lie in the logical development of the debate itself.

There is, after all, nothing basically wrong with Bodelsen's well-known categories—the "optimists" like Grey and Merivale who thought the empire would last; the "pessimists" like Stephen and Sir Frederic Rogers who resigned themselves to the belief that it would not; and the "separatists" like Cobden who hoped it would not—except that separatism was less popular than Bodelsen thought. Like "Little Englandism" it was used as a term of accusation. The pessimists argued that colonies grew, developed, and matured, and when ripe they dropped off the vine as the American colonies of England and Spain had already done. (The separatists merely added that they hoped the parting would happen soon, or even that the mother country should not wait for the colonies themselves to choose to separate.) The optimists disagreed: they argued that colonies grew, developed, and matured, but that, despite the logical development of the vine-fruit metaphor and the experience of the recent past, the imperial framework would somehow hold together.

The mid-nineteenth-century colonial debate rested on the foundation of a common recognition of a process of political development or, as our own generation of social scientists has come to call it, of "modernization." Separatists, pessimists, and optimists all assumed that their European settlement colonies were developing nations that would grow, mature, and be-

21. F. Underhill, *The British Commonwealth: An Experiment in Co-operation among Nations* (Durham, N.C., 1956), p. 3. R. Adams, *Political Ideas of the American Revolution* (3d ed. New York, 1958), pp. 65–83.

come self-governing. The argument dwelt entirely upon what would happen after that. That is, it fastened only upon the uncertain conclusion of an evolutionary process of historical change that was tacitly accepted by all.

This process of developing nationhood was very seldom referred to. It was never systematically analyzed. For the sophisticated understanding of historical change that would have made that possible was only just beginning to emerge—most notably in the thought of Marx. The implicit recognition was no less significant for that. Indeed, the common premise may well have been a good deal more important than the argument it supported.

After all, it made no real difference in Stephen's administrative behavior that he thought Canada would probably opt someday for independence. But the recognition that Canada must be treated as a developing nation, even while she was yet a relatively immature colonial society, was at the heart of the advice he gave to his successive superiors. Such a concept of developing nationhood had not been a common fundamental premise of the debate in Britain at the time of the American Revolution. Its presence in the British mind half a century later would seem to be one of the most important reasons why concessions to colonial self-government were made that allowed the second empire to survive. It would also seem correct to conclude that it was very largely the American experience that had put it there. If the British did learn in this way from their imperial past, then it was a valuable contribution indeed.

The other significant force that was responsible for the liberalization that took place in colonial administration was the influence of economic theory and of Britain's changing commercial policy. In the half-century after 1820 protectionism gradually gave way to free trade, which after 1852 was accepted even by the conservatives. The implications for an empire that had grown up in a mercantilist climate of opinion could not have been more obvious.[22] Those implications have also been explained very thoroughly by historians. If colonies were not to be maintained for the direct economic benefit of the mother country, then it followed that there could be no logical commercial justification for holding them against their will. If the colonies themselves obtained few direct economic benefits from the imperial connection—and with such measures as the repeal of the sugar and timber duties the preferences for colonial products in the British market fell away one by one—then that connection ought to be made as unobjectionable as possible. One did not need to be so devoted a disciple of Adam Smith as Richard Cobden to realize that colonial self-government was the logical corollary of imperial free trade. Members of the "Manchester school"[23] were usually more radical than most of their contemporaries, but on this point they encountered little in the way of opposition. Indeed, this broad principle of colonial policy was never seriously questioned in the mid-nineteenth century. No responsible politician of that period, in power or out, suggested that coercion would be the proper response if the majority of the inhabitants of a settlement colony ever chose to leave the fold.

The coming of free trade reinforced the chastening experience of a century and a half in America. Together they helped to form in England a liberal climate of opinion toward the political development of colonies. This favorable attitude was composed of a common recognition that there was, or very shortly would be, a good deal of pressure for local autonomy, as well as a common belief that such a desire was irresistible and ought not, in any case, to be opposed. The receptive atmosphere did not, however, provide the means of solving the

22. See, for example, H. Grey, *The Colonial Policy of Lord John Russell's Administration* (2 vols., 1853), *1*, 5–6.

23. See the fine book by W. Grampp, *The Manchester School of Economics* (Stanford, 1960).

problem. Concessions must be made: But how? How many? To which colonists? How soon? At what point ought they to stop? When the pressure for liberalization began to become acute, as it did in Canada in the 1830s and in the other settlement colonies in the late 1840s, British administrators had to look elsewhere for guidance.

The solution to the problem would be, of course, "responsible government"—which may be defined at the outset as a system of government by party in which the executive takes advice from ministers able to command the confidence of the legislature. And while it would be incorrect to assert either that Lord Durham and his collaborators ought to receive full credit for the development of the idea, or that it was put into effect in the way that they had intended, it is in the famous Durham Report that the theory of responsible government can best be approached.

Lord Durham plucked the theory of responsible government from a hotly contested constitutional debate that had already been going on in England for several centuries and that was far from being finished. That argument concerned the role, authority, and power in the British government of the crown. The greatest figures in English political theory—from John of Salisbury to Hobbes and Locke, to Blackstone and Burke—had been engaged in it. In the seventeenth century it had spread with the first colonists to America. There, in near isolation, it had tended to rigidify, so that an essentially seventeenth-century constitutional interpretation, drawn largely from the thought of Locke, had sustained the Americans in their rebellion.[24] The colonial agitation for responsible government in the nineteenth century can best be understood in the context of this ongoing constitutional debate.

The precise outlines of this debate, as it existed in the circles in which Lord Durham moved in England and later in

24. See B. Bailyn, *The Ideological Origins of the American Revolution* (Cambridge, Mass., 1967), p. viii and passim.

Canada, must await the study by the reincarnation of Becker. Certainly, the story will be complicated enough to sustain his interest. What was being read? Is it perhaps possible to show who transported the idea to Canada, and how it was rationalized to the point of being plausible in a political environment so different from the one in which it had originated?

These questions cannot be answered here. There is, however, no great mystery about Lord Durham's own general position in the spectrum of constitutional arguments. For he reported that he found in Canada, in addition to "two nations warring in the bosom of a single state," the same "collision between the executive and the representative body" that had dominated English history for centuries. But, continued the Durham Report: "Since the Revolution of 1688, the stability of the English constitution has been secured by that wise principle of our Government which has vested the direction of national policy, and the distribution of patronage, in the hands of the Parliamentary majority."[25] Lord Durham was thus a firm exponent of what has come to be called the Whig interpretation of history.

It was this understood relationship between the executive and the legislature, which was the real essence of the British constitution, that Durham thought must be instituted in Canada. The governor must be elevated, taken out of the melee of colonial politics where his position had been made so untenable. Instead, the governor was to adopt the role of the queen in England, keeping himself above politics. The effective power of the executive must be transferred, in all internal affairs, to a cabinet possessing the confidence of the legislature.

This is not the place to dwell upon the oversimplification of history upon which Durham's constitutional interpretation was founded. Recent scholarship has clearly revealed that the crown retained much of the direction of national policy and

25. C. Lucas, ed., *Lord Durham's Report on the Affairs of British North America* (3 vols., Oxford, 1912), 2, 16, 73, 79.

most of the patronage throughout the eighteenth century.[26] Indeed, the working of that relationship in contemporary English politics was still relatively tenuous: the very government of Lord Melbourne that sent Durham to Canada was to be kept in power until 1841 by a temporary failure of that understanding.[27] Though the historian of the intellectual origins of the Durham Report will have to ponder the question of why constitutional theory should have been so much in advance of practice, Durham's interpretation was common enough. Why, however, should he have thought that responsible government would work in Canada?

The question of who should be credited with suggesting the idea to Durham may never be satisfactorily resolved. It may have been Joseph Howe of Nova Scotia,[28] or perhaps Robert Baldwin of Upper Canada.[29] It may have come through contacts of Durham's collaborator, Charles Buller. But to attempt to trace the origins in this way would seem, in any case, to be the wrong approach. Responsible government was "in the air," the suggestion probably came from several sources at about the same time, and the problem is why Durham was so receptive to it. In order to suggest a possible answer we need to turn to another side of Durham's background. For, in addition to being a Whig interpreter of history, Lord Durham was also a Benthamite.

26. See E. Williams, "The Cabinet in the Eighteenth Century," in R. Schuyler, ed., *The Making of English History* (New York, 1952), pp. 378–91, and J. Brooke, "Introductory Survey," in L. Namier and Brooke, eds., *History of Parliament: The House of Commons, 1754–1790* (3 vols., New York, 1964), *1*, 1–204.

27. The best discussion of contemporary political practice is A. Aspinall, *The Cabinet Council, 1783–1835* (1954).

28. C. Martin, *Foundations of Canadian Nationhood* (Toronto, 1955), p. 132.

29. See Baldwin to Lord Glenelg, 13 July 1836, transcribed from the Durham Papers by K. Bell and W. Morrell, eds., *Select Documents on British Colonial Policy, 1830–1860* (Oxford, 1928), pp. 24–32. See also E. Wrong, *Charles Buller and Responsible Government* (Oxford, 1926), pp. 33–34.

The Benthamites were hardly paragons of consistency. While paying lip service to laissez-faire they promoted a pattern of government intervention that laid the foundations of the modern welfare state.[30] Bentham pronounced himself an anticolonial. But in practice he and his followers were among the most fervent supporters of an active imperial policy. In India they demonstrated their love of outdoor laboratories, appropriately removed from parliamentary scrutiny, where they might apply Ricardian theories of rent and construct whole new legal codes.[31] They were in large part responsible for the annexation of New Zealand and for the colonization of much of Australia. Durham, Wakefield, Buller, Molesworth, Roebuck: some of Bentham's followers became the Colonial Reformers.

The Benthamites, even more than most of their generation, were characterized by what Halévy called "le simplisme."[32] They were magnetized by that attractive quality which Western intellectuals had been attempting to achieve in human affairs at least since Newton had shown mechanical simplicity to be the rule of the natural universe.[33] Locke's second contract, forming the government, had been *automatically* dissolved when the ruler no longer fulfilled his function of protecting property. The theories of Montesquieu and Blackstone of the British system of government, as well as the American constitution which they strongly influenced, had emphasized the me-

30. D. Roberts, *Victorian Origins of the British Welfare State* (New Haven, 1960).

31. See particularly, in J. Bowring, ed., *The Works of Jeremy Bentham* (new ed. 11 vols., New York, Russell and Russell, 1962), his "Principles of International Law," *2*, 546–49; "A Manual of Political Economy," *3*, 56–57; and "Emancipate Your Colonies," *4*, 407–08. See the very interesting book by E. Stokes, *The English Utilitarians and India* (Oxford, 1959).

32. E. Halévy, *The Growth of Philosophic Radicalism*, trans. Mary Morris (Boston, 1963), pp. 6, 491, and passim.

33. I must record my debt to the immensely stimulating book by T. Kuhn, *The Copernican Revolution: Planetary Astronomy in the Development of Western Thought* (Cambridge, Mass., 1957).

chanical simplicity of institutional checks and balances. Adam Smith's model of an ideal economy had run itself, automatically and perpetually, like the common eighteenth-century metaphor of the machine. Despite the excess of the French Revolution and the point-blank denial of Burke that "any simple disposition or direction of power can be suitable either to man's nature or to the quality of his affairs,"[34] the search for simplicity continued in the nineteenth century in the thought of Darwin, Marx, and many others. The tendency to simplify and to systematize was nowhere more strongly emphasized than in the contributions of the Benthamites.

The method of the Benthamites was to reduce problems to their ultimate simplicity. Stripping away such irrelevant complications as how many paupers might starve if the Poor Law of 1834 were applied, they would seek the essence of the matter. Once having succeeded to their satisfaction in isolating the very heart, they would then formulate a correspondingly simple law. Operating thus upon the heart, the law would solve the whole problem automatically. Bentham himself showed the way with his famous felicity calculus, in which one could easily measure the merits of any particular piece of legislation merely by determining the quantities of pain and pleasure that it caused to individuals. (The troublesome objection that "pain" and "pleasure" are qualitative terms did not detain Bentham any more than did the problem of quantitative measurement.) We have already cited Roebuck's admiration for the "well-made watch" of the American statehood system and his "plan" for introducing the mechanical simplicity of the Northwest Ordinance into the British Empire, as well as Molesworth's plea for "system." Wakefield proposed his "sufficient price" as a beautifully simple formula that would sweep away at once the massive complexities of population movement and make irrelevant the stubborn land-grabbing propen-

34. *Reflections on the Revolution in France* (reprinted 1950), p. 67.

sities of sheep. The process of colonization would be entirely self-sustaining, self-regulating, and hence "systematic."[35]

Lord Durham's cast of mind was very similar. In his drafting of the Reform Bill, only a few years earlier, he had proposed what he apparently intended to be the "final" solution to the problems of the British constitution. And, whether or not Durham actually developed the idea himself, responsible government emerges from his Report as the characteristic contribution of a Benthamite.

Responsible government, Joseph Howe later explained, possessed "the merits of being simple and eminently British."[36] Durham also emphasized the quality of simplicity: "It needs no change in the principles of government, no invention of a new sensational theory, to supply the remedy which would, in my opinion, completely remove the existing political disorders."[37] Once implemented, the new system would run itself. It would require no tinkering from London with its mechanical operation. Durham, indeed, was serenely confident of the future. He anticipated none of the difficulties that were to prove to be inherent in the transfer of power. He made no effort to see beyond the introduction of his innovation. Apparently, no further adjustment of the relationship between imperial and colonial authorities would be necessary. Indeed, the list of subjects on which the imperial veto would continue to be operative—including the form of the colonial constitution, foreign relations, tariff policy, and land legislation, a list which became a sort of target for self-governing colonies in their evo-

35. It will be remembered that the price of land (the proceeds from the sale of which were to be used for emigration) was to serve as the sole regulating device. Too high a price would discourage settlement; if it were too low land speculation would set in. The price must be "sufficient." See *A Letter from Sydney* (1829; 1929), and *A View of the Art of Colonization* (1849).

36. "Letters to Lord John Russell," 1840, in H. Egerton and W. Grant, eds., *Canadian Constitutional Documents* (1907), pp. 190 ff.

37. *Durham Report, 2,* 277–78.

lution to dominion status and to sovereign nationhood—indicates that Durham regarded the settlement as final.

If Lord Durham had possessed a more skeptical and less doctrinaire cast of mind, such as Stephen's or even Lord John Russell's, he might never have proposed responsible government seriously. Certainly, it required no small degree of imagination—and possibly even a bit of wishful thinking—to conceive of how the sophisticated British cabinet and party system could be made to work in the alien environment of colonial assemblies that were small and rough, and that possessed no cohesive or really identifiable political parties. From our own vantage point responsible government appears so obvious. Given, however, the situation that actually existed in Canada and the other settlement colonies, it is rather difficult to understand why any half-realistic reader of the Durham Report should have been taken in.

Moreover, as Herman Merivale saw quite clearly in 1861 (looking back over the two decades since the initial publication of his own *Lectures on Colonization and Colonies*), Durham's whole argument contained a serious flaw. To give self-government while at the same time withholding from its exercise such central social problems as the disposal of land was a palpable contradiction.[38] The notion that the mere introduction of a new relationship between a governor and his ministers, important though it would prove, could somehow provide a final settlement of the problem of pressure for colonial autonomy was absurd.

This contradiction is, in fact, common to many of the ideas that were emanating from the little circle of Colonial Reformers. Molesworth's model constitution for the Australian colonies in the 1850s made a similar attempt to separate imperial from colonial areas of legislative control. And his objection to proposals for Australian federation were based, as we shall see, on

38. (Oxford, 1928), p. vii (Preface to the 1861 ed.).

the belief that a federated Australia must soon cut the imperial ties.[39] That is, he was in favor of giving local self-government to immature colonies, but he was opposed to Lord Grey's idealistic attempt to build a nation in the Antipodes. Who then was the "pessimist?"

Similarly, Wakefield seems not to have contemplated that, to quote Merivale, "the first demand of each emancipated community would be to get rid of . . . [a] land system" that penalized one generation of settlers in favor of their successors. Wakefield was a shrewd individual, and he may have thought this through, but he could never have admitted it. If he had tried to take into account such factors as the greed of people, not to mention that of sheep, his "sufficient price" formula would have become far too complicated and unwieldy. It would have lost altogether that rhythmic simplicity which so appealed to its inventor and his converts. It would not have done at all.

The common contradiction in the basic arguments of the Colonial Reformers would seem to indicate that the contention that they were far in advance of their contemporaries in their attitude toward aspiring colonial nationhood needs to be qualified. It is quite true that they were usually more "optimistic" than most, although if Molesworth's opposition to Australian federation is more than an isolated exception, it probably needs to be asked what they were optimistic about. Wakefield did conceive of some sort of continuing relationship between Great Britain and her colonies. So, for that matter, did Merivale and Lord Grey. But the Colonial Reformers did not foresee what actually emerged a century later: the twentieth-century Commonwealth resembles far more closely the vision of the "pessimists" than it does their own. The Colonial Reformers encouraged self-government, but they would also have tried to arrest the progress of political development while it

39. C.O. Confidential Print, n.d. [c. Dec. 1854], Australian Papers, C.O. Library.

was still in embryo. Any attempt by British administrators to adhere very closely to the rules of empire they proposed would have made impossible the evolution of the loose association of independent nations that still belong to the modern Commonwealth.

Durham and the Colonial Reformers ought not, however, to be underrated: with some qualifications they deserve to be remembered as "builders of the Commonwealth." Durham's contribution was to inject into the early-Victorian discussion the idea which, despite its defects and its incompleteness, eventually provided the means by which an evolving imperial framework could accommodate with relative success the challenge of emerging nationalism. He himself, however, was a proud, disdainful, and irascible man, and it is difficult to believe that he could have conducted successfully the delicate and sustained personal relations with colonial politicians that were necessary if his supposedly "automatic" system was going to function effectively. It is probably fortunate that the task of implementing his proposal was left to the less inspired and the more orthodox.

The discussion of colonial questions in the nineteenth century dealt with the grand and the far-reaching. Its participants pondered the universal process of political development in societies of transplanted Europeans, as well as the implications that process might ultimately hold for an imperial structure such as their own. This discussion was by no means wholly insulated from the real world of day-to-day decision making. For, as we have tried to show, at least two important contributions emerged from it. One was the common awareness of the process of political development, which formed the undisputed and unquestioned premise for the argument about the future of the empire. The other was the idea of responsible government, one of a number of theories that were circulating.

Yet the links between theoretical discussion and administrative action were tenuous. British colonial administrators, though undoubtedly aware that their decisions might have broad implications, were attempting to deal with a problem that was far more tangible, far more concrete, and far more pressing. They had to do something about Canada.

The North American colonies presented a profound challenge indeed. In the principal ones—Upper and Lower Canada and Nova Scotia—substantial Reform movements had already developed by the early 1830s. Lower Canada's, led by Louis Papineau, was the most dangerous, for it had the widest following and the deepest roots.[40] It was in fact the first organized voice of French Canadian nationalism, an essentially conservative effort to maintain the inviolability of the separate institutions of French society. Upper Canada's, by contrast, was progressive with a tendency toward radicalism, especially after the capture of its leadership by a militant "firebrand" with Jacksonian democratic sympathies and connections, William L. Mackenzie.[41] Both the Canadas exploded somewhat prematurely in 1837–38 in "rebellions," a term which may be a bit too heroic in regard to Upper Canada. Nova Scotia's movement presented still another variation: a quiet, responsible, thoroughly respectable, and highly disciplined Reform party led by the most capable British American politician of the era, Joseph Howe.[42]

Several basic factors hampered the efforts of British administrators to deal with these movements for self-government. Not the least of the difficulties was that the colonies, as well as the Reform parties within them, were so different. And, as a contemporary Colonial Office minute pointed out, a concession

40. See H. Manning, *The Revolt of French Canada, 1800–1835: A Chapter in the History of the British Commonwealth* (New York, 1962).

41. See W. Kilbourn, *The Firebrand: William Lyon Mackenzie and the Rebellion in Upper Canada* (Toronto, 1956); S. Clark, *Movements of Political Protest in Canada, 1640–1840* (Toronto, 1959).

42. See J. Beck, ed., *Joseph Howe: Voice of Nova Scotia* (Toronto, 1964).

given to one had to be extended to all.[43] Another was that the problem could never be looked at entirely on its own merits, but had to be weighed in the light of democratic developments in the United States. And, in each of the colonies, representative institutions had already been conceded along with a good deal of local autonomy. It had, however, been done unsystematically. Local cliques, such as John Strachan's "family compact" in Upper Canada, had managed to gain the ascendancy by means of the virtually permanent tenure that was possessed by subordinate officials in the colonial governments. The administration at home, as well as the governors on the spot, had become thoroughly identified with them. Thus the problem was not merely the relatively simple one of transferring power. As would happen later in places as diverse as India, South Africa, and Nigeria the question was "which colonists?" And in early-nineteenth-century Canada the dilemma was heightened still further by the fact that power had already in effect been transferred. A door that had been closed had to be reopened. A monopoly of power had to be broken, and the path to its exercise prepared for yet another group of colonists.

It is small wonder, then, that the British government had not been very successful in initiating the fresh approach that was called for by nearly everyone who was at all familiar with the subject. Indeed, as Stephen complained,[44] British policy had been chronically marked by vacillation. British administrators had behaved as though mesmerized. Given the dimensions of the problem and the extent of the encumbrances, it is not altogether difficult to understand why.

It seems probable that the disaffection in Lower Canada had progressed to such an extent that the freely predicted explosion that occurred in 1837 could not have been prevented.

43. Quoted in Martin, *Foundations of Canadian Nationhood,* p. 22.
44. Stephen to Howick, 28 Dec. 1837, Grey Papers.

The problem of French Canadian insecurity, after all, was only temporarily salved by Lord Elgin: nationalism would reappear with increased intensity in the conscription crisis of World War I, and it has not been appeased even yet. In Nova Scotia violence was entirely averted by the maintenance of control over the Reform movement by Howe's moderation. The transfer of power there was perhaps the smoothest example of this process in British imperial history. The same sort of pattern might have occurred in Upper Canada, which also possessed a moderate Reform element, under a governor with the wisdom and the tact of a Lord Elgin or even a Lord Sydenham. Instead, the British government sent Sir Francis Head.

The amusing anecdote about the wrong Head's being dispatched (the invitation having been intended for the Argentine explorer's cousin, later a successful North American governor) need not be repeated here in the face of the somewhat more reliable evidence that is available in Lord Howick's journal. According to him various names were being proposed in 1835: Durham, Stephen, Le Marchant, Sir Charles Vaughan. Howick was honest enough, later, not to strike out the information that his own role had been crucial: "It was with very great difficulty that after we went up stairs [from a cabinet meeting] I got Ld. Melbourne to give a grumbling consent to Sir F. Head's being chosen." Nor was the favorable attitude of this future colonial secretary soon withdrawn. In May 1836 he thought Head's dispatches amusing:

> His manner of carrying on business & managing his affairs is not a little novel & very unlike ye usual formality of a Govr.'s answers to addresses &c. but he seems to be successful, he has put ye Assbly. & Mackenzie clearly in ye wrong about ye *responsible advisers* & ye great agitator seems to have experienced a total defeat at a public meeting of ye county of York.

Head, indeed, won a smashing election victory by taking to the campaign trail himself, managing to identify Reform with republicanism and disloyalty. By July, however, Howick thought the governor seemed to have become dizzy with success, and to be foolishly throwing away his advantage. The situation worsened. Howick reported that his efforts to stir Lord Glenelg, the colonial secretary, into action were all in vain. In October 1837 he noted with fear that in Lower Canada the French were drilling, with the governor Lord Gosford powerless to prevent them. As for Head, he had gone quite mad: "he must either be recalled or made King."

There soon followed the rebellions, and it was decided to send out Lord Durham, whose appointment Melbourne had previously vetoed. Taking Buller and Wakefield with him, he went primarily to Lower Canada, where he acted in a high-handed fashion toward the rebels, Canadian politicians in general, and the Whig government in particular. Howick read his dispatches: "How after writing them he can be allowed by Glenelg & Melbourne to remain I hardly understand, & yet his coming away wd. be so fatal that I think they must try to keep him there notwithstanding the loss of dignity which this will involve."[45] Durham was in Canada only five months, and only a few days of that were spent in Upper Canada. He picked the brains and employed the pens of Buller and Wakefield. He wrote a brilliant report that recommended: a union of the two Canadas, in which he hoped the French would be culturally and politically overwhelmed; a settlement of the clergy reserves, which were tracts of land set aside for the support of the established Anglican church; eventual union of all the North American colonies; and responsible government.

Durham's report was printed in February 1839. It was not received with universal acclaim. Both Lower and Upper Canadians, the former at least with good reason, complained bit-

45. Quotations from journal entries of 18 Nov. 1835, 14 May 1846, 30 Oct. 1837, and 22 Oct. 1838, Grey Papers.

terly. One future colonial secretary, Sir John Pakington, termed the whole document "a tissue of misrepresentation." Another, Gladstone, called responsible government "one of the shallowest of all possible delusions."[46] Russell, who was to take the Colonial Office himself in September, and Melbourne refused to support the recommendation. Even Lord Howick, who together with Elgin would later implement the proposal, never once mentioned responsible government in a long letter that he wrote to Lord Durham immediately after reading the report, a document that illustrates in rather amusing fashion something of the personalities of both men.

Howick enthusiastically approved the Durham Report, for "it strongly confirms the opinions I previously entertained. . . . Your scheme for the future government of these colonies tallies very much with my views upon the subject." Commented Durham in the margin: "except that I mean to propose a perfectly different one." But there were difficulties in the way of a legislative union, and Howick thought some kind of federal arrangement, on the American model, might be better. What, for instance, was to be done about differences in legal systems? Durham: "How did you do it in Scotland and England?" Howick: Wouldn't there be purely local questions that a united legislature could not decide without great inconvenience? Durham: "And leave the French Assembly to govern Lower Canada?" Howick: The want of an intermediate body between the municipalities and the central government "would lead to the vices of the local legislation of this country which is so notoriously defective." Durham: "How is it defective?" Howick: In the United States the vacancy had been supplied by the state legislatures. Durham: "What! did they create State Legislatures to supply this want, & fill this vacancy? In fact if they had not had States, before the Union, would not the general Legislature have done all

46. 3 *Hansard, 52,* 1333; *54,* 716, 732.

the State Legislatures now do?" Howick: Wouldn't Nova Scotia or Prince Edward Island be uncomfortable with a legislative union? Durham: "Why? Is Cornwall? or Northumberland? or Lancashire?" Howick: Would there not be dissatisfaction among those in Upper Canada who wished Toronto to remain a capital? Durham: "They mustn't be minded." Howick:

> But more than this would it be consistent with the opinions in favor of the colonists being allowed to manage their own internal affairs which are so strongly insisted upon in the report to proceed without communication with the inhabitants or knowing their wishes to settle the whole form of their future government and to make the most important changes in their existing institutions? [47]

To this last rather telling point, which was indeed the basic contradiction in his report, Durham gave no answer.

Howick went on to develop his own plan, apparently adopted from a proposal of Stephen,[48] for a convention of delegates from both Canadas, the representatives from Upper Canada to be elected, those from Lower Canada to be appointed in areas still disaffected but to be elected in the rest. The convention would be told to get on with it:

> To this body Parlt. should entrust the power of making such alterations in the act of 1791 as it should think fit. Under this general power it should settle the terms of the future Union whether Legislative or Federal and dispose of various questions which there would be immense difficulty in dealing with directly in this country, among others that of the Legislative Council and of the Clergy Reserves.

Meanwhile, Lower Canada would be governed despotically (as Durham himself had recommended) by "an efficient Gov-

47. Howick to Durham, War Office, 7 Feb. 1839, Durham Papers, PAC, M.G. 24, A 27, XI.

48. Stephen to Howick, 28 Dec. 1837, Grey Papers.

ernor acquainted with the principles of modern legislation" who would "forthwith proceed to the task of amending the laws of L. Canada respecting the tenure of landed property, the constitution of parishes and counties, the administration of justice, &c. &c."

Having identified the contradiction in Durham's plan between giving self-government to the colonies while at the same time dictating what was good for them, Howick had proceeded to introduce the same flaw into his own scheme. Given the context of French Canada in the late 1830s, it is not surprising that there was so little inclination to trust the French. The surprising thing is that statesmen such as Howick, Russell, Peel, and Elgin would be able to overcome their prejudice within the short space of a decade. For the heart of the successful implementation of responsible government would be entirely alien to the scornful condemnation of the French in the Durham Report. Above all, the coming of responsible government would rest upon tolerance and faith.

Durham would not have entrusted the French with so large a share in working out their destiny as that proposed by Howick. In any case he did not comment in regard to the other's plan. As for Howick, fortunately unaware of the rough handling that his letter would receive, he looked forward to talking personally with Durham:

> I think when we do we shall be able to agree very much as to what ought to be done as I entirely concur with you in your leading notions of allowing to the Colonists the most complete self-govt. upon matters of mere internal regulation and local interest, and of binding the different provinces together by the closest and strongest ties which it may be practicable to establish.[49]

Interesting as Howick's reaction may be in the light of later developments, it was Lord John Russell's that mattered at the

49. Howick to Durham, 7 Feb. 1839, Durham Papers, PAC, M.G. 24, A 27, XI.

time. Durham's "practical" proposals for a settlement of the Clergy Reserves and a legislative union of the two Canadas were speedily implemented, their way through the local legislature being encouraged by a promise of a guaranteed loan of £1.5 million for public works. But Russell gave short shrift to the theory of responsible government, he and the new governor Lord Sydenham determining instead on a policy of leadership of the legislature by the governor with the aid of moderate men of all parties.

Russell gave several reasons for rejecting responsible government. One was a thoroughly different interpretation of the practice and historical development of the British constitution from the one that had been argued by Lord Durham. Indeed, it is surprising to find that the position of this future leader of the Whig party was considerably less "Whiggish," as well as much more accurate in the light of modern scholarship, than the Benthamite Radical's. Wrote Russell:

> The constitution of England, after long struggle and alternate success, has settled into a form of government in which the prerogative of the Crown is undisputed, but is never exercised without advice. Hence the exercise only is questioned, and however the use of the authority may be condemned, the authority itself remains untouched. This is the practical solution of a great problem, the result of a contest which from 1640 to 1690 shook the monarchy, and disturbed the peace of the country.

His sophisticated analysis continued: "The power for which a minister is responsible in England, is not his own power, but the power of the Crown, of which he is for the time the organ." To Russell the practical question was whether this same relationship, the product of an organic historical development in England, could exist between the governor and his advisers in a colony.

> It is obvious that the executive councillor of a colony is in a situation totally different. The Governor, under whom he

> serves, receives his orders from the Crown of England. But can the colonial council be the advisers of the Crown of England? Evidently not, for the Crown has other advisers, for the same functions, and with superior authority.[50]

Under responsible government, Russell thought, the governor's position would be an impossible one. He would be pulled between two poles. He might receive advice from his ministers contrary to his instructions—what then? It would be impossible, furthermore, to delineate successfully areas of internal and imperial concern, and in any case there were internal questions on which the honor of the crown could not be compromised by complete delegation to a colonial ministry.

Russell would seem to have been right on several counts. His constitutional interpretation was historically more plausible than Durham's. He was certainly correct in foreseeing the difficult position of the governor under responsible government, for that would remain a problem for decades after its initial concession. He was also right in asserting the impossibility of defining in practice what were to be imperial and colonial questions. That of course was never done. The heart of Russell's objection amounts to this: responsible government would be incompatible with the continuance of the colonial status. It was on this point that Lord Durham and the Colonial Reformers differed with Russell and with most of their contemporaries. And it was on this point that their critics were right. Responsible government proved to be the means not of maintaining the status of dependence, but of facilitating the progress of self-governing colonies toward independence. Russell, then, was mostly right, Durham mostly wrong. It happened, however, that in their stage of political development responsible government was the only way in which the North American colonies could continue to be governed in a practi-

50. Russell to C. P. Thomson [later Baron Sydenham], 14 Oct. 1839, in Lucas, *Durham Report, 3,* 332–35.

cal manner. And so, after a few years of attempting alternatives, the British government gave in.

The story of the attainment of responsible government in the 1840s has been told often, and very well.[51] There is little that can be added to it here. British policy was really directed toward one primary object: to build and maintain the authority of the governor so that he could govern. No one, least of all Russell, ever assumed that he would be able to do so without the close cooperation of colonial politicians—this was made clear in the very dispatch that rejected responsible government. And it was Russell himself who made what turned out to be the crucial step of abolishing the permanent tenure of colonial officials, placing their positions instead at the disposal of the governor. Russell's intention was to strengthen the governor by freeing him from the "family compact," but as is well known his action would have the effect of facilitating the introduction of responsible government.

The first three governors of united Canada had the misfortune to labor under a policy that was self-contradictory.

> I must say [wrote Elgin to Grey in 1847] that when I read Lord Sydenham's despatches I never cease to marvel what study of human nature or of history led him to the conclusion that it would be possible to concede to a pushing enterprising people unencumbered by an aristocracy and dwelling in the immediate vicinity of the United States such Constitutional privileges as were conferred on Canada at the time of the Union and yet to restrict in practice their power of self Government as he proposed.[52]

51. I am following particularly Martin, *Foundations of Canadian Nationhood,* chaps. 5–10; Morrell, *British Colonial Policy in the Age of Peel and Russell,* chaps. 3, 18; and J. Careless, *The Union of the Canadas: The Growth of Canadian Institutions, 1841–1857* (Toronto, 1967), pp. 1–131.

52. 26 Apr. 1847, A. Doughty, ed., *The Elgin-Grey Papers, 1846–1852* (4 vols., Ottawa, 1937), *1,* 29.

The weight of historical opinion has agreed with him. The attempts in the early 1840s to avoid responsible government led inexorably in that very direction.

For a time Sydenham seemed to have succeeded in attaching to himself enough moderates to make rule by a governor's party a practical alternative—but only for a time. Under Francis Hincks's leadership the Reformers were already refusing to serve except under responsible government. Historians have concluded that Sydenham's death came in time to save his reputation. Sir Charles Bagot, Sydenham's successor, felt himself unable to avoid appointing an unpalatable list of ministers that included Baldwin and La Fontaine, the latter a reported follower of Papineau, so that colonial secretary Lord Stanley could claim later that *he* had instituted responsible government.[53] It was hardly so. Stanley complained bitterly enough at the time. And the real question was not whom you accepted as ministers but how you worked with them. Stanley's orders to Sir Charles Metcalfe, who replaced the dying Bagot, were clear enough:

> On one point I am sure it is necessary that you should be firm—I mean in the disposal of Patronage: This is an instrument, effective in all governments, but particularly so in Colonial ones; as long as you keep it in your own hands, and refuse to apply it exclusively to party purposes, it will be felt that you have really substantial power, and I think the Province will support you; but if you let your Council take this out of your hands, they will at once strengthen a party already too compact & too powerful, & tend to reduce your authority, as I doubt not they would desire, to a nullity.[54]

53. 19 June 1849, 3 *Hansard, 106,* 519–22. Debate in House of Lords on Rebellion Losses Bill.

54. Stanley to Metcalfe, 1 Nov. 1843, Derby Papers, PAC, M.G. 24, A 15.

Metcalfe, not surprisingly, soon found himself at complete loggerheads with the whole Reform party. The year 1844, in one historian's opinion, was the low point: "never did Great Britain more thoroughly deserve to lose Canada." [55] The government of the colony was failing, in fact, to function.

The Whigs returned to power in 1846, with the third Earl Grey taking the Colonial Office. Policy was sharply reversed, and the question of responsible government was swiftly decided. When Grey himself had been converted is not entirely clear. He had not been in favor of it in 1837. And though he may have changed his position about the time of the Durham Report, no contemporary evidence has been found that would support this hypothesis. His journal records his approval of Russell's policy with no qualifications.[56] In the early forties the journal begins to be less useful, as his entries become shorter and less frequent—within a few weeks after taking office he ceased to comment in it at all about colonial business. He had several conversations with Elgin, whom he had not met before, including a long visit at Howick while awaiting Elgin's marriage to Mary Lambton, the daughter of Lord Durham (and Durham was Grey's brother-in-law). Once Elgin reached Canada he embarked on responsible government with no hesitation, and his private correspondence with Grey contains no questions or advice about what was to be done. They had obviously settled the whole thing already: but whether Elgin had to be converted, or whether he helped Grey to arrive at a definite conclusion himself, cannot be determined.

Nova Scotia was the first to be conceded responsible government, in November 1846, and thus Joseph Howe's quiet revolution was the first to succeed. In Canada Elgin proved himself a remarkable governor, with whom in that era only Sir George Grey can be compared. Elgin lacked Grey's brilliant, exciting romanticism, but he had a good deal more tact, and in the

55. Morrell, *British Colonial Policy*, p. 63.
56. Entries of 2 Feb. 1839 and 23 Mar. 1840, Grey Papers.

long run (though their positions were very different) he was probably more successful. His letters to Lord Grey reveal him to have possessed a sophisticated sense of history and an accurate appraisal of his place in it. What made his policy work were his tolerance and his courage. He resolutely refused to allow himself to be identified with any particular group of ministers. Reversing the position that had been taken by his father-in-law, he accepted the French as full partners. When the Rebellion Losses Bill, under which former rebels could be compensated for property damaged in the rebellion of 1837, raised the anger of conservatives in Canada and also in England, he refused to panic. And the Whig government, with the assistance of Peel but with the opposition of Gladstone, supported him manfully. It was the only true parliamentary test responsible government ever received.

4: The Transfer of Power in the 1850s

The policy of yielding is the obvious and easy policy.
Sir James Stephen

In the 1840s responsible government had been conceded to communities in North America that were already relatively advanced, not merely in the art of manufacturing troublesome agitation, but also in the possession of leaders—Francis Hincks, Joseph Howe, John A. Macdonald, George Brown—who were fully capable of managing a self-governing colony. The transfer of power to these politicians had been made not so much from the Colonial Office in London as from its appointed officials in the local governments. It had been done with a minimum of friction. The North American colonies, already well along on the road of political development, had been "ready" for the transition.

But what in fact had been conceded? What did responsible government really amount to? Was it merely, as Lord Durham had argued, a simple formula, an easily implemented way that Great Britain might surrender an empty claim to control over local administration, the better to maintain her imperial authority? Or was it more than that? The principle of responsible government had been granted. Its real meaning could only be defined in practice.

It was quite apparent that a process once begun in Canada could not be contained there. No remarkable prescience was required to foresee that the Australian colonies, New Zealand,

and the Cape would demand and in time obtain similar concessions. Prime minister Lord John Russell said as much in his well-attended speech on colonial questions in 1850.[1] And the Whig colonial secretary, Earl Grey, said the same:

> Parliamentary Government . . . is probably on the whole the best plan hitherto adopted of enabling a Colony in an advanced state of its social progress to exercise the privilege of self-government; it may therefore be regarded as the form which representative institutions, when they acquire their full development, are likely to take in the British Colonies.[2]

This statement of Grey's attitude was carefully phrased. He himself would have described it as liberal, and so for the long run it was. But he made substantial qualifications: self-government was a "privilege," not a "right"; and the emphasis was on the future rather than upon the present. Yet in administration as in politics it is the short run that matters most. Grey's good intentions for the distant future were almost irrelevant. It was in the short run that he was confronted with demands for concessions similar to the ones he had already made in Canada. And it was in the short run that he was opposed to them. The urgent question was not "whether" to grant self-government: it was "how much" and "how soon."

Running through Lord Grey's thought on colonial affairs was the same basic contradiction between local self-government and imperial control that so characterized the writings of Colonial Reformers. Grey was a doctrinaire free trader, believing that individual colonies ought not to be allowed to deviate from an enlightened commercial policy best for the empire as a whole. He considered himself a humanitarian, advocating

1. 3 *Hansard, 108,* 565.

2. *The Colonial Policy of Lord John Russell's Administration* (2 vols., 1853), *1,* 33.

the maintenance of enough imperial responsibility in New Zealand and South Africa to prevent mistreatment of the natives. He was a devotee of Wakefield, asserting that unsold land belonged to the people of the empire as a whole, not merely to the first settlers in any particular colony. And he maintained his conviction that the mother country had the right to call upon the colonies to assist her in resettling convicts.

In regard, then, to the degree of self-government, Lord Grey differed with the colonies on most of the things that really mattered to them: with the Australians on the land question, with the Canadians on tariffs, with urbanites in Australia and at the Cape on the convict system. Like the Colonial Reformers he believed that responsible government was not at all incompatible with continuing dependency. No more than they had he fully faced the implications of the new system.

Grey also differed with the colonies on the question of timing, believing that self-government must be prepared for and that it must involve the assumption of responsibility. Political development should evolve by safe and comfortable stages, as it had done in America. As is evident from the abortive New Zealand constitution of 1846 (which he and Stephen drew up with minimal outside influence), he thought that colonial politicians should begin their training in municipal government, graduating after a reasonable interval to a share of power in the colony as a whole. Moreover, self-governing colonies must assume the cost of their own administration and local defense.

In every settlement colony outside the 1867 boundaries of Canada Grey placed the Colonial Office squarely athwart the urge to self-government. He stood firm when the legislative council of New South Wales remonstrated against a continuation of "the exploded fallacies of the Wakefield theory" in the Australian government act of 1850.[3] When Newfoundland's Catholic party agitated for responsible government he simply

3. K. Bell and W. Morrell, eds., *Select Documents on British Colonial Policy, 1830–1860* (1928), pp. 137–40.

refused, explaining curtly that the colony was too backward.[4] In backing Governor Sir George Grey's postponement of the 1846 constitution in New Zealand, on the grounds that the measure would "give to a small fraction of her [the Queen's] subjects of one race the power of governing the large majority of her subjects of a different race," he became a backer of despotism.[5]

Thus, although he was in favor of self-government as an abstract principle, Lord Grey found himself opposed to it in practice. This contradiction is not uncharacteristic, for the man was full of paradoxes. He is usually described as a doctrinaire, which is certainly accurate. But another side of his nature also needs to be stressed: his uncertainty and his agonizing self-doubt.

> I am painfully conscious [he confided in his journal] of faults which make me utterly unfit for any *leading* part in politics. I want altogether ye expertness in ye ways of ye world necessary for taking an active share in its affairs. . . . I am sadly deficient in ye arts by which my views might practically be carried into effect; in short I fear I am infinitely more fit for speculatn. than for actn.[6]

No indictment by a colonial critic can ever have been more devastating. Grey was not merely a doctrinaire: he was an indefatigable perfectionist.

This perfectionism contributed to the attitude of paternalism of which Grey was so often accused. He lacked sympathy with colonial grievances as well as the tact to deal with opposition. Perhaps, as Sir Frederic Rogers observed in a verdict that has often been quoted, his understanding of the historical process was defective:

4. Grey to Gov. Le Marchant, 13 Dec. 1851, CO 194/134.
5. A. McLintock, *Crown Colony Government in New Zealand* (Wellington, 1958), pp. 259 ff.; J. Rutherford, *Sir George Grey, 1812–1898: A Study in Colonial Government* (1961), pp. 71–287.
6. 15 July 1834, Grey Papers.

> Lord Grey was possessed with the idea that it was practicable to give representative institutions, and then to stop without giving responsible government—something like the English Constitution under Elizabeth and the Stuarts. He did not understand either the vigorous independence of an Anglo-Saxon community or the weakness of an executive which represents a democracy. So events took their own course, and left his theories behind.[7]

It is striking how similar Rogers' statement is to Elgin's comment on the naïveté of Sydenham. It must be emphasized, however, that the contradiction in Lord Grey's colonial policy was common to nearly all that small minority of Englishmen who thought the colonial question could be solved within the context of continuing imperial control.

Lord Grey's system of political apprenticeship would have required an inhuman degree of restraint from those he expected to submit to it. So long as the "imperial factor" could be attacked as a means of advancing their own ambitions, colonial politicians could reasonably be expected to do so. Encouraged by what had happened in Canada, they pressed forward. They did not always demand responsible government, for Grey was right in arguing that the base of political parties outside North America was not yet sufficiently developed to support the cabinet system. They demanded freedom from such onerous policies as the transportation of convicts, freedom to manage their lands and minerals, the freedom of popularly representative institutions. The colonial politicians carried the campaign for self-government that had begun in Canada into all the European portions of the empire.

Their techniques are familiar to students of the process of modern political development. In Sydney and Melbourne politicians as diverse in political outlook as J. D. Lang, Joseph Parkes, and W. C. Wentworth harangued large public meet-

7. G. Marindin, ed., *Letters of Frederic Lord Blachford, Under-Secretary of State for the Colonies, 1860–1871* (1896), pp. 297–98.

ings that passed resolution after resolution. Committees of correspondence were formed. Large numbers of pamphlets were produced. In Cape Town John Fairbairn's anti-convict association inspired deluges of identical petitions that were delivered to local government offices just before the mail packet sailed for England, making it impossible for the signatures to be properly authenticated.[8] In that colony's legislative council all but one of the unofficial members resigned, leaving the governor without a quorum. Noisy crowds gathered and boycotts were organized when the convict ship *Neptune* arrived there in 1849. In Newfoundland the legislature refused to vote supplies. In all the colonies a lively torrent of abuse poured out from the press.

These were means which had been employed by the English parliamentarians in their struggle against the king in the seventeenth century. They had been further refined by the American colonists in their conflicts with royal governors. They would be used in turn in India and in Africa—by every people in pursuit of liberty. Moreover, these techniques of agitation were themselves a sign of political development, of ripening, a step toward the responsible exercise of leadership in a representative government. The unhappy focal point of all this wholesome development, Lord Grey, remained unreceptive and impatient, unaware that the hundreds of hostile documents that crossed his desk were but the external evidence of a significant degree of political maturation.

The colonists found considerable support in England. In parliament the remnants of the old Colonial Reform school—C. B. Adderley, J. A. Roebuck, Sir William Molesworth, Joseph Hume—attacked Lord Grey's apprenticeship system as iniquitous and unnecessary: the Americans had never undergone such a period of training. *The Times,* where the former Sydney politician Robert Lowe was writing leading articles,

8. Or so it was charged in John Montagu to C.O., 2 Mar. 1852, Papers re Cape Assembly, PP, 1852–53 [1581], *66,* 142–43.

joined in.[9] As usual it was Stephen who accurately appraised the situation:

> It is inherent in the nature of all such bodies [colonial legislatures] to believe, or at least to act, speak, and write as though they believed, that every accession to their own power is likewise an accession to the public weal. It is inherent in the nature of all local journalists to echo such pretensions. It is scarcely less inevitable that the remonstrances of the Colonial Legislatures and journals, should be re-echoed in our own newspapers and in Parliament. Before that combination the Colonial Office can make no stand. I say 'the Colonial Office' because no member of the Cabinet but the Head of that office can ever be persuaded to devote his time to such repulsive controversies. The policy of yielding is the obvious and easy policy.[10]

Stephen's shrewd advice was taken on the occasion when it was requested, but it was ignored later. And it was on the least defensible of issues, the convict system, that Lord Grey chose to make his stand. The ground could not have been more poorly selected. Public opinion, led by untainted Australians and by Benthamite reformers at home, had been rising against it steadily. As long ago as 1837 a select committee of the House of Commons, of which Grey himself had been a dissenting member, had strongly denounced it. Moreover, the imperial government had already retreated, abolishing transportation to New South Wales in 1840 and even suspending it temporarily to Van Diemen's Land in 1846.

Grey expected opposition to his announcement in September 1848 that New South Wales (which then included Port Phillip) and the Cape were to be added to the list of colonies eligible to receive convicts, but hoped it might be overcome

9. *The History of the Times* (4 vols., New York, 1935–52), 2, 130.
10. Bell and Morrell, *Select Documents,* p. 117.

by an appeal to the colonists' self-interest and sense of imperial responsibility.[11] The colonies, after all, had chronic labor shortages. And since Britain defended them, they should not object to a small gesture in return. Britain's own need was desperate, particularly in connection with the wave of famine-related incidents in Ireland. Despite the Benthamite campaign the government had never seriously applied itself to penal reform, and the responsibility for doing so rested with the Home Office. By dispersing the convicts more widely, while sending them out only after an initial period of confinement, Grey was trying to correct some of the admitted evils of the system. Anticipating that the measure would be unpopular at first, he hoped that once the convicts had arrived and had made themselves useful the colonists could thereafter be persuaded to act in what he regarded as their own best interest.[12] But he was wrong.

There was far more to the issue than the few convicts who were the tangible symbols of resistance. More significant was the fact that Grey was placing the Colonial Office squarely in the middle of the dominant conflict in colonial politics: the struggle between urban and rural interests. In the sheep-raising sections of Australia convicts swelled the squatters' profits; in the cities, where many of them would go after serving out their sentences, they would compete for jobs and perhaps lower the wage levels. Whereas in Canada Grey had wisely withdrawn the imperial government from an involvement in local politics that could only result in embarrassment, in Australia he was tying the Colonial Office to the fortunes of a declining "aristocracy" of squatters.

The issue could hardly have been more convenient for

11. On the transportation crisis see W. Morrell, *British Colonial Policy in the Age of Peel and Russell* (1930), pp. 387–426; J. Ward, *Earl Grey and the Australian Colonies, 1846–1857: A Study of Self-Government and Self-Interest* (Melbourne, 1958), pp. 196 ff.; and E. Scott, "Problems of Settlement: Transportation," *CHBE*, *2*, 415–37.

12. Grey minute of 15 Mar. 1849, CO 48/294.

urban politicians, who swiftly succeeded in building up a rather impressive agitation that was well organized, sustained, and articulate. In Australia the anti-transportation league, based in Sydney and possessing branches in every Australian colony and even spreading to New Zealand, comprised a movement in which some historians have detected the first organized expression of a national attitude.[13] In Cape Town, where Grey sent three hundred Irish political prisoners as a test case in 1849, Fairbairn's machine inspired boycotts and riots to the extent that they enabled Sir Harry Smith to justify sending the convicts on to Van Diemen's Land. Hardly up to the American or even the Canadian standards of political development, the agitations were nonetheless impressive.

Lord Grey was tenacious. "If these convicts shd. be removed from the Cape," he wrote as the news began to arrive, "it will give a stimulus to the spirit of resistance . . . elsewhere wh. will be most dangerous."[14] Thereafter he retreated grudgingly. When he finally bowed to the inevitable in 1851, announcing that the order of 1848 would no longer be applied, he insisted on upholding a principle that was almost certainly not going to be applicable. "This Country is perfectly justified," he wrote later, "in continuing . . . Transportation to Australia; the Colonies being only entitled to ask, that in arrangements for conducting it, their interests and welfare should be consulted as far as possible."[15]

If Lord Grey had really possessed the effective decision-making power in this matter, the results of his attempts to force convicts on the aroused citizenry of Cape Town, Sydney,

13. See particularly the articles of C. Blackton, "The Australasian League, 1851–1854," *Pacific Historical Review, 8* (1939), 385–400; and "New Zealand and the Australian Anti-Transportation Movement," *Historical Studies, Australia and New Zealand, 1* (1940), 116–22.

14. Minute on Smith to S. of S., 29 June 1849, CO 48/296.

15. *Colonial Policy, 2,* 87. He was in fact attempting to leave a loophole in case Moreton Bay (later Queensland) could be persuaded to accept convicts. Grey minute on A. Hodgson to Grey, Brisbane, 29 May 1850, CO 201/437.

and Melbourne might have been rather interesting. It is even conceivable that such stubbornness might in time have galvanized something like the kind of nation-building he was trying, ironically enough, to stimulate on purpose in his proposals for Australian federation.[16] But though the settlement of convicts might well be regarded as an imperial question to be decided in London, that of keeping order in remote colonies had to be left to the governors. When Sir Harry Smith pleaded that the Cape Town mob had left him no alternative but to send the *Neptune* away, a secretary of state might suspect that he was being trifled with, but there was little he could do about it.[17] When Sir Charles FitzRoy warned that Sydney might well become ungovernable, Grey could only give way.[18] As Stephen had observed, "the policy of yielding" had much to recommend it. By February 1852, shortly before Grey left office, the assistant undersecretary T. F. Elliot was offering the judicious if overdue advice that even the principle ought to be dropped, for "in the absence of a substantial difference, it would be very desirable to endeavour to deprive the opponents of Govt. of an opportunity of keeping up the shadow of one." [19]

Along with the Kaffir war in South Africa the transportation crisis dominated Grey's later years at the Colonial Office as the concession of responsible government in Canada had marked his earlier and happier ones. He had presided over one of those comparatively rare attempts in British imperial history to carry into effect a coherent colonial policy conceived at the center. In 1852, disillusioned and convinced that he had failed, he retired from active politics never to hold office again. He had, however, left his mark. Statesmen such as Carnarvon and Macdonald, Chamberlain and Parkes, might one day remember his premature anticipation of their own successful nation-

16. See Ward, *Earl Grey and the Australian Colonies*, passim.
17. Grey minute on Smith to S. of S., 18 Oct. 1849, CO 48/299.
18. Grey to FitzRoy, 10 Apr. 1851, Papers re Transportation, PP, 1851 [1361], *45*, 223.
19. Minute on FitzRoy to S. of S., 5 Nov. 1851, CO 201/443.

building, or acknowledge that to Grey "we all must feel we owe most of the principles by which our colonial policy is guided."[20] More immediately significant were the colonial political movements that had been organized against him and the lessons that colonial administrators learned from his mistakes.

In principle there was little revision after Grey. All administrators either favored or were resigned to the extension of self-government in principle, though qualifications continued to be made in matters of timing and degree. There continued to be little admiration for democracy, as well as dismay at the failure of colonial governments to observe the fundamental axiom that budgets must be balanced. The Duke of Newcastle, fully as devoted to free trade as Lord Grey, could wonder at the folly of a colony's retrogression toward the "exploded fallacies" of protectionism.[21] Nor was there any very sudden surge of faith in the alleged ability of colonial societies to govern themselves. What was learned from the Grey period were more practical lessons.

Most important, there was a common recognition of impotence: "we have no power to enforce."[22] Stephen had realized this. Although Grey had apparently forgotten it, his experience returned it to currency. Without power, paternalism had to be abandoned: "I fear there is no alternative except to shut our eyes to proceedings which seen at this distance wear a most extravagant aspect."[23] Lord Grey's apprenticeship system had demanded patience from the colonists. To refuse to intervene, even in instances that appeared to cry out for corrective ac-

20. Speech of Chamberlain in 1900, in A. Keith, ed., *Selected Speeches and Documents on British Colonial Policy, 1763–1917* (2 vols. in 1, 1948), *1*, 339.

21. Newcastle to Sir Henry Barkly (Victoria), pvt., 25 Nov. 1861, Newcastle Papers, NeC 10,885.

22. Newcastle minute on Acting Gov. Wynyard (New Zealand) to S. of S., 14 Feb. 1854, CO 209/122.

23. Merivale minute on FitzRoy (N.S.W.) to S. of S., 7 Feb. 1853, CO 201/463.

tion, would require considerable restraint from the Colonial Office.

It was also learned that to become involved in local politics could only make matters worse: "indeed our interference is likely to be injurious to the side which we aid." [24] In fact, having been too aggressive under Grey, the office now swung to the opposite extreme: the Duke of Newcastle dealt timidly with Victorian land questions; [25] Sir George Grey did not intervene when the Australian colonies established different railway gauges.[26] It was the Treasury, not the Colonial Office, that had to assume a mediating role in the negotiation of Australian postal contracts. Though Merivale occasionally made halfhearted suggestions about the desirability of federal cooperation in Australia, no secretary of state was willing to exert the slightest pressure to encourage it. If Lord Grey had attempted too much direction of imperial policy, his successors tried too little. The result was a pattern of "drift."

This tendency toward drift was accentuated by the Crimean War and the increasing confusion of politics.[27] Until the creation of a separate minister for the colonies in June 1854 the Duke of Newcastle (who was also secretary for war) was preoccupied with military preparations. Such matters as Victorian land policy and responsible government in Newfoundland were simply neglected. In the fluid state of politics colonial secretaries passed through the office at an alarming rate. Pakington served for less than a year, Newcastle for a year and a half. In the interval between the latter's transfer to the War

24. Molesworth minute on Wynyard to S. of S., 3 Mar. 1855, CO 209/128.

25. See G. Serle, *The Golden Age, A History of the Colony of Victoria, 1851–1861* (Melbourne, 1963), pp. 130–36.

26. Ward, *Earl Grey and the Australian Colonies,* pp. 271 ff.

27. See particularly J. Vincent, *The Formation of the Liberal Party, 1857–1868* (1966); O. Anderson, *A Liberal State at War: English Politics and Economics during the Crimean War* (1967); J. Conacher, *The Aberdeen Coalition, 1852–1855: A Study in Mid-Nineteenth-Century Party Politics* (Cambridge, 1968).

Office and Henry Labouchere's entry into the Colonial Office in October 1855 Sir George Grey, Sidney Herbert, Russell, and Molesworth held the seals, with Grey and Palmerston filling in unofficially during Russell's peace mission in Vienna. With the constant shuffle at the top, where the routine of the office focused so much of the decision making, no coherent administration was possible. In such an atmosphere of confusion and indecisiveness the "revolution" in the second empire that had begun in the North American colonies quickened and spread.

This revolution was very largely administrative. What happened was that the barriers Lord Grey had tried to maintain against too rapid a pace outside Canada were quietly abandoned. There was extraordinarily little excitement, the atmosphere being considerably quieter than in Canada in the thirties or in the other settlements in the late forties. Yet the achievements were significant, leaving none of the established settlement colonies untouched. In Canada the administration of the clergy reserves was handed over to the local government, while the upper house was made elective. Responsible government was conceded in Newfoundland and New Zealand. In the Cape Colony legislative institutions were extended under a constitution that professed to be nondiscriminatory. And in the four colonies of eastern Australia the control of land and gold was given to the colonial governments, new constitutions written, and responsible government conceded. Except in the case of Canada it mattered little who happened at the time to be colonial secretary. Partly from desire and partly from necessity, the Colonial Office abandoned the attempt to control the progress of colonial self-government.

The Spread of Self-Government

In conceding responsible government to Canada Lord Grey had done far more than to permit the establishment of a new relationship between a governor and his colonial advisers. He had in effect removed the last effective barrier standing in the way of Canada's becoming a fully independent nation, the only real question being how long the process would take. These implications were no more apparent to Grey than they had been to Durham, and if the wiser Elgin sensed them he did not say so. Yet the process began at once. In the late 1850s the common imperial tariff would fall; later it would be common defense and Britain's control over Canada's foreign relations. Dominion status would be recognized in 1926. Yet as late as 1949 still another remnant of dependency, the appeals to the Judicial Committee of the Privy Council, would be dropped. The working out of the implications of responsible government was gradual, but it was implied from the start. Durham had proposed a "final solution": instead it had turned out to be a beginning.

With the great drive toward the consolidation of a Canadian national framework still a decade away, in the 1850s it was largely a question of tidying up. The loosest end was the issue of the clergy reserves, tracts of land (bearing an estimated value of £336,000)[28] that had been set aside by the Canada Act of 1791 for the support of the churches of England and Scotland in Upper Canada. They were said to form a barrier against economic development. More important, they were the most visible portion of the larger state-church question, and there was no more heated controversy in English-speaking Canada: Sydenham had called them "the great overwhelming grievance."[29] The settlement of 1840 had permitted several other denominations to receive support, but the "voluntarists" were unappeased and agitation continued. In 1850 an address to the throne from the Canadian assembly asked for

28. Return re Clergy Reserves, PP, 1852–53 (173), *65*, 607.

29. Sydenham to Russell, 18 Jan. 1840, in P. Knaplund, ed., *Letters from Lord Sydenham to Lord John Russell* (1931), p. 42. See J. Moir, *Church and State in Canada West: Three Studies in the Relation of Denominationalism and Nationalism, 1841–1867* (Toronto, 1959).

an act enabling the local legislature to deal with the question, and Lord Grey agreed on the grounds of Canada's right "to regulate all matters concerning the domestic interests of the province."[30] It was to be a test case of responsible government. But, pleading opposition in the Lords and the press of business in the Commons, he postponed the measure,[31] and the fall of the Whig government early in 1852 left the decision to the Conservatives.

Standing on their principles, the Conservatives refused to accept the "obvious and easy" way of graceful retreat which the coming of responsible government had prepared. Although Disraeli was unconcerned, Lord Derby went so far as to say that "no consideration on earth, not even the dismemberment of the empire itself," would persuade him to change his mind.[32] Equally adamant, the colonial secretary Sir John Pakington was wise enough not to attack responsible government directly. Instead he gained time by calling for an election.[33] When it went against him, and addresses arrived from both houses of the Canadian legislature, he stalled further and at length refused to comply, while at the same time claiming that the principle of responsible government was not being violated. His dispatch announcing that no change at all would be made in the settlement of 1840 was canceled by the Derby government's fall in December 1852.

Pakington's successor, the Duke of Newcastle, speedily reverted to Grey's position, ignoring the religious issue in favor of the larger principle of responsible government. Neither he nor Elgin doubted that disestablishment would eventually follow, but as the latter remarked, "it is neither for the interest of the

30. Grey to Elgin, 27 Jan. 1851, Papers re Clergy Reserves, PP, 1851 [1306], *36*, 234.
31. Grey to Elgin, 11 July 1851, Further Papers re Clergy Reserves, PP, 1852 [1448], *33*, 50–51.
32. 22 Apr. 1852, 3 *Hansard, 126*, 291.
33. Pakington to Elgin, 22 Apr. 1852, Correspondence re Clergy Reserves, PP, 1852–53 (85), *65*, 526.

[imperial] connexion, nor for that of the Church itself, that the opponents of the endowments should be able to allege that they are imposed on the people . . . by Imperial authority."[34] The British parliamentary debate was an easier version of the one in 1849 on the rebellion losses bill. Except for Gladstone, who faced the religious issue squarely (reversing his earlier position on responsible government and pointing toward his later disestablishment of the Anglican Church in Ireland), the government speakers refused to discuss the possibility of secularization, maintaining the only relevant question to be the right of a responsibly governed colony to control its own internal affairs. The Conservatives' opposition was little more than token, and some of them were most uncomfortable. "I scarcely know what to do," confessed the younger Stanley to Disraeli. "I am not prepared to support the theory of an Imperial right of interference in the internal affairs of Canada, which is practically a negation of the principle of responsible Govt."[35] In the Lords, where the presence of so many churchmen was cause for apprehension, Newcastle was still more explicit, warning that "colonial freedom will in the end prevail."[36] In fact nine bishops joined the majority, and the question was returned to Canada, where its resolution was to provide the setting for an important turning point in her political history.[37] Britain had succeeded in extricating herself from a potentially dangerous confrontation.

34. Elgin to Newcastle, pvt., 28 Jan. 1853, Newcastle Papers, NeC 9552.

35. 21 Feb. 1853, Disraeli Papers, B/XX/S/593.

36. 22 Apr. 1853, 3 *Hansard, 126,* 257–58.

37. The sequel in Canada saw Macdonald agree in 1854 not to oppose secularization, thus enabling him to outmaneuver George Brown, who had also been attempting to combine with the moderate French and the Upper Canadian followers of Francis Hincks, and thus to form his long-lived Conservative party. See D. Creighton, *John A. Macdonald* (2 vols. Toronto, 1953–56), *1,* 147 ff.; J. Careless, *Brown of the Globe* (2 vols. Toronto, 1959–63), *1,* 116 ff.

Compared with the clergy reserves question, the reform of the Canadian legislative council went almost unnoticed, an exception to the usual pattern of colonial pressure and imperial retreat. For, although the election of members of the upper house had been one of Papineau's most strongly resisted proposals in the 1830s, the measure was conceived and very largely implemented by the imperial authorities through the normal channels of correspondence and without much agitation from the colonists.

The nominated upper house had not proved itself effectual as a check against the democratic leanings of popularly elected assemblies. That much admired quality of institutional balance, which Montesquieu and Blackstone had described and of which Bagehot was to write, was missing from colonial practice. The upper houses lacked the prestige of the American Senate, which became an increasingly attractive model. Thus it was as a conservative that Elgin recommended the reform to Newcastle,[38] who had already arrived at a similar conclusion in regard to New South Wales.[39] Elgin inspired an address to the throne from the Canadian assembly, and there was little difficulty in the English parliament, although Lord Derby rather feebly opposed the drift toward republicanism. The result was an important constitutional change. But it did not of course offset the dominance of the lower house, an institutional imbalance that is apparently quite as inherent in the working of the cabinet system as it is a reflection of democratization.

In the 1850s the substance of the colonial situation was gradually being removed from the relationship between Britain and Canada. The lines of development are so well known that there is no necessity to explore them further here. In 1854

38. Elgin to Newcastle, 26 Mar. 1853, in T. Walrond, ed., *Letters and Journals of James, Eighth Earl of Elgin* (1872), pp. 145–46.
39. Minute on FitzRoy to C.O., 31 Aug. 1852, CO 201/453.

the negotiation of a reciprocity treaty with the United States was carried on through British diplomatic channels, but there was little doubt about who the real parties were.[40] And in 1858 the Canadians succeeded in implementing a tariff against British imports, much to the displeasure of that old Colonial Reformer, advocate of responsible government, and former agent of Lower Canada, J. A. Roebuck, who also happened to be an M. P. for Sheffield. Much as Britain might dislike such measures, explained the Duke of Newcastle in 1859, after Alexander Tilloch Galt's famous declaration of defiance, there was really nothing that could be done about it.[41]

As members of the Colonial Office had observed so often, they had "no power to enforce." The coming of responsible government had provided a graceful means of retreat from confrontation, and its employment by the imperial authorities became increasingly automatic. Many concessions remained to be made. Yet as early as a decade before confederation the contradiction between colonial self-government and imperial control had been effectively removed.

If given to one of the North American colonies, responsible government "must be granted in all." But in the late 1840s Lord Grey had decided: all except Newfoundland. For the system seemed "hardly calculated to answer in a Colony, where the Inhabitants have not been for some time accustomed to the exercise of Representative Govt. in its simpler form." [42] Newfoundland was still economically backward, and

40. See particularly D. Masters, *The Reciprocity Treaty of 1854* (Toronto, 1963); R. Winks, *Canada and the United States: The Civil War Years* (Baltimore, 1960); and J. Careless, *The Union of the Canadas: The Growth of Canadian Institutions, 1841–1857* (Toronto, 1967).

41. See O. Skelton, *The Life and Times of Sir Alexander Tilloch Galt* (Toronto, 1920), pp. 323 ff.

42. Grey to Le Marchant, 13 Dec. 1851, CO 194/134. See R. MacKay, ed., *Newfoundland: Economic, Diplomatic, and Strategic Studies* (Toronto, 1946); A. McLintock, *The Establishment of Constitutional Govern-*

the history of conflict between the predominantly Protestant merchants and the Irish-Catholic lower class (which had already necessitated a suspension of representative government in the 1830s) did not seem promising. But a determined agitation was building up, led by P. F. Little in the Catholic-dominated assembly and encouraged by the Catholic clergy. Though a slight majority in the colony the Protestants were divided and ineffectual. Merivale thought that they "will lean on the Home Government, and its official representatives in the colony, rather than exert themselves, as long as they can." [43] Simply to withdraw would be "obvious and easy," for how could the Colonial Office "continue to refuse to Newfoundland what has been given to Prince Edward Island." [44]

Sir John Pakington too wished not to yield prematurely. He expressed confidence in the governor, repeated Grey's explanation of why the colony was not ready, lectured the Catholic bishop on the impropriety of his meddling in politics, and warned that in the event of a collision with the assembly he would "not hesitate to recommend to Parlt. such measures . . . as the case may require to ensure the better government of the colony." [45] Meant as an only slightly veiled threat to suspend representative institutions entirely, his ambiguously worded statement was seized upon as an invitation to increase the pressure, with the prize of responsible government in the offing should the assembly's tactics prove to be irresistible.

Predictably, the tension increased, with the governor and the appointed legislative council locked in heroic if somewhat Lilliputian conflict with the assembly. The assembly passed

---

ment in Newfoundland, 1783–1832 (1942); and G. Gunn, *The Political History of Newfoundland, 1832–1864* (Toronto, 1966).

43. Minute on Le Marchant to S. of S., 13 Feb. 1852, CO 194/136.

44. Newcastle to Gov. Hamilton, pvt., 7 Oct. 1853, Newcastle Papers, NeC 9552.

45. Pakington minute on Le Marchant to S. of S., 24 Mar. 1852, CO 194/136.

addresses to the throne, and threatened not to vote supplies; Governor K. Baillie Hamilton charged that responsible government would make the colony "a misruled Papal diocese." [46] A delegation soon arrived in London, Joseph Hume sponsoring its visit to the Colonial Office, where the Duke of Newcastle promised a prompt decision. But for nearly two months, "by some unaccountable oversight," the problem resided on his desk, presumably beneath growing piles of paper pertaining to left boots for the Crimea. When at length he got round to it, the answer seemed clear, for how could a concession already made in the neighboring colonies be refused? "Such a position" could not "be long maintained, and if it cannot it at once becomes a clear matter of policy to make the change before such a degree of animosity and antagonism has been produced as must always add far greater dangers to the attainment of popular rights." [47] Reluctantly he made his decision: "It is perhaps the severest test to which 'responsible government' can be exposed." [48] The office having been withdrawn from an untenable position, the assembly and council were left to continue their rivalry, which they did with considerable bravado, the assembly emerging victorious through its control of the purse. But responsible government was not successful enough to prevent Newfoundland's revision, once more, to the status of crown colony, before she finally joined the Canadian confederation after World War II.

As early as 1848 Lord Grey had resigned himself to the decision that representative institutions must be conceded to the Cape Colony. As Stephen explained, the crown-colony system had proved ineffective as a means of governing the sprawling, sparsely populated, and racially diverse area. A more popular

46. Hamilton to Newcastle, pvt., 3 Nov. 1853, Newcastle Papers, NeC 9552.
47. Newcastle to Hamilton, pvt., 7 and 13 Oct. 1853, ibid.
48. Minute of 31 Jan. 1854, CO 194/139.

form of government might not be much worse. Besides, the colonial press was demanding a change, and unless the local politicians should prove to be extremely bad tacticians they would shortly produce a relatively low-keyed agitation that, stopping short of the open rebellion which alone might create support in Britain for resistance, would leave the Colonial Office no practical alternative but to comply. Why not give in gracefully?[49] Lord Grey agreed and, though the convict disturbance delayed the process, by January 1850 a draft constitution was sent to the colony, providing for a bicameral legislature but retaining executive control in the hands of the governor, and leaving to be determined by the local authorities such questions as the machinery of election and the setting of the franchise.[50]

The *Neptune* incident had created a charged atmosphere in which so controversial a question as the vote for nonwhites was unlikely to be approached calmly. By September 1850 the governor was confronted with the resignations of four of five unofficial members of the legislative council, who asserted that they had been elected to draft a constitution, not to act on such "nonessential" measures as the annual estimates.[51] Soon John Fairbairn came to bring pressure more directly in London.[52] Yet despite the heat of the agitation the greatest obstacle was the length of time necessarily involved in drafting a document in two capitals. The measure seemed to be proceeding satisfactorily when the outbreak of a Kaffir war in December 1850, requiring the governor's presence at the front, made postponement inevitable.[53]

49. Minute on Smith to S. of S., 29 July 1848, CO 48/289.

50. Grey to Smith, 31 Jan. 1850, Papers re Cape Assembly, PP, 1850 [1137], *38*, 210–11

51. Smith to Grey, 24 Sept. 1850, CO 48/307.

52. Grey refused to recognize him as having any sort of representative status, deliberately downgrading him by conducting correspondence over the signature of an undersecretary instead of his own. Grey minute [28 Dec. 1850], CO 48/311.

53. Grey minute on Smith to S. of S., 19 Feb. 1851, CO 48/313.

Sir John Pakington readily agreed that the constitution could not come into effect during the emergency. No one, however, had suggested that work should stop on its details. And, as the Cape Town "machine" ground out the petitions, Merivale grew suspicious that the Colonial Office was being blamed for the inactivity of the local authorities. Following the undersecretary's advice, Pakington spurred them on.[54] It was the war, dragging on beyond all expectations, that forced him "reluctantly" to postpone the constitution still further.[55] The problem remained, essentially in the state in which Lord Grey had left it, for the end of the war and for the Duke of Newcastle.

Once Sir George Cathcart brought the war to an end, Newcastle acted swiftly, sending out the constitution in March 1853. His most important decision concerned the level of the property qualification for the franchise. Lord Grey's original draft had put the sum at £25 annual rent, arousing fear in the colony lest too many nonwhite voters should be included.[56] The sharp division in the legislative council and in the colony as a whole had at length been resolved in favor of a £50 franchise, calculated to exclude virtually all African, Cape Coloured, and Asian voters. Beneath the cant of the dispatch announcing Newcastle's decision was an accurate appraisal of its importance.[57] For the 1853 constitution established a safety valve, sharply contrasting with the rigidly exclusionist policies

54. Merivale minute on Smith to S. of S., 18 Feb. 1852; Pakington to Gov. Sir George Cathcart, 14 Apr. 1852, CO 42/324. In fact the legislative council was already sharply divided on the question of the franchise.

55. Pakington to Cathcart, 4 Sept. 1852, Further Cape Assembly Papers, PP, 1852–53 [1581], *66*, 332–33.

56. John Montagu (Cape colonial secretary) to C.O., 28 Feb. 1852, ibid., *66*, 139.

57. Newcastle minute, 7 Mar. 1853, CO 48/277; Newcastle to Cathcart, 14 Mar., 1853, PP, 1852–53 [1581], *66*, 362–64. See S. Trapido, "The Origins of the Cape Franchise Qualifications of 1853," *Journal of African History*, *5* (1964), 37–54, and J. Marais, *The Cape Coloured People, 1652–1937* (reprinted Johannesburg, 1962), pp. 212–15 and passim.

of the Boer republics to the north. The conflict between these two traditions was to have a long history, until the Cape's nonwhite franchise was finally abolished in the 1950s.

As at the Cape, self-government in New Zealand was complicated by the presence of a large and warlike population, who until the late 1850s remained in the majority.[58] Yet the usual clamor arose there, and the "obvious and easy policy" was to yield. Lord Grey with Stephen's aid drew up a "model" constitution in 1846, attempting to strike a balance between the present conditions of wide dispersal and primitive communications, which pointed toward decentralization, and the future circumstances of a small and isolated community that would obviously require centralization. But Governor Sir George Grey refused to put it into effect, pleading that the measure would be premature, unjust, and (in view of the superior strength and numbers of the Maoris) unwise.[59] The embarrassed secretary of state gracefully retreated, doing his best thereafter to shield the governor from the colonists' displeasure.

The governor's reasons for postponing the 1846 constitution are logical enough. It is more difficult to comprehend why he should have decided only four years later to frame a constitution himself. Perhaps he was overconfident of the success of his native policy; perhaps he wished to be the founding father himself. The fact is that the situation in New Zealand had not changed in essentials. Self-government would still be reserved for the whites. As a contemporary critic commented, para-

58. See J. Miller, *Early Victorian New Zealand: A Study of Racial Tension and Social Attitudes, 1839–1852* (Oxford, 1958); A. McLintock, *Crown Colony Government in New Zealand;* W. Morrell, *The Provincial System in New Zealand, 1852–1876* (1932); and D. Herron, "Provincialism and Centralism, 1853–1858," in R. Chapman and K. Sinclair, eds., *Studies of a Small Democracy: Essays in Honour of Willis Airey* (Auckland, 1963), pp. 10–32.

59. Grey to S. of S., 3 May 1847, Bell and Morrell, *Select Documents,* pp. 97–102.

phrasing ironically the governor's own famous language: "Sir George Grey . . . by his own act gave to a minority of Her Majesty's subjects of one race the power of taxing and governing the majority of Her Majesty's subjects of another race." [60]

Having been embarrassed once by a hasty action, Lord Grey was now in no particular hurry. Merivale was able to discover a technical defect or two in the governor's draft, which was sent back to the colony for corrections that might easily have been made in London. By the time the document returned the Russell government was only a few weeks away from its fall. Having been impressed by the governor's arguments that self-government would be dangerous, Lord Grey had carried out a successful delaying action. There were times when the slowness of communication with the colonies was most convenient.

Despite his initial inclination to continue the postponement, Sir John Pakington yielded to the pressure of William Fox, C. B. Adderley, and Edward Gibbon Wakefield, consenting to bring Lord Grey's bill into parliament. There it was greeted by a lively debate that turned more upon abstract theory and the American analogy than upon the circumstances of New Zealand. And thus the constitution was settled, though the governor managed to delay its introduction until after his departure from the colony in 1854. Only then did the colonists themselves begin to play a role. Heretofore, as shown by the debate in the Commons and the tone of the Colonial Office minutes, no one had paid them much attention.

> The truth is [Merivale had written] that the inhabitants of New Zealand are as yet too few, & too scattered, to have formed any definite & valuable opinion on the relative merits of centralisation & federalism as applied to the islands. It is a question of difficulty no doubt, but [one]

60. Dr. A. S. Thompson (a physician in Grey's native hospitals), Papers re Affairs of New Zealand Natives, PP, 1860 [2719], *46*, 438.

which must be decided [i.e., in London] on general views.[61]

This state of comfortable insulation ceased abruptly in May 1854 when, Sir George Grey having made his escape, the New Zealand general assembly was first convened. Within a week the acting governor, Col. R. H. Wynyard, was confronted with a demand for responsible government that was moved by Wakefield, who had emigrated in 1852. Showing no stomach for a fight, Wynyard took advice unofficially from Wakefield who, as Merivale had predicted, "will make governing the colony no easy task for any one who will not take him as his unavowed prime minister." [62] Swiftly Wynyard gave way, appointing three members of the House of Representatives to his executive council, and obtaining promises from the official members to resign with compensation pending the approval of London. It was a de facto acceptance of responsible government. Wakefield and the New Zealand politicians in little more than a month had accomplished what Joseph Howe had spent years to achieve.

In view of the heated discussion that took place later over what, in the context of the wars of the 1860s, would then appear to have been a serious mistake, it is surprising that the Colonial Office in 1854 dealt with the matter perfunctorily. Sir George Grey of Falloden was inexperienced, and the permanent staff failed for some reason to bring the implications to his attention. There were complaints that the temporary governor had overstepped his authority, and that the home govern-

61. Pakington to Grey, 10 Apr. 1852, CO 209/94; Fox to Pakington, London, 25 Mar. 1852, and Pakington minute; Wakefield to Pakington, 2 June 1852; minute on Fox to Pakington, 28 Apr. 1852; CO 209/113.

62. Minute on Wakefield to Newcastle, Wellington, 21 May 1853, CO 209/121. See W. Swainson, *New Zealand and its Colonization* (1959), pp. 282 ff., for a firsthand account of the maneuvering; also Correspondence re Establishment of Responsible Government in New Zealand, PP, 1854–55 (160), *38*, 555–600.

ment was being treated shabbily. A good deal of attention was paid to pensions for the Colonial Office's appointees who were to be replaced by responsible advisers. Merivale discussed the constitutional basis of the system:

> 'Responsible government' in this country rests on no law, but simply on recognized usage . . . it [is] not established by any law, generally speaking, in the Nth. Am[erica]n colonies, where it is best understood . . . the danger of legislation on such subjects is that the necessary arrangements & modifications on a subject which must often require them are thus rendered more difficult.[63]

Not one word, however, was written about the complications legislative power would cause for native administration, over which the governor would remain responsible though he would be utterly dependent on the assembly for funds. Nor was any effort made to arrive at some sort of settlement with regard to the colony's share of its defense costs, before the lever of conceding responsible government was abandoned. These implications were completely ignored. The Colonial Office based its dissatisfaction, instead, on the technical details of how the question of responsible government had been presented.

In the Australian colonies (hereafter the exception of Western Australia may be assumed) what had been a relatively gradual political advance was greatly stimulated by the gold discoveries of the early 1850s. Scholars have recently been emphasizing more continuous factors: the primacy of wool in the economy, and the role of the cities rather than the goldfields in the formation of democracy. More a catalyst than an initiator, gold speeded the operation of forces that had been lead-

63. Minute on Wynyard to S. of S., 10 Aug. 1854, CO 209/124.

ing toward self-government for decades.[64] Yet the social effects of the discoveries should not be underrated,[65] while their immediate psychological impact was enormous. Projects that had been languishing or advancing slowly were stepped up. The rate of assisted and unassisted immigration spurted. A steam postal service was suddenly if fitfully established. Convict transportation, "disarmed of its terrors," was summarily abolished,[66] while even Grey's last hope for a renewal of it at Moreton Bay was abandoned.[67] British policy toward Australia in the 1850s was very largely dominated by the psychological reaction to the gold discoveries, which influenced significantly the timing and degree of changes that would eventually have come about in any case.

In the Australian government act of 1850 Lord Grey had brought the other colonies up to the level of limited representative government that was then in effect in New South Wales, and then had tried to call a halt. Much of the continent was only a generation removed from the "founding fathers": Australia had better develop her municipal government and let more ambitious undertakings come in good time. He had refused to concede responsible government and, what was more germane, administrative control over land policy and revenue. How Grey intended to hold the line is not entirely clear, for of

64. See the articles by R. Hartwell, "The Pastoral Ascendancy, 1820–1850," and I. McNaughtan, "Colonial Liberalism, 1851–92," in G. Greenwood, ed., *Australia, A Social and Political History* (Sydney, 1955), pp. 46–144.

65. Victoria increased in population from 87,000 in 1850 to 540,000 by 1861; between 1851 and 1853 her revenue increased from £392,000 to £3.2 million, her imports from £1 million to £15.8 million, and her exports from £1.4 million to £11 million. Even if a correction were made for inflation the statistics would still be impressive. Statistical Abstract, PP, 1866 [3709], *73*, 193–215.

66. Pakington to Sir William Denison (Van Diemen's Land), 14 Dec. 1852, in Bell and Morrell, *Select Documents*, p. 320.

67. Pakington to FitzRoy, 9 Dec. 1852, Papers re Transportation, PP, 1852–53 [1601], *82*, 131; Newcastle minute on FitzRoy to S. of S., 11 Aug. 1852, CO 201/453

course the Australian politicians had available all of what Merivale dryly referred to once as the "approved modes of agitation."[68] It was left to Sir John Pakington to form Australian policy in the "golden age," and however much Disraeli may have belittled him he was a distinct relief from the cranky stubbornness of Lord Grey.

In January 1852 the legislative council of New South Wales renewed the attack, calling for control of the colony's land and now gold revenue and for a constitution similar to Canada's. Once more, however, as in the Declaration and Remonstrance of 1851, responsible government was not a prominent demand: for the Australians were backing off.[69] More was involved than the demands of one colony. Partly from habit and partly because she remained the leader in the ability to agitate, New South Wales continued to be the focal point, but she could not be considered apart from "the neighboring colonies placed in similar circumstances."[70] As had been the case in North America earlier, a concession made in one colony "must be granted in all."

The result of the deliberations, in which Merivale played a prominent part, was the famous "golden dispatch" of December 1852,[71] in which Pakington gracefully conceded on all im-

68. Minute on Denison (N.S.W.) to S. of S., 28 Jan. 1856, CO 201/487.

69. Encl. in FitzRoy to S. of S., 15 Jan. 1852, CO 201/450. On the point that New South Wales did not press for responsible government, see J. Ward, *Empire in the Antipodes: The British in Australasia, 1840–1860* (1966), pp. 73–87.

70. Pakington to FitzRoy, canceled dispatch of 25 Sept. 1852, CO 201/450.

71. On Merivale's role see A. Melbourne, *Early Constitutional Development in Australia: New South Wales, 1788–1856* (1934), pp. 398–99. In my view the evidence (contained in CO 201/450) is not quite so conclusive in regard to Merivale's influence as Melbourne suggested. My reading of it is that Merivale probably did persuade Pakington to make concessions on self-government and land, in addition to the one on gold contained in the original draft. But the possibility remains that Merivale was responsible for no more than an adjustment of routine—i.e., the

portant points. Though agreeing with Lord Grey that local control over land revenue must be considered a question not of right but of expediency, he concluded that the recent increases in wealth and population had made it expedient. He conceded the management of the gold, and reaffirmed the discontinuance of transportation. And he invited the colonists themselves to frame a new constitution, "more closely assimilated to British institutions," with an elective assembly and a nominated upper house. New South Wales had asked for no more.

Pakington's graceful yielding was continued by the Duke of Newcastle. For the latter, determined at the outset to "avoid all irritating topics," [72] reaffirmed the abolition of transportation as well as the other pledges of his predecessor: only on the vexing question of Victoria's Convict Prevention Act did he permit himself to be drawn into a quarrel.[73] Indeed, he went Pakington one better by advising that responsible government would be the most appropriate means of exercising those legislative powers that had already been promised. That the legislative council of New South Wales had not pressed for the system did not trouble Newcastle, any more than the fact that none of the colonies yet possessed anything like political parties.[74] The decision was illustrative of the attitude that dominated the office after Lord Grey: the colonies would certainly demand responsible government; there would be no means of withholding it when they did; so why not deprive them of the opportunity for further agitation?

---

timing of dispatches. The crucial document, a private letter from Merivale to Pakington, is missing, and is not listed in the catalogue of Pakington's papers in the National Registry of Archives.

72. Minute on FitzRoy to S. of S., 31 Aug. 1852, CO 201/453.

73. Victoria was setting aside the crown's prerogative of mercy by prohibiting the entry of ticket-of-leave men, who were supposedly free to move so long as they did not return to England. As each act was disallowed the colony passed a new one, and finally succeeded in getting its way. See Serle, *The Golden Age,* pp. 126–30.

74. Ward, *Empire in the Antipodes,* pp. 73–87.

Primarily, however, Newcastle's secretaryship was a time of waiting. The colonies were making constitutions, a process largely dominated by a conflict between urban and landed interests that was crucial in Australian history.[75] By the time the constitutions arrived, the Duke had moved on to the War Office, his place having been taken by Sir George Grey. The documents themselves can be summarized in terms of the few main points that occupied the authorities in London: the form of the upper house, the extent of self-government, and the advisability of a federal assembly. All three acts—the one from Van Diemen's Land arrived too late to be considered with the others—provided for bicameral legislatures. Only Victoria's went beyond Pakington's instructions by proposing an elective upper chamber. She and New South Wales had accepted Pakington's rash invitation to draw up a list of "imperial interests" to which the royal veto would be restricted.[76] Although the select committee in Victoria had urged federation, nothing to encourage it was included in any of the documents.

As was usual in the handling of colonial acts, the draft constitutions were first considered by the legal adviser to the Colonial Office, Sir Frederic Rogers. And, although he may have jokingly referred to his task as one of drawing up Australian

75. See particularly J. Main, "Making Constitutions in New South Wales and Victoria, 1853–54," *Historical Studies, Australia and New Zealand, 7* (1957), 369–86; Serle, *The Golden Age*, pp. 188–215; Greenwood, *Australia*, pp. 99 ff.; D. Pike, *Paradise of Dissent: South Australia, 1829–1857* (Melbourne, 1957), pp. 461 ff.; Melbourne, *Early Constitutional Development in Australia*, pp. 417 ff.

76. The lists had been taken from a speech of Molesworth of 1850. See H. Egerton, ed., *Selected Speeches of Sir William Molesworth on Questions Relating to Colonial Policy* (1903), pp. 392–401. New South Wales listed allegiance of the colonists to the crown, the naturalization of aliens, foreign treaties made by Britain, foreign relations between the colony and other powers, laws pertaining to British military and naval forces within the colony, and high treason. Victoria added divorce. For copies of the constitution acts see Further Papers re Australian Constitutions, PP, 1854–55 [1927], *38*, 67–79, 81–92.

declarations of independence,[77] it was a difficult job which he took seriously. For he had to strike a delicate balance. He could not be casual about the formal soundness of such important legal foundations as written constitutions, but he fully appreciated that they must be considered in their historical and environmental settings. They must be framed in such a way as to permit the successful absorption within the political structure of social change that was obviously going to be rapid and massive.

Rogers found most objectionable the limitations upon the royal prerogative, though some restriction was inevitable in practice. Responsible government had been conceded on the assumption that the colonists were capable of managing their affairs with justice toward one another; the crown was therefore relieved of any obligation to protect the colonists from their own mistakes or to defend minorities against the legislation of the majority. Two of the bases upon which disallowance had rested had been abolished, and it was probably unimportant (though not the British way) that the change was being stated formally. The third object, to protect the crown itself against acts of dependencies for which it was responsible, was also being set aside. Great Britain would indeed be placed in the position of having possibly to defend colonies over which she exercised no real control, but this contradiction was "inherent in the nature of responsible government, and is only increased, not created, by extending Colonial self-government from matters of administration to matters of legislation." Only the fourth object remained, that of protecting the empire "against legislation which is injurious to the general interest." The list was not long enough: native affairs and tariffs, for example, were not included. Moreover, such an attempt to separate colonial and imperial areas of jurisdiction

77. Rogers to R. W. Church, 15 Sept. 1854, *Blachford Letters,* pp. 157–58.

would result in a good deal of unnecessary strife. In practice the royal veto was seldom exercised, and there was no good reason why the Australians should resent its being retained. But if such a separation of spheres of competence were really thought necessary, he suggested that such a body as the Judicial Committee of the Privy Council might be used to arbitrate in cases of conflicts of interpretation.

In considering the legislative council, Rogers hoped to achieve some sort of constitutional balance. The upper house should provide a check against democracy, but not too formidable an obstacle lest the constitution itself should be threatened in time of crisis. None of the drafts seemed to have solved the problem. New South Wales had proposed a nominated council so that, in the absence of party, a neutral body above politics might be appointed. It was at least as likely, thought Rogers, "that responsible government . . . may at once result in a determined struggle between the squatting and other interests," the nominee council becoming "a mere instrument of the party having the upper hand." Victoria had adopted the elective principle with a £5,000 freehold qualification, but this seemed too restrictive. The council would almost certainly be controlled by the squatters, and a serious conflict with the city-dominated lower house (to be elected by universal suffrage) would be almost inevitable. "Supposing a collision probable, and assuming that if it occurs the deliberate wishes of the larger constituency will by force or otherwise finally prevail, it is a question of whether or not a mode should be provided for enabling them to prevail constitutionally." [78]

It is this discussion of constitutional balance that reveals the subtlety and shrewdness of which Rogers was capable. His grasp of the role of political institutions in a young and rapidly modernizing society is rather striking. Not that he thought

78. Rogers to Grey, 6 Sept. 1854, no. 7 of C.O. Australian Papers, C.O. Library.

he could achieve the ideal formulation himself. He examined possible alternatives, only to discard them as impractical in the Australian environment. The prestige of the U.S. Senate, which had so attracted Grey and Elgin to the elective principle, had resulted from indirect election by state legislatures: a small Australian colony could not provide such an intermediate electorate. The same objection would militate against an electoral college, which in Australia "would run the risk of reflecting too accurately the very feelings which an Upper Chamber is intended to check." Reluctantly, Rogers concluded that institutional checks against the lower house and the triumph of democracy were futile in Australia.

Colonial secretary Sir George Grey next submitted the documents to interested members of the cabinet, suggesting that the forms of the upper chamber preferred by the colonies should not be tampered with, even though they were not uniform; that restrictions on the royal veto should be rejected; and that the occasion might or might not be a favorable opportunity for encouraging federalism.[79] Russell, Gladstone, Molesworth, and Sidney Herbert submitted position papers, so that the Australian constitutions were considered rather carefully.

Although he had accepted responsible government, Lord John Russell's opinions had undergone little change in the fifteen years since he had rejected the system. He wished in general to be liberal: yet "there is a limit at which this liberality must stop, or it will degenerate into waste." Once, he went on, executive council members had been appointed by the crown: under responsible government this power would belong to the assemblies. Once, legislative councils had been appointed as a check against popularly elected lower houses: now Victoria's council would also be elected. "Thus one by one all the shields of authority are thrown away, and the body of the Monarchy is left exposed to the assaults of democracy." To the crown re-

79. No. 8 of C.O. Australian Papers.

mained only the powers of appointing governors and freely instructing them, and these must be retained. Restrictions against the royal prerogative "could not be submitted to. The independence of the Australian Colonies, with no obligation to defend and protect them, would be a preferable alternative." But in fact, he gibed at Molesworth, there was no evidence to suggest that the colonies really wanted such restrictions: they were "a reflexion from debates in the House of Commons." His conclusion was the same as the instructions he had given long ago to Lord Sydenham. The attempt to separate imperial and colonial jurisdiction would not work: "Either you would limit the Crown too strictly, or you would include subjects which, in nine cases out of ten, ought to be left to the Colonial authorities." [80]

Sir William Molesworth defended the principle of jurisdictional separation that had played so prominent a role in the Durham Report as well as in his own speeches: it was absolutely essential if the imperial relationship were to be maintained. The nominee councils of New South Wales and South Australia ought to be changed to the elective principle that the colonists really favored, only Pakington's instructions having persuaded them to adopt anything else. And on the question of adding something to encourage federation he was adamant: "Our policy should be to bind the Colonies to the mother country, and not to each other. It should be rather to divide the Colonies from each other, than to divide them in any way from the mother country, '*Divide et impera.*'" [81] The contrast is sharp: whereas Lord Grey had tried to delay responsible government in the hope of granting it eventually to a mature Australian nation, Molesworth favored giving responsible government prematurely with the object of preventing the achievement of federation. He was a man of little faith.

Gladstone, though agreeing with Russell that the limitations

80. No. 9 of C.O. Australian Papers.
81. No. 14 of C.O. Australian Papers.

on the royal prerogative were objectionable, thought they must be retained since Pakington and by implication Newcastle had already agreed to them. Nor, as could be demonstrated by analogy with the separation of powers between the central and state governments in the United States, was such a proposal necessarily impractical. There would be differences of opinion, but conflict was the essence of the judicial process, and could be resolved "with no intolerable grievance, or hazard of confusion to the general movement of the machine of Government." [82] He disagreed with Russell that the nominee councils had constituted effective "shields of authority": on the contrary the independent executive and its appointees had been "sources of weakness, disorder, disunion, and disloyalty." Finally, he thought the federal question premature.

In the end Sir George Grey settled upon compromise. He left the upper houses as they were: the Australians could modify them if they wished. Maintaining his earlier position he agreed with Russell that no specific prohibition against the exercise of the royal veto would be included. And he reserved the federal question "for further consideration," [83] thereby effectively postponing it for half a century.

Compared to the executive government's careful consideration of the Australian constitutions, parliament's role was perfunctory. In the Commons colonial secretary Russell had only to deal with the attempt of Adderley, who carried the Colonial Reform banner in Molesworth's conspicuous absence, to revive the separation of local and imperial powers and the attack of Robert Lowe against the New South Wales squatting interest, a continuation of his earlier career as a Sydney politician.[84] In the end the bills emerged from the lower house unscathed and, sailing through the Lords without so much as a single no-

82. No. 16, C.O. Australian Papers, Dec. 1854. I have not seen the paper of Sidney Herbert, but Serle, *The Golden Age,* p. 198, says that it was worthless.

83. No. 17, C.O. Australian Papers, 30 Dec. 1854.

84. 17 May 1855, 3 *Hansard, 139,* 80–81.

tice of their existence, received the royal assent in July 1855. In sending them on to the colonies Russell quashed any hope that, as Wentworth and the Australian Association in London so much desired, the imperial government would use the period of constitution-making to spur on Australian nation-building. "The present," concluded Russell, "is not a proper opportunity." [85]

Conclusion

By 1855 the "revolution" that had begun in the North American colonies in the 1830s had swept through the second British Empire. Only Western Australia and the Cape Colony among the established settlement colonies had failed to demand and receive responsible government: the first because it wished to continue convict labor, the second because it wished to avoid the responsibility of defending its frontier. The constitutional structure of the empire was much altered, though how much was not yet fully apparent. The transfer of power in the 1850s was a strangely quiet affair, seldom involving violence or even much direct coercion.

For the most part the campaign for responsible government was carried out in tiny colonial assemblies by politicians employing the ancient legislative techniques that had been invented and exported by the mother country herself. To the student of the transfer of British political institutions, those techniques are as significant as the spread of more formal structures and theories. For without the sophisticated use of political tactics that were successful enough to absorb social tension, the transfer of institutions must have been devoid of substance and body, as transitory as the many attempts have been to import the U.S. constitution into Latin America. And the fact is that, however imperfectly the cabinet system might

85. Russell to Denison (N.S.W.), 20 July 1855, Further Papers re Australian Constitutions, PP, 1856 [2135], *43*, 15–18.

function in the absence of political parties possessing ideological or organizational bases (which the British system itself had lacked through much of the eighteenth century), this crucial aspect of the political practice of Westminster was already in working order.

The revolution of the early 1850s was largely administrative. It rarely went beyond the normal Colonial Office routine. And it was by no means finished. Indeed, the evolution of an empire of internally self-governing colonies through dominion status toward the free association of fully independent nations that is the modern Commonwealth had scarcely begun. What had happened by 1855 was that, in defiance of the rigidity of mind of a Derby, a Durham, a Wakefield, or a Molesworth, room within the imperial structure had somehow been made for the force of colonial nationalism. Responsible government had made that framework flexible.

This "transition from the groping, reactionary uncertainty of 1837 to the generous recognition of full self-government (with responsible ministers and elected legislatures) as the panacea of discontent in colonies of settlement was the most important change in British colonial policy during the nineteenth century."[86] Why did it happen? In general there is nothing wrong with the traditional answers: free trade, the desire not to repeat the mistakes of the American Revolution, the gathering momentum once a breakthrough had been made in Canada. We have suggested that a common recognition of the process of political development, implicitly undergirding the debates of the mid-nineteenth century, may have been important. Yet once the level is reached at which policy decisions were actually being taken, the logical sequence of cause and effect becomes less certain. The general causes had little to do with determining answers to the more specific and probably more crucial questions of the timing and degree of self-government. For the fact is that responsible government in Canada

86. Ward, *Empire in the Antipodes*, p. 74.

grew in large part out of a series of decisions that were supposed to avert it. Once the system had been conceded there it significantly narrowed the range of alternatives available to administrators who had to respond to pressure elsewhere, but it did not define the decisions of Lord Grey. After him the transfer of power speeded up, but in an incoherent set of responses to particular circumstances.

The transfer of power in the 1850s may be compared to Macmillan's "winds of change" policy toward Africa in the 1960s. Of course there are wide differences. The earlier event was not greatly complicated by external factors; the latter had to be carried on in the context of the Cold War. Earl Grey never visited a colony and worked with information that was months old; Macmillan had access to instantaneous communications, and could reach any colony himself in a matter of hours. British political institutions blended easily with the cultural mores of Englishmen overseas; in Africa those political forms had only begun to work their way into the social fabric of the communities.

There are, however, striking similarities. In both instances one crucial test case was fought out: in Canada in the 1840s, in Ghana in the 1950s (or possibly it came in India in the 1940s). In both the resolve of the imperial authorities to insist on an adequate period of preparation, once having been abandoned in regard to one part of the empire, was swiftly given up with regard to the rest. In both there was a favorable attitude in Great Britain toward the general principle of self-government. But in both the conflict revolved around the more short-term questions of timing and degree. In both there was substantial sentiment in Britain and substantial pressure in the colonies: in both it is hard to determine whether the imperial authorities were pushed or pulled.

Whether or not the withdrawal in the 1950s from Africa was actually as orderly a process as it would appear on the surface to have been, that for the present may be regarded as a fundamental point of contrast. As Gordon Gairdner, the senior clerk of the Australian department, explained it for Lord Grey:

> Whether it [responsible government] could have been much longer withheld by the Home Government I believe is very doubtful. . . . In fact the agitating colonists pointed to the Canadian Constitution as containing the measure of self Government to which they had a right to look, and their advocates in this country adopted the same tone, without considering that time had matured the societies in the North American Colonies for the enjoyment of that for which the new societies were not fitted; and the Home Government appear simply to have receded before the pressure which they were not prepared to withstand.[87]

87. 28 Nov. 1857, quoted from Grey Papers by Serle, *The Golden Age*, p. 194.

5: The Working of Responsible Government

We are still in the infancy of our experience in the working of responsible government.
Sir William Denison

Responsible government is one of the looser terms. In retrospect it has acquired a certain orthodoxy, but in the period of its making it was imprecise. It was employed in the mid-nineteenth century to refer to all sorts of positions along a continuum that ranged from the barest degree of home rule to a state of things only a shade removed from independence. To Lord Durham it meant primarily a means of ensuring the supremacy of Anglo-Canadians over their French compatriots. To Lord Elgin it contained the hope of reconciliation. Edward Gibbon Wakefield saw in it a way for the New Zealand colonists to seize from the governor the effective control over native affairs and land policy. Gladstone hoped its institution in the Cape Colony would enable Britain to throw upon the colonists the responsibility and expense of border conflicts.[1] The system was defined as it was made. It meant different things to different persons, in various places and at various times.

Responsible government had several levels of activation and implementation. Of these the most apparent was the political: a group of permanent colonial officials, appointed by the Colonial Office and responsible to the home government as well as being subordinate to the governor, was replaced by a group of extraordinarily impermanent ministers who possessed for the

1. See Rawson W. Rawson to Gladstone, Cape Town, 18 Aug. 1859, Gladstone Papers, Add. MS. 44,263.

time being the confidence of the legislature and who advised the governor on matters of domestic concern. Even within this relatively restricted focus the system was not instituted all at once. How, if not by the favor of the governor (which was supposedly ruled out) or by support of party (which had yet to be developed), was the confidence of the legislature to be won and retained by a relatively stable political leadership? If party did not exist (and with the doubtful exception of Canada its development came after the winning of responsible government [2]) then it had to be created. Yet the evolution from the inward-looking personal faction to the outward-oriented modern political party was a gradual process in the colonies as it had been in England. So long as politicians exchanged ministerial chairs every few months on no other basis than that of personal antagonism, the governor retained the influence that went with continuity. In such circumstances responsible government could not be said to be "in working order." [3]

And what, indeed, was meant by "domestic" legislation? As was so amply demonstrated in the controversies over Victoria's Convicts Prevention Act, Canada's tariff, and New Zealand's native policy, there could be no hard lines between colonial and imperial areas of interest. There was plenty of room for maneuver and redefinition. Responsible government was a gradually evolving thing.

The political side of responsible government is the most familiar, but there were others. One of them had to do with the development of increasingly autonomous centers of administrative authority overseas, a process inspired as much by the hope of greater efficiency as by colonial pressure. Local land

2. See P. Cornell, *The Alignment of Political Groups in Canada, 1841–1867* (Toronto, 1962); P. Loveday and A. Martin, *Parliament Factions and Parties: The First Thirty Years of Responsible Government in New South Wales, 1856–1889* (Melbourne, 1966).

3. The phrase is taken from a minute of Robert Lowe on Australian federation, 8 May 1857, CO 201/500.

departments worked themselves free of the Colonial Land and Emigration Commission. Colonial treasurers and auditors ceased to submit their accounts for authentication by the British Treasury. Colonial legislative acts were no longer reviewed by the legal adviser to the Colonial Office, or even "left to their operation" (in the contemporary phrase) by the queen in council. Eventually, appeals in civil and finally in criminal cases were no longer submitted to the Judicial Committee of the Privy Council. The Colonial Office itself gave up the attempt to control the flow of events at the peripheries. Lines of bureaucratic authority shifted: sometimes imperceptibly, sometimes with the dramatic swiftness of Sir John Pakington's "golden dispatch." But in the course of time such transfers of authority decentralized the administrative structures and procedures of an empire.

The pace of transition in these two spheres was very different. Responsible government at the political level came quickly at least in principle, while the development of autonomous centers of administrative authority was gradual. Some of that evolution long preceded any recognition of the right of self-government. Much of it directly or indirectly accompanied the immediate political transition, so that a contemporary might have supposed that the transfer of power was virtually complete. But in fact there was enough administrative lag, enough tidying up to keep colonial bureaucrats happily occupied for decades.

Responsible government also involved important internal adjustments within these increasingly autonomous colonial administrative centers. Lines of authority had to be redrawn and channels of communications shifted. Existing procedural patterns had to be altered and new ones introduced. Methods of interdepartmental coordination had to be revised. The effective working of responsible government was no more compatible with the traditional colonial bureaucratic framework than it was with a political milieu marked by the absence of party.

In particular, two features of responsible government required significant administrative adjustments. The first was a change from a single executive authority exercised through a group of permanent and unequal subordinate officials to a cabinet whose members for the time being approached a state of administrative equality. In theory responsible government changed little. The power of the executive continued to belong to the governor and not to his advisers. Yet in practice the ministers responsible for advising the governor had also the authority while in office to implement that advice. Somehow, new means of achieving coordination and control had to be devised within the matrix of executive departments. For the old ones, depending as they had upon the direct or delegated intervention of the governor, would no longer serve.

The second feature was the novel necessity of submitting the actions of the executive, especially in matters of finance, to the scrutiny of the legislature. It had not only to be done: it had to be done in advance. For without the presentation of regular, accurate, and detailed budgetary estimates for the government as a whole, as well as for its individual departments, responsible government could be little more than fiction.

The internal reorganization of the executive involved, again, a gradual development that began long before the coming of responsible government. It was given considerable momentum by the political transition, but it continued long afterwards. The drive toward more efficient administrative patterns in the executive had been initiated by earlier governors with the object of strengthening their own positions. They had built up the base from which, antiquated though it later appeared when responsible government was instituted, the new system could ultimately proceed. And, at the other end of the time scale, it was only very gradually that executive departments devised new modes of working together or learned new techniques of preparing adequate budgetary estimates.

It is in the perspective of the interacting political and administrative levels that the working of responsible government needs to be approached. To see it merely as the fruits of a struggle over principle and personality is greatly to oversimplify. To see it entirely as a set of changes in the legislative branch is to neglect its equally significant implications for the executive. The coming of responsible government has been treated as a customary breaking point in colonial history; it is remarkable how many studies of other subjects either begin or end with it. The establishment of responsible government in its various aspects was itself a process of considerable complexity, and it deserves to be studied as such.

Fortunately J. E. Hodgetts has already written a fine book on the subject with respect to Canada.[4] In it he answers most of the pertinent questions about how the ground was prepared, how responsible government was introduced at the lower levels, what it meant in terms of immediate administrative consequences, and how it developed at length into a working system. I have already drawn upon his work in the earlier introductory paragraphs, and I intend to employ it further as a basis for comparison with my own much more limited investigation in New South Wales. It cannot be stressed enough, however, that the vast amount of local research upon which a thorough and systematic comparative analysis of the working of responsible government in the mid-nineteenth-century empire could alone be based—and each colonial archive would provide enough material for a weighty graduate thesis—simply does not exist.

Like the personalities of the individuals who compose them, bureaucracies undergo formative periods in which their basic patterns of behavior are established for what may be years to come. Such patterns comprise an interlocking system of procedures and techniques, of channels of communication and lines of authority: habitual ways of getting things done. Some parts

4. *Pioneer Public Service: An Administrative History of the United Canadas, 1841–1867* (Toronto, 1955).

of the system grow up gradually. Others may be initiated in response to the injection of a technological innovation: a typewriter, a telephone, or a computer. Still others may come about by means of rational evaluation. But the time of consolidation into an interlocking behavioral system is usually a comparatively brief one, often associated with a man or perhaps with a regime. In this moment rational reforms and inherited procedures jell together into what can be called an institution. It is accepted because it is compatible with the prevailing climate of opinion, at least to the extent that it enables the bureaucracy to withstand the attacks of outsiders, and because it serves at least tolerably well the smooth internal operation of the bureaucratic machine. Once consolidated the system develops a momentum and even a dynamic of its own. Thereafter the paper continues to flow. The organization responsible for circulating it alters slowly, according to its own internal needs, until some massive change in the conditions within which it operates—an increase in work load, an important technological innovation, a shift in the climate of opinion—makes it desirable to recast the system as a whole, as opposed to the more ordinary adjustments among its parts. Some such process, at any rate, may be adopted as a sort of working model.

A formative period, followed by a relatively long period of comparative quiescence, has already been observed in the Colonial Office, where Stephen's administrative system that took effect in the late 1830s remained essentially unaltered until it was severely challenged about 1870. Such a time of consolidation is highly applicable to the reforms of Governor Sir Ralph Darling in the late 1820s in New South Wales, for it was essentially his creation that provided the jumping-off point for the establishment of responsible government in the 1850s. And, according to Hodgetts, some such description is appropriate for the government of Lord Sydenham in the United Canadas of the early 1840s.

There had been other formative periods in Canadian administrative history, notably the one that occurred during the regime of Dorchester and Simcoe. Yet the state of things encountered and condemned so harshly by Lord Durham indicated that a massive recasting of the system was long overdue. He detected inefficiency and weaknesses that made effective executive action virtually impossible, whether by a governor or by a cabinet of responsible advisers. There was a sad want of centralization and little interdepartmental communication. He could find no heads of departments who were actually responsible either for advising the governor or for regulating the actions of their subordinates. No one agency had the power of control. Financial affairs were in a particularly deplorable condition. There was no budget. There were no means of keeping accurate accounts. Many offices were corresponding directly with their counterparts in England, bypassing the governor completely. The executive council, far from reinforcing the governor's position and prestige, weakened him by usurping his patronage and his authority. The Durham Report was thus a forceful indictment against the Canadian public service. But it was Sydenham, backed by Lord John Russell at the Colonial Office, who initiated what was to be the brief but crucially formative period of administrative reform and consolidation.

Neither Sydenham nor Russell, it will be recalled, thought responsible government theoretically or practically desirable. Both wished to forestall it by asserting the governor's authority, making him the most influential politician and the most powerful administrator in the colony. As Stanley was later to instruct Metcalfe so explicitly, the most effective weapon in the governor's arsenal was that power of the patronage which through the years had been so sharply curtailed. Russell intended to restore it, primarily by reorganizing the public service along the lines of Durham's recommendations. Heads of departments, Russell announced in his well-known dispatch of

October 1839,[5] were hereafter to be responsible directly to the governor and were to be removable from their offices at pleasure. The governor would also be strengthened, he thought, by the establishment of a more effective working relationship with the legislature. Hence the General Assembly should "check and control abuse, profusion, or misapplication" of the public revenue. Further, the proceedings of the various executive departments must be systematically recorded so that they could be submitted upon the request for papers by the Assembly. As in the English system, legislative scrutiny would help to keep the executive offices from flagging, and would therefore place at the governor's disposal a far more smoothly functioning administrative machine.

Russell's instructions were intended to prevent or at least postpone the coming of responsible government. But reform in the executive branch was in fact an essential prelude to the establishment of an effective government of any type. And it was particularly necessary for a system that would require such a close coordination of executive and legislative branches as government by cabinet. Russell's objections to responsible government as being incompatible with the essence of the colonial relationship were genuine enough, and it has been argued here that in the long run his arguments were valid. But if in 1839 he had been convinced of the inevitability of the system, and had set out with a flood of constitutional arguments to win the time in which to lay a proper administrative basis for its ultimate adoption, he could hardly have operated more effectively.

Russell provided the instructions and the backing, Sydenham did the work. Only the short space of a year and a half was allotted the governor before his tragic death. Yet, though he did not accomplish as much as he was sometimes wont to

5. Printed in H. Egerton and W. Grant, eds., *Canadian Constitutional Development* (1907), pp. 190 ff.

boast, his contribution to the development of the Canadian bureaucracy was considerable. In place of a dozen rambling and overlapping agencies, he established a single board of works. He instituted crown land departments for both provinces. He strove to make Russell's instructions regarding the need for heads of departments to be responsible to the governor into a practical reality. It is usually concluded that his political system was already crumbling before his death, and his administrative reforms were by no means as effective or as sweeping as he had hoped. His achievement, however, was that the Canadian government service did not therefore return to the state of limbo in which Lord Durham had found it.

Sydenham was far less successful in establishing really effective interdepartmental communication. What centralization existed was concentrated almost entirely in his own person. Canada's principal administrative problem, then as now, was to deal with two distinct linguistic communities whose interests and needs were often different. And the perennially ineffective but probably inevitable answer has been: separately. Strive as one might, departments tended to split into virtually autonomous divisions that were presided over precariously by a head whose primary object was to smooth over their rivalry. Agencies that communicated only fitfully and intermittently within themselves could hardly maintain a close degree of coordination with one another.

This extreme lack of effective channels of interdepartmental communication was naturally a tremendous handicap to successive governors, as well as a fundamental obstacle in the way of the effective working of the cabinet system as a pattern of administration. In the 1850s what coordination there was tended to be carried out almost entirely at the ministerial level. Depending as it did upon the uncertain tenure and the varying degrees of dedication with which the individual ministers approached their departmental duties, it was necessarily uneven and discontinuous. At a lower level, to be sure, permanent subordinate officials were gradually evolving more effective methods and channels of communication that came in time to fill the vacuum. Hodgetts concludes, however, that as late as the eve of confederation the system had only really begun to jell into an institutionalized pattern of administrative behavior. Responsible government, which by then had been in existence for two decades at the political level, had been operating in the meantime under a serious burden of bureaucratic inefficiency underneath.

Even so the system might not have been quite so cumbersome if some institutionalized focus of centralization had been present. But, once again, the dual nature of the supposedly united Canadas was a difficult obstacle. In the highly centralized system of New South Wales, as we have seen, Governor Darling had elevated the colonial secretary's department, assigning to it the function of checking and controlling the activities and expenditures of offices that were to be explicitly subordinate. No such solution could be readily adopted in Canada. There had to be two provincial secretaries, and two distinct departments: and someone had to coordinate *them.*

Aside from the governor himself (and no system ought to be dependent upon the chief executive to perform routine administrative duties) the logical candidate for such a role was his private secretary, who was called the "civil secretary." Up to 1840, indeed, the correspondence to the governor from below had normally been directed through his office, which had handled routine patronage as well. Sydenham, however, objected to using the civil secretary in this way. For, he argued, since the civil secretary came and departed with the governor, the practice would deprive the government of knowledge of local affairs. He preferred, instead, to handle the local correspondence and patronage through the two provincial secretaries, leaving his private secretary to assist him in such correspondence as that with the Colonial Office and the British embassy in Washington. The Colonial Office, perhaps perceiving that if the private secretary did not provide coordination none was to be had, did not agree, and Bagot and Metcalfe attempted to use the office as a focal point of colonial administration. But Elgin, who found the practice unpopular with Canadian politicians, gave it up again. Thus what centralization there was resulted from the informal activities of the governor. In practice there seems to have been little enough of it.

Since there was little or no centralized administrative communication before responsible government was established at the political level, the principle of control within the executive had to be instituted afterwards. When it gradually evolved in the late fifties and early sixties it centered on that fundamental artery of government, finance. The development of financial responsibility was encouraged by the influence of William Lyon MacKenzie, who in addition to his more explosive youthful activities had steeped himself in the writings of British "economists." It rested primarily, however, on the work of John Langton as auditor general. Methods of keeping accounts were revised. (In 1840 there had actually been two important financial departments, belonging to the inspector general and the receiver general, whose work greatly overlapped but whose books and accounting procedures did not match.) Centralized issues of money to the various departments and audits of their expenditures were instituted. Finally, a detailed budget was provided to parliament, an ex post facto affair until 1864, when estimates began to be submitted in advance. Thus the control of the purse by the legislature, without which in theory there can be no responsible government, was only beginning to be a working reality by as late as 1867.[6]

Canada, then, presents the pattern of a bureaucratic system plagued by divisive tendencies and remaining decentralized, partly because of and partly in spite of the formative efforts of Lord Sydenham. The lack of effective interdepartmental communication and control hampered the introduction of the cabi-

6. Hodgetts, *Pioneer Public Service,* passim.

net system, having to be gradually created from within the bureaucracy after responsible government had been instituted at the political level. The primary limiting factor was the dual nature of the legislative union, which indeed appears never to have worked. The larger framework provided by confederation, which frankly recognized that the provinces *were* to be administered separately in local matters, was probably as desirable from the administrative standpoint as it was from the political.

It was otherwise in New South Wales. There the problem to be encountered in implementing responsible government was rather too much centralization than too little. For Sir Ralph Darling's creation, relatively suitable as it may have been as a means of diffusing the governor's authority throughout the small colonial bureaucracy, simply had to be overthrown. Since Darling it had been improved by the hard-working and judicious colonial secretary Edward Deas Thomson, who had brought it up to a peak of efficiency in the late 1840s. But even then, as he readily admitted later, it had already become a cumbersome anachronism in the enlarging government of an expanding society. Still it went on, unreformed in essentials, until a significant alteration in conditions—the coming of responsible government—made it necessary to change.

At bottom the weakness of the Darling system was the same fundamental flaw that had been revealed in it at the outset. His campaign to relieve the colonial secretary's department from the burden of unnecessary detail, thus freeing it to exercise a more general supervisory role, had not succeeded. And the reason is fairly evident. He who can grasp the threads of detail is master of the administrative process. It was by the meticulous scrutiny of the transactions of other departments, if at all, that the governor's authority could in practice be exerted on them. In this sense Darling's program was self-contradictory. His effort to strengthen the colonial secretary's department was countermanded in practice by his wish to control the routine of government. Instead of reducing the workload of that office he increased it.

Comparatively speaking the system worked well. One need only compare the administrative position of the governor in New South Wales to that in Canada of the 1830s to perceive what a difference centralization made. Yet the constant routing of business of all sorts through the colonial secretary's office created a kind of bureaucratic logjam: the result was delay and dissatisfaction within the government and among the public at large. Deas Thomson, indeed, thought it necessary to explain that such an admittedly awkward system had been indispensable:

> All authority was vested in the Governor alone. His decision could only be obtained through the recognized organ of the Government [i.e. the colonial secretary's department]. Hence the circuitous, operose, and unsatisfactory course necessarily adopted. It is only just to bear in mind that the delays and inconveniencies which resulted from it were attributable to the system, and not to the Officers concerned.[7]

Whether the Darling system, deprecated as it was even by those who ran it, could have been substantially improved without destroying it is doubtful. For the essential dilemma—how to exercise the governor's authority save by an inevitably cumbersome scrutiny of detail—would probably have defeated any intended reformer. A way out was presented by the need to implement the new constitution. Politicians who were also heads of departments would hardly submit to the degree of control that had previously been focused in the colonial secretary's office. Nor could such a quasi-despotic system be de-

7. Deas Thomson to Denison, 2 July 1856 (report on administrative arrangements), N.S.W., *Votes and Proceedings 1* (1856–57), 877–84.

fended theoretically, once the governor had ceased to rule directly. Hence the coming of responsible government to New South Wales provided a favorable opportunity for basic administrative reform.

Little attention had been paid to the implications that the working of responsible government would have upon the organization and functioning of the executive. The Australian constitutional debates had dwelt upon the powers that would belong to the responsible advisers, not upon how ministers would exercise those powers or arrange themselves administratively. A skeleton scheme of which ministers might compose the cabinet had been tacked onto the draft constitution as something of an afterthought, but it was abruptly discarded by the first expert, Deas Thomson, to think the matter through. The imperial government's deliberations were no more helpful. Neither Rogers nor any members of the British cabinet had so much as mentioned the matter. The string of Colonial Office dispatches had been devoid of recommendations, although an analysis of how the system had been implemented in Canada would have been useful. Responsible government had simply not been seriously considered as a working system of administration. It had been regarded by the colonists as a suitable slogan for agitation, and by the Colonial Office (who in fact had anticipated the cry) as a graceful means of ending it. Beyond these vague generalities no one, either in England or in Australia, had bothered to go.

Some day it would all come down to earth. Getting responsible government had been relatively easy. The Australians had even managed to do it without strongly demanding it. Working it would be far more difficult. The Australian politicians were very much like new bridegrooms, whose problems were just beginning.

The coming of responsible government in 1856 was awaited from several viewpoints. Governor Sir William Denison, who had argued unavailingly that the colonies were not ready, had mixed emotions. Much as he might dread a difficult period of transition that would demand the utmost skill and tact, and much as he might regret the reduction of his own authority, he could not but relish the coming discomfort of colonial politicians who would be confronted not mainly with glory but with drudgery. Well, he confided to a friend in England, it would serve them right! "However, we are in for it now, and the only question is, how one can work the new system with most comfort to oneself, and benefit to the Colony." [8]

For their part the politicians were happily occupied in the usual pastime of criticizing the governor. James Macarthur thought Denison lacked "caution & deliberation in arriving at conclusions & tact in submitting his plans to those [in the legislative council] who are to decide upon them." [9] Charles Cowper agreed that the governor wanted discretion, while for Charles Nicholson "the more I see of H. E. the *less* faith I have in his judgment—the less hope that he will be able to cope with the events with which the political history of the Colony will for some years be associated." [10] The imminence of constitutional change had not altered the normal current of colonial political conversation. The politicians would soon be falling on each other, but as responsible government approached the focus was still upon the governor.

As it neared its demise, the old regime slowly ground to a halt. One by one its members submitted their resignations, retiring to the handsome pensions which it had been one of the Colonial Office's chief objects to secure for them out of the colonial revenue. Deas Thomson, at least, would put his leisure

8. Letter to Mrs. Stanley, 15 Sept. 1855, W. Denison, *Varieties of Vice-regal Life* (2 vols., 1870), *1,* 315.

9. James to Edward Macarthur, 14 Sept. 1855, Macarthur Papers, ML–A2931.

10. Cowper to James Macarthur, 22 Sept. 1855, and Nicholson to James Macarthur, 15 Sept. 1855, ibid., A2923.

to good use by building a racetrack.[11] Stuart Donaldson, correctly predicting that he would be chosen to lead the first responsible ministry, began to contact prospective colleagues from what he was pleased to refer to as the "liberal conservative" group.[12] As Denison had observed, "in these colonies there is but little of the instinct of party."[13]

The legislature was convened in April, and by the end of the month Denison had chosen Donaldson as the first premier. There was a lull while the new cabinet sought reelection, so that not until June did they begin to settle into their administrative duties. As Denison had dryly anticipated, they were shocked and discomfited. There was a sudden surge of respect for the governor. "I was agreeably surprised," the new treasurer, Thomas Holt, reported after a briefing, "to perceive the accurate knowledge His Excellency appears to have of our financial position."[14]

The new ministers were left to fret and grope, with no clear guide for their behavior. Nothing at all had been done to prepare for an orderly transfer of power: the old regime had just summarily departed. And so they drifted, while Denison prodded. "You must allow me to press upon you," he wrote to the premier, "the utter impossibility of conducting a Govnt. upon the system or rather no system under which we are now suffering." Arrangements must be made swiftly for dividing up the work among the cabinet members. Otherwise, "I see very clearly that you will not be in a state of preparation to meet the Council."[15] Donaldson complained at the lack of advice —"Thomson has never come near me nor do I believe that any

11. Denison, *Varieties, 1,* 485.
12. Donaldson to James Macarthur, 4 Apr. 1856, Macarthur Papers, ML–A2923.
13. Denison to his mother, 30 Dec. 1855, *Varieties, 1,* 326.
14. Holt to Donaldson, 18 June 1856, Donaldson Ministry Papers, ML–A731.
15. 2 July 1856, Denison Letters, ML–B205.

one of *the highly paid pensioners has offered one iota of assistance to any of my colleagues their successors in office*"—and issued an urgent plea for help:

> In the meantime my particular position has become so embarrassed by arrears & by the accumulation of foolscap & red tape which Thomson's centralising system has entailed upon this office that it is impossible I can go on. Some subdivision of labor *must* take place & if you are to take charge of a bureau I really wish you were in Town.[16]

At length the floundering ministers were rescued by a lengthy and very able memorandum on the reorganization of the executive that was prepared at the governor's request by Deas Thomson. In it he admitted the defects of the former system and just as tactfully predicted that the new order would be a distinct improvement: "Mere matters of detail will be immediately decided by the Minister to whose departments they belong. Measures only of general policy or regulation will have to be submitted to the Cabinet or to the Governor General and Executive Council." He proposed a cabinet of six members: the principal secretary and premier, attorney general, solicitor general, minister for finance and trade, minister for public instruction, and minister for crown lands and public works. Save for the two legal members, who would be served by one office, each minister would be assisted by a clerical staff with a permanent head who would carry on routine business during ministerial changes or absences. Ranged beneath these five executive departments and subject to their control would be the various offices that made up the working bureaucracy of government, grouped together as much as possible according to function. To the minister for finance and trade, for example, would be assigned the Treasury, customs

16. Donaldson to James Macarthur, Col. Sec. Office, 4 July 1856, Macarthur Papers, ML–A2923.

department, chief inspector of distilleries, immigration agent, portmaster, and shipping master.

With respect to relations between the governor and cabinet, and among the ministers themselves, Deas Thomson presumed that English practices would be followed as much as possible. Each minister would be responsible to his colleagues for the performance of the departments under his charge, and he would convey to his subordinates the collective decisions of the cabinet. Save for the higher levels of the public service, he would be responsible for matters of patronage, promotion, and discipline within those offices. Normally, matters requiring joint administrative action would be settled by direct communication between individual ministers. Most of the business of government, then, would go no further than the appropriate minister, or would be settled by means of informal negotiations among members of the cabinet.

Some matters would transcend these ordinary channels of communication. If more formal collective deliberation were required, then the proper way to achieve it would be through cabinet meetings. The cabinet, he quoted from Murray's *Official Handbook of Church and State,* would come together "on the summons of any one of its Members . . . its business and deliberations are [secret] . . . it is unattended by any Secretary, or other Officer; its resolves, of which no formal record is kept, are carried into effect by those of its Members to whose Departments they appertain."[17] The cabinet, he emphasized, was solely a deliberative body; as in England it would be "unknown to the law," possessing no collective authority to act or to proclaim. If formal proceedings were necessary the appropriate minister would submit a minute to the governor, who would consider the subject in executive council and act accordingly. To the council would be submitted for the information of the cabinet copies of all but confidential correspond-

17. Report dated 2 July 1856, printed in N.S.W., *Votes and Proceedings, 1* (1856–57), 877–84.

ence with the Colonial Office. Thus the cabinet was to model itself as closely as possible upon its English counterpart, while the executive council (where alone the governor would meet with his advisers on a formal basis) would resemble the Privy Council.

The resemblance was not to be complete, however, for the Privy Council had long since degenerated through enlargement of its membership into an organization that was almost entirely honorific. In England this trend was not particularly destructive, since the personal role of the sovereign had declined as well. But for those whose business it was to consider the working of responsible government, such as Deas Thomson and members of the Colonial Office, a similar enlargement of the colonial councils would be unfortunate. If the governor's authority were not to be undermined completely, then his executive council must remain functional and therefore fairly small. Who then should belong to it? Only current members of the cabinet? Distinguished colonists, hopefully above partisan or factional conflict, whom the governor might appoint? Former ministers? The Australian constitutions had left the question open. Deas Thomson, though apparently favoring the first solution, left it ambiguous and unresolved. It was to become a fairly serious problem in the late fifties as former ministers, sometimes on the basis of only a few weeks in office, claimed the right to retain their positions in the council as well as their titles of "Honorable." The question was finally decided against them, but only after considerable controversy.[18]

Finally, the monarchical principle of administration was to be retained. "As in England the Minister is presumed not to act on his own authority, but on that of the Sovereign, so in

18. See particularly Denison to S. of S., 8 Sept. 1856, CO 201/495; Sir Henry Barkly (Victoria) to S. of S., Conf., 8 May 1858, CO 309/45, and 14 Jan. 1859, CO 309/48. The subject is treated very fully in G. Serle, *The Golden Age: A History of the Colony of Victoria, 1851–1861* (Melbourne, 1963), pp. 308–19.

this Colony the Minister will act on the authority of the Governor General as representing Her Majesty." In theory all executive authority would continue to reside in the crown's representative. In practice that authority was now to be diffused. How to do this was the question that had so perplexed Lord John Russell. The governor would continue to receive instructions from the imperial government, and Deas Thomson acknowledged that some of his transactions would not even be laid before the executive council. What if those instructions conflicted with the wishes of his responsible advisers? Deas Thomson did not attack this problem, thus implicitly recognizing the correctness of Russell's theoretical objections. Instead, he wisely ignored it. If responsible government were to work, the conflicting claims upon the governor had to be presumed not to exist.

All in all the plan was a good one, a rational and relatively comprehensive approach to the problems of transferring power under responsible government. Deas Thomson had considered the subject in the light of his long years of experience, first as clerk of the executive and legislative councils and then as colonial secretary. He had conferred with his opposite number in Victoria, finding that the approaches of the two neighboring colonies were much alike.[19] Both the governor and the ministers reacted favorably. Denison began at once to urge that all important business should be brought before the executive council, a practice that by enabling the governor to make known his views would reduce misunderstanding and the chance of collision with his ministers. But he insisted only that military and naval correspondence must remain with the governor instead of being transferred to the principal secretary's office.[20] Deas Thomson's plan was settled upon as the

19. Hugh Childers to Deas Thomson, Melbourne, 6 Mar. 1856, Deas Thomson Papers, ML–A1531.

20. Denison to Donaldson, 5 Aug. [1856], 1 Aug. 1856, Denison Letters, ML–B205.

crucial starting point: other problems would "have to be worked out by degrees." [21]

The kernel of Deas Thomson's plan was thus decentralization. The administrative authority formerly exercised through the colonial secretary's department would be diffused and delegated. Instead of forcing the whole business of government into one increasingly clogged channel of communication, there would now be five of them. Each would possess to a high degree the ability to adjust and control itself. The stifling accumulation at the top of the structure would be avoided. What would be lost in unity, especially at first, would be more than repaid in greater flexibility and a freer flow of information. The cabinet, relieved of the burden of detail, would be able to exercise more general supervisory power. The plan thus promised a way out of the dilemma that had plagued the Darling system throughout its life.

So favorable an appraisal of Deas Thomson's plan must, however, be qualified. He assumed that there would be no necessity for ministers to work with details. In fact, it would remain true that any administrator who meant to have some control over the flow of water at the lower levels would have to get his hands wet. The report also assumed that most business would be settled directly by the appropriate minister, and that the rest would be negotiated informally at the top. The channels of communication would thus be autonomous and virtually self-contained, coming together only at the ministerial apex.

Now the trouble with this is that governments do not work that way. Many matters, routine as well as important ones, would involve more than one department and more than one ministerial division. Almost every decision made anywhere would involve money and therefore consultation with the Treasury. How often would the ministries for crown lands and

21. W. M. Manning to Donaldson, 4 Aug. 1856, Donaldson Ministry Papers, ML–A731.

public works have to call for legal opinions? The analysis to which much of this book is devoted of how the British government departments interacted with respect to colonial policy is a relevant analogy to the functional patterns that were emerging in colonial bureaucracies as they became more complicated. A vast and sustained flow of interdepartmental negotiation was inevitable, and no more than a small fraction of it could possibly have been handled at the ministerial level.

Deas Thomson developed a plan for the organization of the cabinet and for the arrangement of departments under the supervision of its members. He did not deal with the far more subtle transition that would be required in the way the bureaucracy worked underneath. Functioning governments normally operate within recognized and habitual patterns of communications. The Darling system's pattern had focused on the colonial secretary's department, through which virtually all of the government's correspondence had been routed up and down. Now that network was being deliberately cast aside. What would evolve to replace it?

The historian who eventually comes to write the definitive history of the evolution of responsible government in New South Wales into an effective machine at the administrative level will have to answer all sorts of additional questions. How did the jelling of the bureaucracy into a working organization occur? What were the peak periods in the process? Who were the principal actors? How did the communications system work? Can case studies of central problems be isolated in order to reveal how the departments interacted? How did the executive bureaucracy's relationship to the legislature develop? Precisely how and when did the active administrative role of the governor decline? Such questions have provided the framework for Hodgetts' fine book on Canada. Presumably they would do as much for studies on the Australian colonies.

The first line to follow, given the centrality of finance in the working of any government, would be the Treasury. If the new system was going to develop some sort of focus of decision making, the Treasury was the logical contender for that role. Indeed, the shifting of the controlling function from the colonial secretary's department to the Treasury had probably already begun with an improvement in the latter office. In April 1855, in a development that was apparently entirely unconnected with the imminence of the new constitution, a board of enquiry was appointed to investigate the Treasury and the office of audit. In June 1856, even as the first responsible ministers were beginning their ordeal, the board made its report. It had found much overlapping and rivalry between the two departments in function and jurisdiction, a want of precise accounting procedures, and an overabundance of detail, much of which could more properly be handled by the other departments themselves. It recommended reduction in size and a precise demarcation of authority between the two offices. A year later a second board investigated and recommended still more streamlining of the work and interrelation of the two departments.[22] It is a reasonable inference, if no more than that, that the role and prestige of the Treasury continued to grow with time and that a study of that office's development would have much to reveal about how responsible government gradually evolved over a number of years into a working administrative system.

In the immediate period of transition, however, most of the cement that prevented the framework from coming to pieces entirely was supplied by the personality of the governor. It is true enough that governors frequently complained about the strictures that were placed against their authority. In the last half of the nineteenth century they greatly preferred the semi-despotic positions in crown colonies, wanting like Sir William Denison "something to do." But such a view is by no means the whole story, as a few quotations from Denison's own private correspondence with his ministers make clear.

22. Printed in N.S.W., *Votes and Proceedings, 1* (1856–57), 1171–78, 375–77.

[2 July, 1856] Dear Donaldson—I see some grumbling among the people on the Hunter as to the project of the Harbour improvements—call for a report . . . as to the steps to be taken to carry out the work which has been sanctioned, namely the Breakwater and the works for deepening the shoals—we shall then see what grounds of complaint they have, and may feel ourselves called upon to accept.[23]

[24 October 1856, Denison memorandum] Let me have the correspondence between this Govt. & that of Victoria relative to the arrangement of an uniform system of Light House Management. . . . [They] were transmitted to the Secretary for Lands & Public Works on 14 Instant.

[25 February 1857] My dear Donaldson—For Heaven's sake get your Loan Bill & all other Bills over as fast as you can, or we shall have the Legislature constitute itself a permanent Body.

[4 March 1857, Denison to Donaldson] I hope the Govt. is going to press for the Railway loan as placed upon the Estimates. The Govt. has made up its mind to carry out certain Railroads and the mere fact that a select committee does not choose or is not capable of making up its mind upon the subject of Railways in general should not deter you from carrying out your own proposition—if you do not press the loan you will have on your back the whole of the advocates of Railway extension, & you will be accused of having asked for a loan of £400,000 without having made up your mind whether you wanted it or not. The responsibility which rests upon you is that of deciding such matters, not of bringing them before the Assembly to be decided by a select committee.[24]

As both the tone and content of these extracts illustrate, the governor was far from being an administrative cipher in the

23. Denison Letters, ML–B205.
24. Donaldson Ministry Papers, ML–A731.

early years of responsible government. While ministers came and went with alarming rapidity, he stayed on for long periods. The really important shift was not a simple diminution of his former influence, but a profound change in the ways he had to exercise it. He had to be more subtle, giving way gracefully before an incident could develop, planting an idea in the mind of a politician only to feign surprise when it was suggested to him a few days later. In such subtle and informal ways a successful governor like Lord Elgin provided most of what continuity and purpose remained in an era of such massive administrative and political transition. The government of colonies became if anything a more difficult and exacting job. It did not, at least at first, become less important.

Nor did the governor's political role immediately evaporate. In theory Lord John Russell's objection that the governor could not be bound by two possibly conflicting seats of authority, valid as it was, had had to be ignored. Otherwise responsible government could never have been introduced. In practice, however, the governor's dilemma could not be avoided. There were several subjects—defense, native affairs, church matters—on which the imperial government had not yet entirely abdicated. Since each of these areas was also an important domestic concern, each remained a source of tribulation for the governor. In theory he had a veto. In practice, confronted as he was with legislative control of the purse and with the need for either getting along with his ministers or finding new ones if he could not, he seldom used it. And yet he could not avoid responsibility.

In many ways the governor under responsible government resembled an ambassador, serving as a link between autonomous centers of administrative authority. His role in the negotiations that went on between them—on defense, postal contracts, and so forth—was often crucial. His importance ought not to be discounted merely because the nature of his authority and the ways he had to exercise it had so altered.

The governor remained in a position which, though normally elevated above the tensions of colonial politics, could easily bring him under fire. He retained the authority to grant or refuse dissolution of parliament, a power which could easily work to the advantage of one contestant. "It is one in which," wrote Herman Merivale, "by the very nature of the case, he cannot be bound under all circumstances to take the advice of his ministers—the same rule, I apprehend, applying to him as to the Crown here."[25] He should of course attempt to be strictly neutral. As the Duke of Newcastle observed (the irony was apparently unintentional), the governor "should endeavour to imitate the conduct . . . of our good Queen who has never throughout Her reign allowed any whisper to be raised that she was the Sovereign of a Party."[26] But there were cases, such as the one that confronted Sir Edmund Head in 1858,[27] in which any action was bound to give offense. The governor's position under responsible government ranged from the difficult to the impossible, and the Colonial Office was well aware of it.

25. Minute on Sir Edmund Head to S. of S., 9 Aug. 1858, CO 42/614.
26. Newcastle to Sir Charles Monck, 29 Nov. 1862, Newcastle Papers, NeC 10,887. On the general subject of the Colonial Office's attitudes toward governors under responsible government see D. Clarke, "The Attitude of the Colonial Office to the Working of Responsible Government, 1854–1868" (unpublished Ph. D. diss., University of London, 1953).
27. See C. Martin, *Foundations of Canadian Nationhood* (Toronto, 1955), pp. 244–57; J. Careless, *Brown of the Globe* (2 vols. Toronto, 1959–63), *1*, 209–80; D. Creighton, *John A. Macdonald* (2 vols. Toronto, 1953–56), *1*, 238–72.

6: The Implications of Responsible Government

Whether Canada belongs nominally or not to England is comparatively immaterial.
Sir Edmund Head

In the early 1850s Lord Grey's scruples against premature concessions of full responsible self-government outside Canada had been precipitously abandoned. A swift succession of events in the colonies created what the collective mind of the Colonial Office, prepared by theory and by the experience in North America, interpreted as an imperial crisis. The range of alternatives sharply narrowed. The Colonial Office all but ceased to inquire into whether European settlement colonies were really prepared for constitutional advancement. The relevant question became instead whether their demands for it could any longer be resisted. Rather suddenly it appeared that they could not. And the result was a transfer of power: to any colony that asked for it, ready or not.

The primary motive for this retreat was negative: what else was there to do? The attempt to maintain an independent colonial executive in the face of legislative control of the purse was an admitted failure, a source of little strength and much embarrassment. Indeed, the colonies seemed likely to become ungovernable unless that anomalous situation were corrected. The intensity of their resistance against Lord Grey's convict transportation policy in the late 1840s had revealed a vision of a troubled future for which the Colonial Office had no stomach. Power was transferred largely in the attempt to solve or avoid what had become a pressing administrative problem.

The increasingly predictable but essentially negative response to a narrowing range of alternatives is, however, but one dimension of the policy-making process. What might be called the horizontal flow of day-to-day calculations is shaped by its interaction with a vertical dimension composed of ideas and positive motives that contribute a sense of rationality and coherence. Neither dimension is ever entirely absent, but their relative significance and their relationship to each other are variables. In the spread of responsible government the vertical side played little part in comparison with the necessity to respond to specific events and with the momentum of an administrative process already in motion. Yet long-term motives of a positive nature were never wholly absent, and as the crisis passed they played an increasingly important role.

One of the reasons that had long been advocated for extending self-government was the belief that it would foster the development of a morally wholesome and financially advantageous habit of local self-reliance. This argument could be traced to Adam Smith, as well as to Bentham and his followers. Cobden, Bright, and Joseph Hume brought it up in parliament at every opportunity. Others took up the theme. "I should like," asserted Gladstone, effortlessly reconciling moral and financial considerations, "to see the state of feeling restored to the Colonies, which induced the first American Colonists, when they revolted, to make it one of their grievances that British troops were kept in their borders without their consent." [1] How in the age of Samuel Smiles could such an argument be refuted? The attitude had been widely accepted long before a resolution of the House of Commons endorsed it in 1862. Once responsible government had been conceded, its

1. Testimony before select committee on colonial military expenditure, PP, 1861 (423), *13*, 357.

implications pointed toward carrying colonial self-defense to its logical conclusion.

The prevailing military theory pointed in the same direction. Although the Russian menace to India was frequently imagined, it was the more tangible French threat to the security of the empire that was emphasized by such recognized experts as General John Burgoyne and Admiral Sir John Colomb.[2] To meet it they favored a concentration of forces. For the advent of steam power (and soon of ironclads) seemed to have increased the danger substantially, though by how much was a matter of conjecture. Presumably French ports would be more difficult to blockade, the British fleet's effectiveness in home waters would be reduced, and it would be harder to prevent a temporary loss of command of the sea. Britain herself was far more open to attack than she had been during the Napoleonic wars. In these altered circumstances the traditional policy—and no one seemed able to provide good reasons why it might have been adopted in the first place—of dispersing the army widely in a large number of colonial garrisons ought to be sharply revised.

The lack of concentration, it was argued, had already contributed substantially to the nation's inefficiency in the Crimean campaign, when France had fortunately been an ally. Next time Britain might not be so lucky. And what, after all, was being gained in compensating advantages? The colonies in fact could be protected only by sea power, and they could not be defended at all if the metropolitan power should be successfully invaded. The small garrisons stationed in them merely provided vulnerable targets rather than effective arms

2. J. Burgoyne, "Popular Fallacies with Regard to our Security against Invasion," W.O. Confidential Print, Nov. 1858, WO 33/5; J. Colomb, *Colonial Defence and Colonial Opinion* (1877). Among secondary authorities see C. Bartlett, *Great Britain and Sea Power, 1815–1853* (Oxford, 1963), pp. 250–93; C. Stacey, *Canada and the British Army, 1846–1871: A Study in the Practice of Responsible Government* (reprinted Toronto, 1963), pp. 52–63; W. Tunstall, "Imperial Defence, 1815–1870," *CHBE 2*, 806–41; and R. Preston, *Canada and "Imperial Defense": A*

of resistance, while their presence made it easier for colonists to adopt a false sense of security, contributing to their neglect of harbor defenses and militias which they could form and maintain themselves. Thus in literally every detail, the experts argued, the security of the empire was being undermined by an unwise distribution of its strength.

In their predictions the experts were of course mistaken. It was to be a series of small and scattered colonial wars—on the Gold Coast, in the Sudan, in Afghanistan, in Burma—that would occupy the army, not the direct defense of the British Isles. For despite repeated war scares the invasion never came. The arguments in favor of concentration, however, were widely accepted. A select committee of the Commons overwhelmingly adopted them in 1861, concluding that the army ought to be consolidated into two effectively positioned striking forces. Some of it would have to remain in India, where the Mutiny had shown a sizable percentage of European troops to be necessary and where the Indian revenue would pay for it. But the remainder ought to be stationed at home.[3]

The theory of concentration had two logical corollaries. One was the extension of self-government. An imperial power that no longer intended to garrison her colonies could hardly expect to continue to control them administratively. The repeal of the Navigation Laws had removed one prop of the theoretical edifice on which imperial domination of settlement colonies had once rested, and the adoption of the prevailing military theory would destroy another. The second logical implication was that if Britain herself were not to provide for the military (as distinguished from the naval) protection of individual colonies, then they ought to be encouraged to combine themselves as much as possible into large regional units that could look forward in time to defending themselves.

These were positive reasons why responsible government

Study of the Origins of the British Commonwealth's Defense Organization, 1867–1919 (Durham, N.C., 1967).

3. PP, 1861 (423), *13*, 75.

ought to be conceded, but of course it had already been done. And the generation of colonial administrators who had presided over the transfer of power had rarely if ever made the connection between what they wished to do and what they thought they had to do. The process was reversed: responsible government having been given up, what was now to be made of it? In the cumulative answer which over a period of time the Colonial Office gave to this question the positive motives —the vertical dimension of policy making—played a larger part.

Logically speaking, the fact of responsible government might be expected to have resulted in a deliberate and sustained drive to develop groups of small and rival colonies into large cooperative nations on the federal model. If indeed it had ever existed, the day of effective imperial domination of settlement colonies was over. Molesworth's somewhat impractical preoccupation with "separation" apart, there remained no very good reason for trying to maintain them as tiny, isolated, and helpless dependencies. Finance, strategic theory, and paternal pride in colonial self-reliance all pointed in the same direction. "Whether Canada belongs nominally or not to England," asserted Governor Sir Edmund Head, one who *did* make the connection, "is comparatively immaterial."[4] For an "independent existence," as he called it, Canada and eventually the other settlement colonies must have. Hence the crucial question was not really "separation." It was whether self-governing colonies could be treated in such a way that their independence, when it should inevitably come, would prove to be a source of strength to the former imperial power. Thus, he concluded, "the duty and the interest of England . . . seem to coincide."[5] The long-run solution to the implications of re-

4. Head to G. C. Lewis, 23 Dec. 1853, Head Papers, PAC, M194.

5. Quoted by C. Martin, ed., "Sir Edmund Head's First Project of Federation, 1851," *Canadian Historical Association, Annual Report* (1928), p. 17.

sponsible government would be a campaign of nation building.

Over the course of the next century it was precisely this logical policy that the imperial government would attempt to put into effect. In retrospect, the encouragement of federalism comes close to being that rather rare thing, a constant goal of British policy makers. A recent authority's unqualified generalization that British policy ever since the Durham Report has consistently opposed federalism would seem to be a somewhat inadequate explanation of the role of the imperial authorities in regard to Canada in the 1860s, South Africa in the 1870s, and Australia in the 1890s, as well as in the West Indies, Malaya, Nigeria, and central Africa in our own era.[6] Moreover, their motives would appear to have been those outlined above: finance and strategy, often accompanied and rationalized by expressions of the virtues of "self-help" that might, but probably ought not to be, dismissed as mere cant.

The day-to-day calculations were rarely affected directly by such clarity of vision. Although Merivale for one regarded federalism as being ultimately necessary and desirable, the Colonial Office at first did nothing to encourage it in the long run and even on occasion opposed it in the short run. There are several reasons that could be offered in extenuation of such "unheuristic" behavior: the administrative routine was itself so self-justifying that it discouraged long-range planning; the colonies were of course so small and powerless that to regard them as great nations of the future might have seemed fanciful; earlier attempts at federation, notably in the West Indies in the 1830s and in Australia in the late 1840s, had already failed; and the obviously impending schism in the United States was casting temporary doubts upon the success of federalism in Tocqueville's America and hence upon the principle itself. Thus, obvious though the encouragement of federalism may seem in retrospect, policy makers did not adopt it at once.

6. W. Livingston, ed., *Federalism in the Commonwealth: A Bibliographical Commentary* (1963), p. xi.

Instead they groped uncertainly. There was policy formation rather than policy, the lines of which came together only gradually.

As in so many areas, Lord Grey's years at the Colonial Office were formative. It was he, carrying on a campaign of reform he had started earlier at the War Office, who took the first rational look at the way the army was being dispersed. It was he who first attempted to persuade self-governing colonies to contribute toward their own defense costs. And it was he who tried to federate Australia. Though there is no evidence to indicate that he saw much of a tangible connection between them, a discussion of the themes of colonial self-defense and colonial nation building must begin with Lord Grey.

In seeking to establish the principle that self-governing colonies ought to pay their own way Grey chose the easiest test case: the Australian colonies, which were comparatively secure against external danger and, unlike New Zealand and the Cape, under no need for internal protection. Grey simply announced that the imperial government would maintain small guards for the governors in the capital cities but no more. If additional troops were wanted, they might be sent if they were available, but the colonies must pay for them.[7]

Simple as the Australian case was, it set important precedents. One of them had to do with method. Grey did not undertake to negotiate with the local authorities, but simply announced his terms. Over the next two decades no other tactics would ever be successful. As the Canadian politician, Francis Hincks, himself once advised: "Nothing will be done by negociation. . . . The British Government . . . must take the responsibility of declaring that they will withdraw the entire forces from Canada and then we *must* deal with the

7. Grey to FitzRoy (N.S.W.), 21 Nov. 1849, in H. Grey, *The Colonial Policy of Lord John Russell's Administration* (2 vols., 1853), *1*, 362.

question."[8] The other precedent was a basic inconsistency in the imperial government's position. For Grey did not assert that troops were unavailable because they were needed elsewhere, but that the colonies must pay for them. It was financial not military arguments that would dominate Anglo-colonial relations until the very eve of the "recall of the legions" in the early 1870s. A more forthright emphasis at the beginning on the doctrine of strategic concentration might have precluded much of the bitterness that so characterized defense negotiations. Basing its case on financial considerations laid the imperial government open to charges of pettiness that were difficult to refute.

In Canada Grey and Elgin moved more cautiously, fearing not so much a direct American invasion (in which case the *number* of British regulars on hand would be comparatively immaterial in what would be primarily a Canadian struggle[9]) as the possibility of strengthening the annexationist fad that swept through Quebec in 1849. Any reduction, advised the governor, ought to take place quietly, with a minimum of dogmatic utterances that might remind Canadians that the potential enemy was more Great Britain's than their own. Discussions having begun in 1848, the decision to call upon the colonists "to take upon themselves a larger share than they have hitherto done, of expenses which are incurred on their account, and for their advantage" was delayed until 1851.[10] By then the mood had changed, and the apathetic reaction to Grey's announcement made the earlier caution appear slightly ridiculous.[11]

8. Hincks to Col. R. Bruce, 10 Sept. 1853, Newcastle Papers, NeC 9552.

9. Elgin to Grey, pvt., 6 Dec. 1848, A. Doughty, ed., *The Elgin-Grey Papers, 1846–1852* (4 vols., Ottawa, 1937), *1*, 266–69.

10. Grey to Elgin, 14 Mar. 1851, in Grey, *Colonial Policy, 1*, 260.

11. Stacey, *Canada and the British Army*, pp. 84–85.

By the time Grey left office in 1852 he had reduced the colonial garrisons by nearly ten thousand men.[12] He had carried out a policy of self-defense in Australia, and had announced the intention of doing so in Canada. Although he had left untouched the far more sensitive problems in New Zealand and South Africa, his efforts were a distinct beginning.

In the area of nation building Lord Grey's period was also a seedbed. No federation was in fact formed anywhere. In North America, like Lord Durham before him, he looked toward some sort of federal union as being inevitable and desirable. Like Durham, however, he did not consider it essential for the present. There was so little commercial and cultural intercourse among the colonies; the recent union of Upper and Lower Canada ought to be given a chance to jell before being enlarged once more; and the tone of events in the United States, though ominous enough for the future, as yet provided no sufficient motive for urgency. Lord Elgin advised that any overt move by the imperial government would be premature. Agreeing, Lord Grey strove instead (though in the end unsuccessfully) to guarantee a loan for a railway from Halifax to Quebec, hoping to establish effective communications for the nation of the future.[13]

In Australia, where there was still less of a tangible reason for urgency, Grey's attitude paradoxically was firmer and his actions less cautious, for he went so far as to provide for a general assembly in the government act of 1850. But the Australians were not ready. Their reaction ranged from apathy in New South Wales and Victoria to outright hostility in South Australia, which felt threatened by the bigger colonies. In the British parliament the remnants of the Colonial Reformers argued that federation, a thing unwanted by the colonists, would shortly lead to separation. And in the end Grey gave up the attempt without a great deal of resistance. He was ahead

12. Return of army, PP, 1857 (79, Sess. 2), 27, 124.
13. Grey to Elgin, pvt., 8 Aug. 1849, *Elgin-Grey Papers, 1,* 437–38.

of his time, swimming against the tide of sectionalism that would dominate Australian political life for another half a century.[14]

After Grey there was a lag. Although the Duke of Newcastle tried to maintain the pressure for colonial self-defense, after the Crimean War the policy was in effect abandoned. Only the cumulative effect of the succession of crises—the Indian Mutiny, the war in China, and the struggle for Italian independence—in the late 1850s succeeded in reviving it. Meanwhile, partly as a result of Grey's failure in Australia, federalism temporarily fell from favor. The subject was deliberately avoided when the Australian constitutions were being discussed in 1855. The Colonial Office waited for pressure to build in the colonies. And even when it began to do so the imperial authorities were hard to move.

Although Sir John Pakington made significant concessions to colonial self-government he left it to others to deal with their implications. It was the Duke of Newcastle, harder working and more deeply interested in the colonies, who returned to the subject of the colonial garrisons. Canada's, "whilst it is ludicrously inadequate for defence in case of a war," seemed far above what Britain should maintain there in peacetime.[15] So long as reductions were made quietly, replied Lord Elgin, without any "ostentatious adoption of new principles,"[16] they would be advisable. Working cautiously, Newcastle by the end of 1854 had taken out 1,300 men, or one fourth of the garrison. In the same period he had reduced the force at the Cape by one third. But now caution had to be abruptly discarded in the frantic effort to form an expeditionary force for the Crimea. By the end of 1855 the colonial garrisons had

14. See J. Ward, *Earl Grey and the Australian Colonies, 1846–1857: A Study of Self-Government and Self-Interest* (Melbourne, 1958).

15. Newcastle to Elgin, pvt., 1 Jan. 1853, Newcastle Papers, NeC 9552.

16. Elgin to Newcastle, pvt., 4 Feb. 1853, ibid.

fallen from 40,000 to 27,000, with Canada's dropping to less than 1,900.[17]

These emergency reductions might well have served as the logical conclusion to the efforts of Lord Grey. After the war, however, the Palmerston government, unwilling to demobilize too quickly and therefore finding itself with a sudden excess of troops, sent the forces back again. It was decided to make a display of power against the United States by "properly reinforcing . . . our North American colonies."[18] Over the objections of Elgin, who had returned to the Lords, against the negation of "a policy deliberately adopted and steadily and consistently carried out,"[19] the careful efforts of himself, Grey, and Newcastle were abruptly set aside.

In fact no such reversal was intended. The Palmerston government had thrown the entire financial responsibility for the forces sent to quell the goldfield disturbances entirely on the Victorian government,[20] and in announcing the decision on Canada colonial secretary Henry Labouchere contended that "the policy of Her Majesty's Government continues the same" in regard to self-defense.[21] Canadians and other colonists would, however, draw their own conclusions. British policy at the close of the Crimean War, an occasion that might have been used to settle the colonial defense question, instead destroyed much of what had already been accomplished. The doctrine of strategic concentration had not been fully accepted by the War Office or, more importantly, by Palmerston. A foreign policy decision had been made with little or no at-

17. Select committee on colonial military expenditure, PP, 1861 (423), *13*, 367.

18. Palmerston to Panmure (Sec. of State at War), 30 Mar. 1856, C. Douglas and G. Ramsay, eds., *The Panmure Papers; Being a Selection from the Correspondence of Fox Maule* (2 vols., 1908), *2*, 172.

19. 18 Apr. 1856, 3 *Hansard, 142,* 682.

20. G. Serle, *The Golden Age: A History of the Colony of Victoria, 1851–1861* (Melbourne, 1963), p. 169.

21. Labouchere to Head, 2 May 1856, quoted by Stacey, *Canada and the British Army,* p. 101.

tention to its implications for colonial affairs. By failing to assert itself the Colonial Office was building trouble for itself in future colonial defense negotiations.

Proposals for Federation

In the late 1850s there came proposals for the federation of Australia, Canada, and South Africa. None of them originated in the Colonial Office. Two were chiefly the work of governors, while the third emanated from a group of Australian expatriates who, widely separated as they were in London from the scene of sectional collisions, were able to think in terms of larger issues. Two, again, were attempts to deal forcefully with the implications of responsible government by forming federal structures before sectionalism could become an even stronger force. The third was a governor's personal effort to find a more realistic framework in which to confront South Africa's frontier and race problems. The Colonial Office resisted them all.

Most Australians greeted apathetically Lord John Russell's decision of 1855 not to encourage federalism. A few were disappointed. The *Sydney Morning Herald* complained: "These colonies would probably have taken their cue from the British Government; but they will never, under ordinary circumstances, take it from each other." [22] In Victoria an Irish nationalist, Charles Gavan Duffy, chaired a select committee that recommended a federal convention. Sir Edward Deas Thomson supported the idea in New South Wales. But the strongest proposal came from the General Association of the Australian Colonies, a group in London led by W. C. Wentworth, who in March 1857 urged the Colonial Office to carry through parliament an act that would enable the Australians to form a federal union.

The reaction was hesitant. Gordon Gairdner, senior clerk of

22. Quoted by Ward, *Earl Grey and the Australian Colonies*, p. 348.

the Australian division, advised that such a course would be "hazardous," since the Association had left the imperial government to decide such delicate issues as the representation to be given each colony and the subjects on which the proposed assembly would be empowered to legislate. Robert Lowe, the former Sydney politician who was now at the Board of Trade, was still more hostile. Probably influenced by contemporary problems in America, he argued that "history teaches nothing with more uniformity than the failure of federations." Federal machinery was unnecessary among colonies that were like "foreign countries" to one another, and they should be left to themselves.

Such was colonial secretary Henry Labouchere's decision: he could not act, he told Wentworth, without a more decided opinion from the colonial legislatures.[23] Deprived of British leadership, the federation movement quickly faded. The local press spoke in favorable but comfortably detached terms, while the governors merely observed and reported.[24] Nothing happened. "Federation in 1857," concludes the foremost authority, "would have required an act of choice that the Australian colonies were politically incapable of making." [25] Thereafter, intercolonial rivalry deepened and intensified, and the chances in favor of federation decreased.

Durham, Grey, and Elgin had all talked vaguely of North American federation, but it was Sir Edmund Head who formed the first concrete plan, building a movement out of the materials of a Canadian political crisis that occurred in the summer of 1858. For him the encouragement of federalism was by no means new. As early as 1851, while serving in New Brunswick, he had drawn up a preliminary sketch for the union of British North America in which he revealed himself

23. Memorial, 31 Mar. 1857 (registered in C.O., 12 May), and minutes, CO 201/450.

24. See for example Sir Henry Barkly (Victoria) to S. of S., 9 June 1858, CO 309/45.

25. Ward, *Earl Grey and the Australian Colonies,* p. 467.

as one of the few statesmen of his generation who thoroughly grasped the implications of responsible government.[26] Unlike the Colonial Reformers he assumed that the new system would be neither static nor a final solution, but that it must lead the colonies toward what he called an "independent existence." His aim was constant: to build a nation that could resist encroachment from the south. But his means were flexible, and he bided his time.

In 1856, as governor of Canada, he returned to the subject more forcefully. He had been responsible for the colony's safety when the withdrawal of troops during the Crimean War had left her exposed, and he had been impressed by the dangerous absurdity of having to obtain winter shipments of arms by way of a railway running through the territory of the only potential enemy. He had watched anxiously the deterioration of the American situation.[27] He corresponded privately with secretary of state Labouchere and, while in London during the summer of 1857, held conversations and wrote a lengthy memorandum on the subject.[28] Considering impractical at present the more ambitious project of North American federation, he concentrated instead on a smaller union of the maritime colonies which might conceivably serve as a "stepping stone." From Labouchere he received encouragement if not action and, having learned on his return to Canada that Lord Stanley (who succeeded Labouchere in February 1858) was also favorable, he determined to strive for the wider North American federation he had always wanted.[29]

26. Martin, *Canadian Historical Association Report* (1928), pp. 14–26. See D. Kerr, *Sir Edmund Head, A Scholarly Governor* (Toronto, 1954).

27. His correspondence with G. C. Lewis (PAC) is predominantly concerned with developments in the United States.

28. Head to Labouchere, 3 Sept. 1857, quoted by Kerr, *Sir Edmund Head*, p. 167; A. Stewart, ed., "Sir Edmund Head's Memorandum of 1857 on Maritime Union: A Lost Confederation Document," *Canadian Historical Review, 26* (1945), 406–19

29. No record was kept of the conversations, but according to Merivale: "Mr. Labouchere particularly requested him to take it in hand, when he (Sir E. H.) was last in England. . . . Mr. Labouchere's view

The local political crisis which Head contrived to use may be summarized briefly.[30] The Act of Union, passed in 1840 when Lower Canada had the larger population, had given equal representation to each province. By the early 1850s, however, the balance had shifted, and in 1853 the leader of Canada West's reform party, George Brown, came out in favor of "rep. by pop.," which became the chief issue in the bitter election of December 1857. Indeed it threatened to blow the fragile union apart. Then, as later, the Anglo-French problem seemed to call for a larger and looser framework.

The governor maneuvered shrewdly. He kept the Macdonald government in office by means of a questionable exercise of the power of dissolution.[31] He brought an avowed pro-confederationist, A. T. Galt, into the cabinet, and succeeded in converting it. In early July Galt moved a resolution in favor of confederation, and in August Head proposed to communicate officially with the imperial government and the other colonies. The Colonial Office, unaware of the extent of the involvement of its own representative, was suddenly presented with an opportunity for decisive action.

Head had apparently received enough encouragement from Labouchere and Stanley to convince him that he was safe, but he had not prepared the ground carefully enough among the permanent officials, nor bothered to ascertain the attitude of Sir Edward Bulwer Lytton, the popular novelist who stepped in when Stanley moved to the India Office in May 1858. Arthur Blackwood, senior clerk of the North American division,

---

was, not that it was a thing to be urged from this side, but that we ought to be prepared for its proposal & rather encourage it than otherwise." Minute on Head to S. of S., 16 Aug. 1858, CO 42/614. For Stanley's opinion see Carnarvon minute on Head to S. of S., 22 Oct. 1858, quoted by W. Whitelaw, *The Maritimes and Canada before Confederation* (Toronto, 1934), pp. 122–23.

30. See C. Martin, *Foundations of Canadian Nationhood* (Toronto, 1955), pp. 244–74; J. Careless, *Brown of the Globe* (2 vols. Toronto, 1959–63), *1*, 209–80; D. Creighton, *John A. Macdonald* (2 vols. Toronto, 1953–56), *1*, 238–72.

31. See Merivale minute on Head to S. of S., 9 Aug. 1858, CO 42/614.

declared the proposal "startling," confessing an ignorance of past proceedings that is surprising.[32] Lytton, characteristically impetuous, wished to censure the governor at once, but was advised by Merivale that the measure had indeed been discussed beforehand. He received a Canadian delegation courteously and tactfully. Advised by undersecretary T. F. Elliot that federation would divert but not solve the Canadian representation problem, while it would not materially add to the colonies' "union and strength" and very probably turn them against the Colonial Office, Lytton decided against it. Only one political party had committed itself to the idea, he argued, so that by acting the imperial government would appear to be taking sides. To encourage federation now would be both "premature and unwise."[33] Without British support, the maritime colonies' fears of domination by Canada were allowed to prevail. Federation was postponed for yet another decade.

In South Africa, even more than in North America, the drive for federation was engineered by the governor. Sir George Grey had arrived fresh from a celebrated but controversial tour in New Zealand, charged with carrying out a recently instituted policy of disengagement from the interior. Stung by the expense of Kaffir wars and convinced of the futility of attempting to keep pace with the trekking habits of the Boers, Britain had resolved to stay clear of internal commitments. To that end she had signed neutrality treaties with the Orange Free State and the Transvaal. Her policy, after decades of indecision, was for the moment fixed: order was to be maintained within the enclaves of Natal and the Cape Colony, but a strict impartiality was to be observed toward the rest of southern Africa, black and white.[34]

32. Minutes on Head to S. of S., 16 Aug. 1858, CO 42/164, and 9 Sept., CO 42/615

33. R. Trotter, ed., "The British Government and the Proposal of Federation in 1858," *Canadian Historical Review, 14* (1933), 285–92.

34. See J. S. Galbraith, *Reluctant Empire: British Policy on the South*

Why anyone should have supposed that the aggressive Grey was the man to follow such a timid policy is not apparent. Echoing the charges being made by missionaries,[35] he was soon complaining that Britain's neutrality was a sham: to permit the sale of ammunition to the Boers but not to the Africans meant in practice "that we abandon the colored races to the mercy of the two Republics."[36] Humanitarianism was motive enough for him to urge greater flexibility, at the least, and to recommend by December 1856 that a federal union was the ultimate solution.[37] Soon strategic arguments could be added. Such events as the threat of war between the Basutos and the Free State late in 1856 and the cattle-killing disaster among the Xhosa in 1857 enabled him to explain that turbulence within British territory was inevitably linked to pressures beyond it. Asked to treat the symptoms instead of the causes, he chafed and sought to remove the restrictions on his freedom of maneuver.

Grey's efforts came to a head in 1858–59. His campaign had succeeded at least to the extent of causing the Colonial Office to doubt the wisdom and morality of its stated policy, if not to adopt his own. He had won the right to arbitrate, and with it a degree of latitude. Receiving considerable evidence of indecision on the part of the secretary of state, Sir E. B. Lytton, he tried to nudge him further by entering negotiations with the Orange Free State. Only after Grey had committed himself did Lytton decide against him, recalling him from office in April 1859. In turn the Duke of Newcastle, colonial secretary in the Palmerston government, sent him back to continue his work among the Africans, but on the understanding that federation was not to be mentioned again.

African Frontier (Berkeley, 1963); and C. de Kiewiet, *British Colonial Policy and the South African Republics, 1848–1872* (1929).

35. See particularly J. Wallis, ed., *The Matabele Journals of Robert Moffat, 1829–1860* (2 vols., 1945), *1*, 377–78.

36. Grey to S. of S., 22 May 1856, CO 48/374.

37. Grey to S. of S., 20 Dec. 1856, CO 48/377.

From the pages of the late James Rutherford's brilliant account of this famous episode emerges a classic case of a governor's conflict with imperial bureaucratic officialdom. There is Grey: headstrong, imaginative, and forceful; seeking through one bold stroke to solve his local problems and to build a great and lasting nation overseas. There is Lytton: timid and vacillatory; neglecting his work for months on end, leaving the governor on the end of a rope; trying to avoid problems instead of solving them; worrying most about how the correspondence would look in the parliamentary blue book; in effect, and perhaps in intention, setting a trap for Grey. There is the under-secretary, Merivale, knowledgeable and willing to offer advice, but refusing to become involved. There are misunderstandings, messages that cross, and plenty of intrigue. And there at the end is Grey's brilliant dispatch, written at white heat, tearing Lytton to shreds, describing as if for all time the position, role, and dilemma of the man on the spot:

> Can a man who, on a distant and exposed frontier, surrounded by difficulties, with invasions of Her Majesty's territories threatening on several points, assumes a responsibility which he, guided by many circumstances which he can neither record nor remember as they come hurrying on one after the other, be fairly judged . . . by those who, in the quiet of distant offices in London, know nothing of the anxieties or nature of the difficulties he had to encounter? [38]

Thus three opportunities for nation building confronted the Colonial Office in swift succession in the late 1850s. Just as swiftly, all of them were rejected. Explaining that nothing like a groundswell of colonial opinion existed in favor of any of them, the imperial authorities refused to pursue a policy that

38. Grey to S. of S., 20 July 1859, Papers re Grey's recall, PP, 1860 (216), *45*, 22–30. J. Rutherford, *Sir George Grey, 1812–1898: A Study in Colonial Government* (1961), pp. 406–26.

smacked in the slightest degree of coercion or interventionism.

None of the movements was in fact very strong. Support was probably most broadly based in Australia. But South Australia, at least, would have had to be coerced; apathy was more prevalent than strong conviction in any of the colonies; the governors were opposed; and no compelling reasons were brought forward to show why action was necessary. In North America, Sir Edmund Head had only just succeeded in lining up a base of support in Canada, having built no comparable foundations in the maritimes. And in South Africa there was only Sir George Grey. No mandate, then, existed in any of them.

Yet to conclude that the imperial power did not act merely because it had no strong support from the colonies does not seem sufficient. Lord Grey had tried to act without it in Australia, while the local enthusiasm for Lord Carnarvon's South African scheme in the 1870s may not have been significantly stronger than it had been for Sir George Grey's.[39] The most important variable factor would appear to have been the inclinations of the Colonial Office.

Several reasons have already been suggested why there was hesitancy in the late 1850s: events in America were casting doubts on federalism; Lord Grey's overeagerness was remembered; the Colonial Reformers thought nation building would lead to separatism. An obvious point of contrast is that ten or twenty years later, when federalism came once again to the fore, such figures as Carnarvon and Sir Frederic Rogers had been through it all before. And it is probably true that, in the years just after responsible government was conceded, the office was being unusually cautious. To federate by fiat would have flown in the face of the self-government that had just been granted. Probably most important, however, in explaining Britain's lack of motivation in the 1850s is the fact that the

39. See C. de Kiewiet, *The Imperial Factor in South Africa: A Study in Politics and Economics* (Cambridge, 1937), and C. Goodfellow, *Great Britain and South African Confederation, 1870–1881* (Cape Town, 1966).

intimate connection between colonial nation building and imperial defense that was being urged for the first time by Sir Edmund Head and Sir George Grey had not yet penetrated the official mind.

The Implications Realized

In the 1860s Great Britain gradually worked out a policy for dealing with the implications of responsible government. That policy was a unilateral disengagement from settlement colonies, hopefully leaving behind as much order and good feeling as possible, but with the emphasis being placed on withdrawal. The process under which this policy came to fruition was rather comparable to the earlier pattern in the coming of responsible government. In both cases the basic forces had been working and the essential ideas had been in circulation for some time. In both there was a focus of opinion—on the Durham Report in the first instance, on the select committee on colonial military expenditure in the second—that pointed the way. But there were periods of groping uncertainty, with cautious attempts at implementation. At last there were short climactic periods in which the barriers came down with a rush. In both cases it is difficult to determine where uncertain policy making ended and settled policy began.

British imperial administrators became increasingly concerned with the themes of colonial defense and nation building which have been traced back to their beginnings under Lord Grey. Of these the former emerged first and was the controlling element in shaping the policy of withdrawal, which was foremost a measure of economy. The realization of the latter, as well as of the interconnection between the themes, came more gradually and as a by-product.

Palmerston had administered a temporary setback to the colonial defense agitation at the close of the Crimean War. Pressure soon revived, concentrated primarily as before upon financial arguments rather than upon the broader concept of military concentration. Within the government reform was urged by the Treasury and the War Office, the latter department being now the charge of a minister who bore no responsibility for the colonies and who was therefore able to display a singlemindedness that had been impossible for Grey and Newcastle. In the Commons the old voices—Cobden, Bright, Adderley—were raised. Agitation was also directed against the stragglers by colonies that had already been brought into line. By 1861 the campaign had led to the formation of an interdepartmental committee and to an important select committee of the House of Commons.

The chain of events that eventually led to the parliamentary committee began in Australia, where the neighboring colonies of New South Wales and Victoria were being regulated according to different defense arrangements, a situation that naturally led to recriminations. After receiving numerous complaints the Colonial Office concluded "that we cannot long go on without some definite & intelligible rule." [40] Soon a scheme was submitted by Governor Sir William Denison of New South Wales, who proposed that the cost of fortifying Sydney harbor should be divided equally between the colony and the mother country. That document was forwarded to the two service departments with the observation that Denison's suggestion might well serve as the basis for "some definitive understanding" with other self-governing colonies.[41] Thus the search within the British government for a universal rule on colonial defense began in the Colonial Office.

For most of the next year the Denison plan went unnoticed, and only after the Colonial Office pressed for an answer was the matter taken up at all. Then the War Office raised the

40. Merivale minute on Acting Gov. Macarthur (Victoria) to S. of S., 28 May 1856, CO 309/40.

41. Denison to S. of S., 14 Aug. 1856, and C.O. letters to W.O. and Admiralty, 23 Dec. 1856, CO 201/495. See also W. Denison, *Varieties of Vice-regal Life* (2 vols., 1870), *1*, 346–48.

ante: the colony would pay half the expense for those troops the imperial government might decide were necessary, as well as the entire cost of any additional forces that might be provided at the colony's request. Now it was the Colonial Office's turn to back away. Merivale had feared from the beginning that colonies would naturally claim ownership over any troops they paid for, an event that would be incompatible with the requirements of imperial strategy. Parliamentary undersecretary Chichester Fortescue agreed, and secretary of state Henry Labouchere decided to leave things as they were. The imperial government would continue to determine the necessary amount and pay the entire cost of military and naval protection against external danger, while internal security would be charged to the colonies.[42]

But an idea once implanted in the War Office was not so easily displaced, especially when Denison continued to send home so many helpful suggestions that Merivale came to wish "Sir W. D. instead of sending us able arguments on questions incapable of accurate solution, would apply himself to using his influence to obtain from his legislature some reasonable contribution towards the classes of expenditure here discussed."[43] In fact there was no stopping. In March 1859 the reluctant Colonial Office agreed to an interdepartmental committee to examine "the difficulty and embarrassment occasioned . . . by the absence of any fixed and recognised principle."[44]

Although assistant undersecretary T. F. Elliot resisted them as well as he could, George Hamilton of the Treasury and John Robert Godley of the War Office delivered the expected highly critical report. They found that of a total expenditure of £1.4 million in 1858, the colonies had contributed a mere

42. W.O. to C.O., 16 Nov. 1857, and C.O. minutes, CO 201/500.
43. Minute on Denison to S. of S., 26 Oct. 1858, CO 201/504.
44. W.O. to C.O., 14 Mar. 1859, Report of committee on colonial defense, PP, 1860 (282), *41*, 573–74.

£150,000, the worst offenders being New Zealand, paying nothing toward an expenditure of £110,000, and the Cape Colony, paying only £40,000 of £680,000.[45] They found flagrant inconsistencies and inequities: Victoria, for example, which paid a good deal, had once been punished by the removal of troops to Tasmania, which paid nothing at all. Most of the old arguments were brought up, Hamilton and Godley objecting to the existing situation on the grounds of finance, strategy, and "most important . . . the tendency which this system must necessarily have to prevent the development of a proper spirit of self-reliance amongst our colonies, and to enfeeble their national character." Though they spoke favorably of Lord Grey's plan, they preferred Denison's, under which the colonists would properly assume the initiative for their own defense. Elliot dissented. If they must adopt a plan, then Grey's would be better. It at least would avoid negotiations. But he doubted whether "one self-acting rule, which shall be a substitute for the judgment and firmness of the Ministers of the Crown" could ever be devised for so diverse a collection of societies as the British Empire.[46] He argued forcefully, but the tide was against him.

From the interdepartmental committee it was an easy step to the select committee of the Commons, a body which did so much to crystallize British attitudes toward the implications of responsible government. That committee met in a charged atmosphere. For though it was the logical conclusion to many years of parliamentary agitation, it speedily became a focal point of the British reaction to two conflicts—the American Civil War and the Maori wars in New Zealand—the one a real danger, the other a distinct annoyance.

Schism, rebellion, and military build-up in the United States posed a major threat to the North American colonies, while it

45. Appendix to report of select committee on colonial military expenditure, PP, 1861 (423), *13*, 393.

46. Committee report, 24 Jan. 1860, Elliot memorandum, WO 33/9.

was clear that the damage to Britain's cotton industry might be severe. Britain would find it hard to remain neutral. Palmerston quickly reinforced the Canadian garrison, overruling Gladstone and ignoring questions about whether colonies were worth defending, so that by the spring of 1862 there were 18,000 British regulars in North America.[47] Yet those whom Palmerston contemptuously dismissed as "theoretical gentlemen" were not easily brushed aside. Goldwin Smith and others, regarding Canada's continuing state of dependency as an unhealthy anomaly, neglected few opportunities to say so.[48] How deep this current of separatism ran is difficult to determine. It has almost certainly been overemphasized in the older accounts, but to deny its existence would be just as mistaken. It was a frequent question: would the Canadians exert themselves? If not, why should Britain bother?

The Maori wars, which though not so serious had a high adrenalin content, made plain the failure of both native and defense policies. They undermined the reputation of Sir George Grey and the Treaty of Waitangi, and provided substantial evidence to support the thesis—which would receive additional documentation in southern and eastern Africa—that the safeguarding of native interests by an imperial power is incompatible with the enjoyment of self-government by the settlers.[49] What was more to the point at the moment, however, was the bill that was about to be presented to the imperial treasury: "we have the troops there, and some one must pay for them," admitted the Duke of Newcastle fatalistically, "and we know pretty well what generally happens" in such colonial wars.[50]

47. Palmerston to Russell, 9 Sept. 1861, Russell Papers, PRO 30/22/21. Stacey, *Canada and the British Army,* p. 122.

48. See G. Smith, *The Empire* (1863). Also the testimony of Robert Lowe, PP, 1861, (423), *13,* 313.

49. See K. Sinclair, *The Origins of the Maori Wars* (Wellington, 1957), and B. Dalton, *War and Politics in New Zealand, 1855–1870* (Sydney, 1967).

50. PP, 1861 (423), *13,* 292.

Ever since the great potential lever of responsible government had been thrown away to no advantage, the colonists had successfully evaded equitable defense arrangements. Now that the crisis was at hand, it would be harder than ever to reach an agreement.

The question of New Zealand's contribution to her own defense had first been broached late in 1855, when Sir William Molesworth had reasoned that since the colony had received "the sweets, it ought also to bear the burdens of self-government." More concretely, "all disputes with the natives about land are *local* questions with which the Imperial Govt. has no concern." [51] It all seemed forthright enough. But the very dispatch that announced this principle also approved the stationing of three hundred men at British expense in Taranaki, where land disputes were in fact most likely to occur. Moreover, the strategy of negotiation was adopted, so that Merivale's question was highly pertinent: "how are we to enforce it." [52] In the years that followed only Lord Stanley proved resolute enough to propose that if the colony should refuse to pay then "the troops should be withdrawn." [53] But with the indecisive Lytton the situation reverted to the earlier proposition that the colony *ought* to pay,[54] which it mostly would not. And by 1861 a series of extremely tortuous negotiations had finally yielded a colonial contribution of a mere £5 per man, out of a total maintenance cost of £80. Having acted throughout on the very questionable assumption that to withdraw imperial troops would be inhumane, the Colonial Office had been playing with an exceedingly short trump suit.

New Zealand and North America were largely responsible for the sense of urgency with which the select committee collected its statistics, examined its witnesses, and framed its re-

51. Minute on Acting Gov. Wynyard to S. of S., 19 Apr. 1855, CO 209/129.
52. Minute on W.O. to C.O., 18 Dec. 1856, CO 209/140.
53. Minute on Gore Browne to S. of S., 11 May 1858, CO 209/141.
54. Minute on same to same, 26 June 1858, CO 209/145.

port. Surrounded by a worsening international situation, Britain herself did not feel secure, and her empire seemed to be becoming increasingly burdensome. No one knew when another colonial war, in South Africa for example, might erupt. A rational defense policy seemed long overdue.

The report of the select committee reveals the extent to which by 1861 the implications of responsible government had become widely apparent. Following the Hamilton-Godley report, the imperial dependencies were divided into two classes: colonies and military outposts. The latter would of course continue to be maintained at the discretion and at the expense of Great Britain. In the former, and particularly where self-government had been conceded, both "the responsibility and cost of military defence . . . ought mainly to devolve upon" the colonists themselves. Lord Grey's plan of dictating terms was preferred over the Denison scheme which would involve negotiation. The committee supported its recommendations with two main arguments. One of them was strategic: since "the tendency of modern warfare is to strike blows at the heart of a hostile power," [55] British forces ought not to be spread too thinly. Yet the committee stressed far more heavily the financial argument, which continued in the 1860s to lend an air of unedifying pettiness to the whole affair.

In March 1862 the select committee report was duly ratified by a resolution that passed the House of Commons without a division:

> This House, while it fully recognises the claim of all portions of the British Empire on Imperial aid against perils arising from the consequences of Imperial policy, is of opinion that Colonies exercising the rights of self-government ought to undertake the main responsibility of providing for their own internal order and security and ought to assist in their own external defence.[56]

55. PP, 1861 (423), *13*, 116, 74, 75.
56. 3 *Hansard, 165,* 1060.

By adding parliamentary prestige to the Colonial Office's efforts the resolution was a significant turning point, helping to transform what had sometimes been irresolute into a fixed principle and hastening a process of disengagement that was already in motion. Yet the resolution was a guideline, not an attempt to deprive ministers of administrative flexibility. At the moment contrary measures were plainly necessary: there was a rebellion to be put down in New Zealand and a threat to British North America to be averted. The British might grumble, but so long as there was real danger they would pay. Steadily and deliberately though the Colonial and War offices attempted in the 1860s to apply the doctrine of colonial self-defense, it was only by the end of the decade that it had been implemented throughout the self-governing portions of the empire: and then South Africa remained a significant exception.

Although the resolution was a stimulus toward clarity of purpose, it did not remove entirely the inconsistencies that had plagued British defense policy. The last phrase, for example, called upon the colonies "to assist in their own external defence." Yet when Victoria attempted to do so, by advocating a small navy of her own, the Duke of Newcastle was indignantly hostile, convinced that separatism would inevitably follow such a devolution of imperial protection. It is one of the ironies that Victoria's persistence at length helped British statesmen begin to make the transition from the concept of "colonial" to that of "imperial" defense.[57]

As yet there was little explicit discussion of the corollary: that colonies would be better equipped to defend themselves if they could be formed into cohesive national units. That subject was not much considered by the select committee on colo-

57. Newcastle memorandum, 25 Mar. 1862, Palmerston Papers, Naval Correspondence. B. Knox, "Colonial Influence on Imperial Policy, 1858–1866: Victoria and the Colonial Naval Defense Act, 1865," *Historical Studies, Australia and New Zealand, 11* (1963), 61–79.

nial military expenditure. Newcastle would admit only (and that most unenthusiastically) that confederation might perhaps facilitate *Britain's* defense of Canada. And Merivale dismissed the topic as a purely political question that was therefore irrelevant to the committee's line of inquiry. The risk of involving the Colonial Office in local politics was still the overriding concern.[58]

The increasingly transparent curtain between political and military aspects of colonial nation building was shortly to be lifted. The decisive event was the American Civil War, a crisis which showed British statesmen how much their own national interests were bound up with what happened in Canada. It succeeded in reconverting them, after what had been a temporary fall from favor in the 1850s, to the virtues of bigness as contained within the federalism of which Tocqueville had written. British colonial policy, said Edward Cardwell in a crucial parliamentary speech of 1867, was frankly directed toward the formation "of great and powerful communities" overseas that could defend themselves and stand on their own feet.[59] That had been Sir Edmund Head's position. It was the full realization by a generation of British statesmen of the implications of responsible government that formed the mainspring of the colonial policy of the late 1860s. It was a conscious policy of rapid disengagement. There were two main test cases, both of which have been treated very extensively in recent acounts: Britain's role in the confederation of Canada and her military withdrawal from New Zealand.

The origins of Canadian confederation were largely colonial, as indeed they had to be in the era of responsible government when the Colonial Office's powers of intervention in

58. PP, 1861 (423), *13*, 281, 220–21.

59. Quoted by D. Creighton, *The Road to Confederation: The Emergence of Canada, 1853–1867* (Toronto, 1964), p. 429. See also Martin, *Foundations of Canadian Nationhood;* W. Morton, *The Critical Years: The Union of British North America, 1857–1873* (Toronto, 1964); and Stacey, *Canada and the British Army.*

local politics had been so sharply curtailed. As in the abortive attempt of Sir Edmund Head in 1858 the campaign that bore fruit in 1867 grew largely out of the need of the united Canadas for a larger framework in which to face their representational difficulties. Its other root was a movement among the maritime colonies for a union of their own, onto which the Canadian effort was successfully grafted. Colonial statesmen are rightly regarded as the founding fathers. Yet the role of the Colonial Office was important. Without Cardwell and Carnarvon the provincial jealousies of the maritime colonies might well have been allowed to prevail as before. The curbing of Lieutenant Governor Arthur Gordon of New Brunswick, who along with old Joseph Howe of Nova Scotia provided the most articulate opposition to the Quebec plan, was particularly crucial. Without the active encouragement of the imperial government Canadian confederation might have had to be postponed for perhaps another generation.

Confederation was a prelude to withdrawal, over the protests of John A. Macdonald and other Canadians, of all remaining imperial troops by 1871. Only two years earlier colonial secretary Lord Granville, in an official dispatch, had asked the governor "to bring to my notice any line of policy or any measure which without implying on the part of Her Majesty's Government any wish to change our relations, would gradually prepare both Countries for a friendly relaxation of them": as if it had not already been found! [60] Now he was withdrawing from New Zealand, over even louder protests than the Canadians had raised, leaving the colonists themselves to deal with the last phase of the Maori wars and removing the last shadow of a pretext for talk of the imperial government's responsibility to the natives.[61] The troops were being brought home from the Australian colonies, and a substantial reduction was being made in the garrison at the Cape,

60. Quoted by Stacey, *Canada and the British Army*, p. 216.
61. See Dalton, *War and Politics in New Zealand*, pp. 206–59.

which received responsible government in 1872. It was all of a piece: a conscious and swift attempt to bring to a logical conclusion a process of disengagement that had been implicit in the initial concessions of responsible government and, ultimately, in the Durham Report. The implications of responsible government had been realized at last.

The mid-Victorian generation of British policy makers have sometimes been chided by imperial historians for their lack of faith in empire, for their pessimism, and for their separatism. The most widely accepted thesis has been that the "Little Englanders" helped to preserve the empire in spite of themselves by removing the source of its unpopularity at home.[62] Thus only after reaching its nadir could the imperial idea regain its vitality and respectability.

There is in fact much truth in this view. Empire, or at least some aspects of it, *was* unpopular in Britain in the 1860s. It was not only the exceptional crank who thought that colonies added little to her strength and that their independence would probably make very little difference.[63] It is, however, somewhat easier now than it was between the world wars to perceive that the mid-Victorians were realists as well as pessimists. For the colonies did become independent, the continuing Commonwealth membership of most of them detracting not a whit from the complete exercise of sovereignty. It is not the realism of the 1860s that needs to be explained. It is the rise in the late nineteenth century of the belief that some other outcome, such as imperial unity, was really a practical possibility in the long run.

In his Crystal Palace speech of 1872, abandoning his metaphors of "millstones" and "colonial deadweights," Disraeli took to task Liberals past and present for their failure to develop a

62. Stacey, *Canada and the British Army*, pp. 257–59.

63. Cf. A. Thornton, *The Imperial Idea and Its Enemies: A Study in British Power* (1959), p. 8.

coherent plan of empire. Instead they had drifted, expecting the colonies to depart. The colonies had not chosen to do so. The time for drifting was past: it was a time for imperial achievement. And, although he himself thereafter took but little interest in the empire outside India,[64] his castigation of British colonial policy in the mid-nineteenth century has tended to stick.

There was drift indeed. But there were also responsible, progressive decisions. The achievement of the mid-Victorians ought not to be overlooked. In the twentieth century decolonization has been shown to be a process at least as dangerous and as complex as colonization. Between 1840 and 1870 Great Britain peacefully disengaged herself from a substantial portion of her empire. There was no precedent for this: no imperial power in modern times had ever done such a thing before. The graceful way in which she did it, leaving behind her a residue of goodwill instead of bitterness, ought rather to be the cause of admiration than contempt.

64. See R. Blake, *Disraeli* (New York, 1967), p. 665. S. Stembridge, "Disraeli and the Millstones," *Journal of British Studies*, 5 (1965), 122–39.

PART III

Interdepartmental Relations

Introduction

One characteristic of a modern bureaucracy, suggested Max Weber, is that the spheres of administrative competence belonging to the departments within it tend to be defined with increasing sharpness and precision. At first glance the administrative system of the British Empire in the nineteenth century seems to bear him out. It possessed more or less clearly delineated areas of primary jurisdiction. India was administered by a separate set of authorities and, after 1858, by a single government department. The Foreign Office dealt with areas where British influence was being exercised informally, the Colonial Office with territories that had been annexed by the crown. There was a marked trend, as well, toward a more rational distribution of responsibilities: the transfer of former dependencies of India to the Colonial Office and the gradual abandonment of Treasury control over local colonial financial operations being good examples. The progressive narrowing of the British colonial secretary's duties after the eighteenth century has been described in an earlier chapter.

Yet to emphasize the trend toward departmental autonomy is misleading. British imperial policy making remained a collective process, a pattern of constant interaction among the departments that composed the government complex in London, and stretching out to the other centers of administrative authority in colonies throughout the world. Not all problems had to be processed through that formidable array of offices. Some were purely local matters that could be handled entirely on the spot. Others could be dispatched without ado by the Colonial Office. But many problems, and often the most important ones, had to be coordinated with other departments. Anything involving money had to be worked out with the Treasury. The War Office had to be consulted in matters concerning troops, the Board of Trade in those concerning commerce, the Admiralty in those concerning sea communications. Nor was it always a simple matter of the Colonial Office's obtaining the approval of another department before acting on a subject that properly belonged to it. In many cases the question of which department should take charge could not have been worked out in advance. Was imperial finance the responsibility of the Colonial Office or the Treasury? Did colonial defense belong to the War Office or the Colonial Office? Should the extent of the activities of naval captains off West Africa be decided by the Admiralty or the Foreign Office? Interdepartmental negotiations were often carried on among parties that were virtually equal.

All this is elementary enough, but it may bear stressing. For while the Colonial Office has been subjected to the most microscopic scrutiny, interdepartmental relations have usually been handled as an aside, relegated to a short but sweeping chapter in a book devoted to some other subject. The focus seems distorted. And the methodology has been far from systematic or satisfactory.

What has chiefly been done is to gather quotations, lifting the succinctly phrased office minute from the back of an incoming dispatch. On its face, such evidence is often unreliable, fragmentary, and exaggerated, frequently written for the sake of humor rather than of accuracy, and rarely describing the complex. To quote Stephen and Merivale on the behavior of the Treasury, or George and Edward Hamilton of the Treasury on that of the Colonial Office, is frequently to transfer the oversimplifications of contemporaries to the conventional wisdom of historical interpretation.

Now the purpose of these introductory remarks is merely to suggest that the student of interdepartmental relations in British imperial administration is confronted with a serious methodological problem that has not yet been satisfactorily resolved. What, in fact, is to be done? The whole subject cannot be undertaken over long periods by one person: it is far too big. Nor is the task made easier by investigating the whole cross section over a comparatively short period, for then it is difficult to detect the elements of continuity and change. So the problem must be broken down.

One way is to isolate the relations between the Colonial Office and other departments on an individual basis. The time period can be relatively extensive, which is an advantage. And it should be possible to restrict the range of inquiry within manageable proportions. A series of monographs employing this approach would be most welcome. The only important disadvantage—and all the possible strategies have shortcomings—is that the process of interdepartmental interaction must remain somewhat distorted so long as the analysis is restricted to combinations of two offices. Much policy making involved three or more departments, and the increase in complexity as each is added is probably geometrical.

The other potentially fruitful approach, the case method, is the one that will be followed in the next two chapters. The idea behind it is simple. Instead of beginning with the departments, and then proceeding to the subjects that concern them, the student begins with a preselected problem and lets it lead him through the bureaucratic maze. The offices that pertain to it are thus fixed in a specific, substantive context and in a manageable time period, so that the process of day-to-day decision making can be followed in some degree of complexity. Combinations of three or more departments become practical objects of attack. And, at the end, the question can be asked: do the generalizations of the conventional wisdom appear to be verified in terms of this case? If not they must be questioned and perhaps modified or even discarded.

The case method too has disadvantages. The most serious is

that, since the range in time and subject matter must be restricted, difficulty may be encountered in constructing substitutes for the generalizations that may be challenged. There is no systematic way of accurately distinguishing between what is unique and what is part of a more general pattern of behavior. Conclusions that are drawn in connection with one case study may simply be invalid when applied to another.

The most difficult part of the method is the initial selection of cases. There are not as many good ones as might be supposed, and it is not always easy to predict which problems will produce the fruitful meshing of public and private documents that is so desirable. Problems that appear to be relatively obscure may well turn out to be the most productive, while the yield from such obvious examples as that of the negotiation between the Treasury and the Colonial Office of colonial guaranteed loans may be disappointingly slight. The first of the two case studies that follow was the result of an accurate prediction (made after several notably less successful ventures that fortunately need not be disclosed) that potentially fruitful material was likely to be uncovered. The second was discovered quite by accident. Neither case study is without substantive significance in its own right. Both of them are being offered here, however, as examples of the process of interdepartmental relations in the making of British imperial policy.

TELEGRAPH TO INDIA
1857

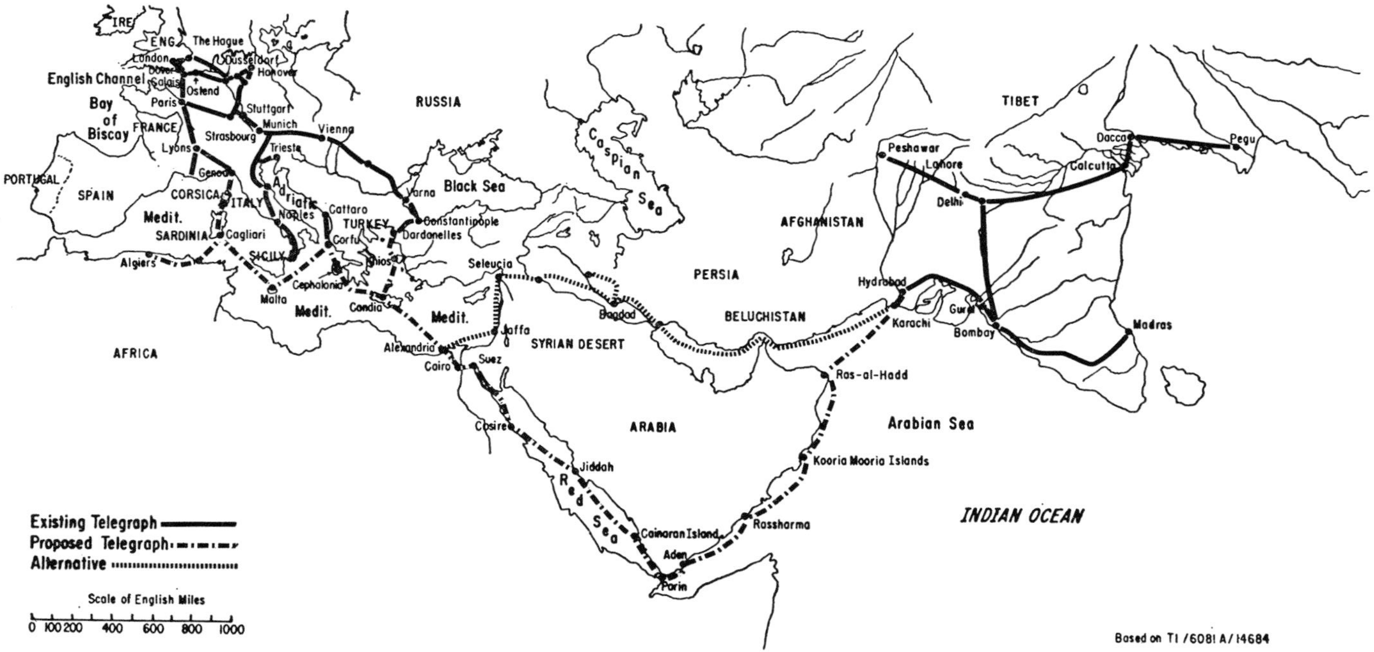

Based on T1 /6081 A/14684

7: The Management of Eastern Communications, 1855–1861: A Case Study of Treasury Control

The Treasury is the center of the government.
James Wilson

One of the most fundamental aspects of British expansion and administration was communications. Soldiers, settlers, missionaries, traders, administrators, goods, money, and information all flowed along lines of communications that had, themselves, a powerful dynamic of their own. It has already been suggested that changes in the base of communications which occurred over the course of the nineteenth century exerted a significant impact upon the working of the Colonial Office and the administrative system of the empire as a whole. But the consequences were larger than that. It is a truism: without communications no empire could have existed. A map of the lines that were in operation about 1870 reflects at least as well as investment charts the directions in which Great Britain would be expanding formally in the two great waves of acquisitiveness—1882–95, and at the close of World War I—that lay ahead.[1] She would be filling in the links of an already existing

1. See particularly R. Robinson and J. Gallagher, *Africa and the Victorians: The Official Mind of Imperialism* (1961); W. Louis, *Great Britain and Germany's Lost Colonies* (Oxford, 1967); and D. Platt, *Finance, Trade, and Politics in British Foreign Policy, 1815–1914* (Oxford, 1968).

network of administrative, commercial, and political communications.

The obvious often merits analysis, and the subject of imperial communications deserves further study in its own right. How were they established? How were they managed? How did they work? What effects did they have? In this chapter the problem is reduced to the manageable proportions of the lines proceeding in a single direction within a relatively short period of time. The years from 1855 to 1861 were crucial ones for British communications with the East, encompassing the consolidation of the regime of the Peninsular and Oriental Steam Navigation Company (as they did Cunard's on the Atlantic) as well as the pioneer age of submarine telegraphy. They were years of crisis when Britain's Eastern interests were being emphasized by the Crimean War, the Indian Mutiny, and the wars with China, as her interests in the West were being underscored by the American Civil War.

Important as the subject of communications is, however, it is being employed here primarily as a framework within which to assess the role of the Treasury in the making of British imperial policy. This too is a problem that deserves much serious study.[2] It may be observed at the outset that the field of communications has certain advantages over some other types of case study—notably that of imperial guarantees of colonial loans in the London money market—that have sometimes been suggested as strategies for "opening up" the Treasury. The main one is that the management of communications was an area in which the Treasury's jurisdiction was primary, the Colonial Office's distinctly secondary. The Treasury can therefore be met on its own ground. Further, since this problem was one of the Treasury's principal concerns—the subsidies it

2. See J. S. Galbraith, "The Empire since 1783," in R. Winks, ed., *The Historiography of the British Empire-Commonwealth* (Durham, N.C., 1966), p. 52, who also speaks of the need for more attention to the subject of communications.

paid to steamship and telegraph companies in the early 1860s amounted to no less than a million pounds a year—it was not dealt with as a side issue by some junior official on an occasional basis, as was so often the case in colonial matters. Instead, it engaged the constant attention of the department's most important members. Moreover it created in abundance the kind of informal material which the historian values most and which, again, is so often lacking in the Treasury's records of its relations with the Colonial Office.

The Treasury did not of course manage alone the network of communications with the East. For the character of that problem brought together a vast array of government departments, individuals, and unofficial agencies in a complex process of collective decision making. It was a postal question, involving the Post Office. It was a commercial question that brought in the Board of Trade. But until the creation in 1860 of that office's marine department, only the Admiralty was competent to survey the ships as to their size, speed, and engine capacity, and to certify that contract specifications were being met. Again until 1860 when the task was transferred to the postal authorities, the Admiralty carried out the negotiations with the shipping companies. The overland route to the East passed through France and Egypt, and the troublesome arrangement of concessions and security measures was the responsibility of the Foreign Office. Through the India Office (the Board of Control until 1858) were funneled the loudly voiced and competing pressures of commercial interests in such places as Bombay, Madras, Calcutta, and Singapore. Through the Colonial Office came those of Hong Kong, Ceylon, Mauritius, the Cape, New Zealand, and the Australian colonies. Beyond the London bureaucracy there was a government of India, and there were governments of Indian presidencies, not necessarily of one mind with each other or with the home authorities. There were colonial governors and, at the Antipodes, legislatures that had recently won responsible

government, anxious to assert themselves. Located primarily in the City of London and in Liverpool there were the established shipping companies and the banks that financed them, as well as a myriad of investors and entrepreneurs attempting to raise themselves into competitive positions. And all these interests had their spokesmen in parliament and in the press.

A more complex array it would be difficult to imagine. But the common denominator of it all was money, and the British Treasury's role was therefore central. As William Stephenson, principal clerk of the contract division of that office, explained, only in the Treasury were there "the means of collecting the opinions of all the different departments that you require, and of getting into your hands all the threads which enable you to deal with them in a comprehensive spirit." [3]

At the Treasury authority was not precisely defined. Stephenson knew his business thoroughly, worked at it enthusiastically, and moved confidently in the City. His rank, however, was too low to admit of his making decisions. The First Lord, who rarely concerned himself with department business, was too high. Of the Chancellors of the Exchequer only Gladstone (partly because he was abnormally meticulous, and partly because Frederick Peel's capacities were somewhat limited) took the contract operations into his own hands. Before Gladstone, and one would think as a general rule, decisions were made one step lower by the financial secretary, a political appointee though not of cabinet rank.[4] As a former holder of that office explained, though he consulted the chancellor, particularly with regard to new subjects, "the Financial Secretary . . . is, in practice, the executive of the Treasury," its being "usual for him to act upon his own responsibility." [5] The Treasury Board, the oft-invoked "my Lords" of the department's stilted corre-

3. Testimony before select committee on telegraphic contracts, PP, 1859 (180, Sess. 2), *6*, 30.

4. On the role of the financial secretary see T. Heath, *The Treasury* (1927), pp. 80–96.

5. James Wilson, Testimony before select committee on telegraphic contracts, PP, 1860 (328), *14*, 50–51.

spondence, was but a rubber stamp. In connection with the contract business, then, "the Treasury" until 1859 means the financial secretaries (Wilson, Stafford Northcote, George Hamilton, and Samuel Laing), assisted by Stephenson and occasionally given directions by chancellors G. C. Lewis and Disraeli. After 1859 the phrase means Gladstone.

Early Cables to the East

Behind the romance of the pioneer age of submarine telegraphy lay the development of an applied science as well as considerable entrepreneurial activity. Behind it too lay tremendous implications for British wealth and power. A telegraphic link with her Mediterranean possessions, for example, would effectively double or treble Britain's naval strength in the area by enabling it to be brought to bear quickly where it was needed. No more need a Nelson search desperately for a Villeneuve. Speedy knowledge of events of commercial importance in India could make investment there less risky and more profitable. Even those who, like Sir George Clerk of the India Office, might scoff at particular ventures regarded the establishment of telegraphic communications with the East as a great national object.[6]

The development of telegraphy had been amazingly rapid.[7] In the decade after Morse's invention of 1835 land lines were put into operation in Britain, Europe, North America, and even in parts of the Near East. Dover and Calais were connected by submarine cable as early as 1851. Six years earlier the idea of a transatlantic cable had been broached to the British government by the brothers Jacob and John W. Brett. And in 1856 the latter formed with Cyrus Field and Charles Bright

6. Minute of May 1857, India Office, Board of Control Letters, no. 6.

7. There has been surprisingly little study of this subject. The best overall treatments are still C. Bright, *The Life Story of the Late Sir Charles Tilston Bright* (2 vols., 1908), and his *Submarine Telegraphs: Their History, Construction, and Working* (1898).

the famous Atlantic Telegraph Company. It would be surprising if the Anglo-American venture had not been matched by a simultaneous drive to the East.

That drive began in the summer of 1855 in the midst of the Crimean War. Four main proposals were put forward, of which the government seriously considered two. For the Eastern Telegraph Company Lionel Gisborne, a former government engineer in Ireland, proposed to lay down a cable from Alexandria to the Red Sea, his offer being made attractive by virtue of an exclusive firman, or concession, from the Porte to extend the line from Constantinople. John Brett, whose Mediterranean Electric Telegraph Company had obtained exclusive concessions for fifty years from France and Sardinia, offered to build a line from Cagliari to Malta and then to extend it along two branches, one going to Corfu and Constantinople, the other to Alexandria and on to India via the Red Sea. Brett's terms were that Britain should pay an annual subsidy of £10,000 toward the construction and operation of the line as far as Alexandria, with additional support for the European section to come from France and Sardinia. For its part the East India Company had already responded favorably to the idea that it should assist in taking the line on to Karachi, where it could be connected with the Indian land network.[8] Even though the situation in the eastern Mediterranean remained uncertain, prime minister Lord Palmerston was cautious: "it remains to be shown," he observed to chancellor G. C. Lewis, "that we shall not get that Communication without so large an annual Contribution as £10,000." [9]

The telegraph proposals came initially to the Foreign Office. Permanent undersecretary Edmund Hammond circularized

8. F.O. précis of telegraph proposals, 10 Sept. 1855, T1/6016A/9108 (1856). I shall normally omit the year at the end of the citation except when it varies, as it does in this case, from that of the document itself. Papers were sometimes carried forward into the next year's correspondence.

9. 7 Sept. 1855, Palmerston Papers.

those departments whose opinions would be pertinent. Yes, the Board of Control tentatively agreed that the Indian government would assist in financing the Indian portion of the line. No support, said the Board of Trade, ought to be given Gisborne until his exclusive firman from the Porte had been withdrawn. In fact, it would be eminently more satisfactory for the British government and the East India Company to construct and manage the whole network themselves. The cost, perhaps a million pounds, would probably be no more than the government would eventually pay out in subsidies, and in a pioneering venture of this kind it would be desirable to bypass the private promoters. The Colonial Office agreed, stressing the necessity of being able to transmit secret messages. The Foreign Office itself disclaimed any responsibility in the area. Hammond sent a précis to Palmerston informing him that the Treasury had already taken the problem in hand. The prime minister, still cautious, advised that "the Matter ought to be well considered." [10] And—it must be remembered as we go deeper into what can only be called a fiasco—so it was.

The government having formally expressed an interest, the various competitors for its favor scattered to promote their efforts. To Paris went Brett, but he was unsuccessful there in obtaining assistance. His luck would improve in Vienna. To Egypt went Francis Gisborne, younger brother of Lionel, to acquire a firman for a monopoly of entry into that country from any source whatever, aiming to shut Brett out of Egypt. The good wishes of the Treasury naturally did not go with him: financial soundness, read its didactic minute, not concessions bribed from oriental potentates, ought to form the basis of business enterprise.[11] By methods that can only be imagined—and whether they were helped or hindered by the re-

10. Palmerston minute, 11 Sept. 1855, T1/6016A/9108 (1856).

11. Treasury minute, 4 Dec. 1855, Correspondence re Telegraphic Communication with India, PP, 1857–58 [2406], *60*, 317–18.

sourceful and independent British ambassador to Turkey, Lord Stratford, is unclear—the Gisbornes by February 1856 obtained the coveted monopoly from Egypt. By October Francis added another triumph: a firman from the Porte for the ninety-nine year right to build and use telegraph stations on the Red Sea. The Gisbornes had a right to celebrate. Fume though it might, if the Treasury wanted the line to follow the usual commercial route through the Red Sea, then it would have to deal with them.

There was still a way around, however, and the Treasury tried to take it. For the government had already opted for Brett. Having failed in Paris, he had proposed a conditional guarantee of five per cent for a line from Cagliari to Malta and Corfu, where it would connect with an Austrian line to be built from Ragusa (i.e. Dubrovnik) to Alexandria.[12] The Chancellor of the Exchequer, the financial secretary, and the president of the India Board had met and had decided to accept, agreeing that Alexandria would be the point through which the telegraph would pass. In February 1857 the Treasury concluded a preliminary agreement with the European and Indian Junction Telegraph Company. The line would go overland across Turkish territory and on to Karachi via the Persian Gulf.[13] The Treasury was trying to bypass the Gisbornes.

The comparatively leisurely pace was considerably quickened by the outbreak of the Indian Mutiny. It was too great a

12. That is, the government would agree on condition of the line's proper functioning to supplement if necessary the company's earnings so that an annual dividend of 5 per cent could be issued to holders of paid-up stock.

13. Under the agreement the government and the East India Company would pay, for twenty-five years from the date of completion of the line, up to £12,000 or as much as would enable the company to pay a dividend of 6 per cent. But the stock must be fully subscribed, 20 per cent of the capital must be paid up within a month of the agreement, and the necessary firmans for passage through Turkish territory must be obtained. E. & I. J. T. to Treasury, 3 Feb. 1857, T1/6097B/2079.

shock to be resisted. Too many important families had relatives in danger. Too many businessmen were losing fortunes as the financial difficulties of India's government and commercial houses rebounded in Lombard Street. In the late summer of 1857 an empire was obviously at stake.

Also at stake were the fortunes of promoters engaged in the attempt to bring India nearer. Two groups were still in the running. One was the European and Indian Company (introduced above), an offshoot of a railway enterprise. Backed by a proposed capital of £200,000 the E. and I. offered to construct a line overland from Seleucia to the head of the Persian Gulf, thus connecting the Austrian network with a cable to be laid by the East India Company from Karachi. Since the object was the rapid establishment of a connection this one would be the best. For though the land line would have to be strung through some very wild country, where superstitious tribesmen might well cut down the poles, less deep-water cable would be involved. But by the crucial month of July 1857, despite the efforts of Ambassador Stratford, the company had not succeeded in obtaining a firman from the Porte. And so the company stood: no firman, and hence no capital.

Its competitor was the Red Sea and Indian Telegraph Association (later incorporated). For the Gisbornes had sold their concessions to an imposing group of financiers who claimed to be able to raise a base of £800,000. The Red Sea group was pressing for a government guarantee. Without it, claimed its chairman John Marshman, the present highly disturbed state of the money market would make the necessary capital impossible to raise. "Our object," he continued, "is a public one; we are not seeking the aid of the public authorities to enable us to get up a Stock Exchange project. We are anxious to provide for a great national object with promptitude and zeal."[14] Charles Bright, the highly respected chief engineer on the At-

14. Marshman to India Office, 28 July 1857, encl. in I.O. to Treasury, 28 Aug., T1/6081A/14137.

lantic project, gave his opinion that the Red Sea's coral banks and unusually deep water would not prove to be insuperable obstacles. It was enough for Palmerston. Abandoning his earlier caution, he wished to close with the Red Sea group at once: "Even if we get two Strings to our Bow what is the Harm." [15]

Two strings—but in fact there was one. Stratford soon telegraphed that the pro-French party in the Turkish government had blocked the concessions to the E. and I. Company. Financial secretary Wilson urged the Foreign Office to obtain a reversal. But even Stratford's considerable powers were to no avail. By October 1857 Wilson had to give up on the company. And he was emphatic enough in rejecting pleas for compensation. Risk was the essence of business; a gamble had been made on success in obtaining the firman, and it had lost: "it appears to My Lords that the Co[mpan]y have no just grounds for complaint." [16]

Meanwhile the Red Sea group had raised the heady prospect of laying its line at once from Suez as far as Aden, employing two thousand miles of unused cable that had been left over from the Atlantic project. The linkup with India might be only a matter of a few months away! On 24 August, as the news was being circulated of the Porte's refusal to grant concessions for the Persian Gulf project, a high-level meeting at the Board of Control brought together the Red Sea promoters, the Treasury, and the Indian authorities, No firm decision was reached. A week later Wilson drafted a Treasury minute designed to test the financial soundness of the company, thus removing the most immediate obstacle.[17]

15. Palmerston to Lewis, 7 Aug. 1857, Palmerston Papers.

16. Minute of 26 Oct. 1857, T1/6097B/16308.

17. 31 Aug. 1857, T1/6081A/14137. By seeking competitive bids Wilson had already determined that in the current state of the money market Marshman's offer was reasonable. The British government was to contribute so much of a maximum annual subsidy of £20,000 as would permit the payment of a 6 per cent dividend. The company's capi-

The crash program fell through, but the delay was at the India Board, not at the Treasury. At the meeting of 24 August the Red Sea promoters had proposed that the East India Company place the submarine telegraph enterprise on a similar footing with the Indian railways by guaranteeing an annual interest of five per cent on a capital outlay of £300,000 for the line between Suez and Aden. This the Indian authorities, both because of the financial straits of the Indian government and the high-risk nature of a venture that had not yet been successfully carried out anywhere, were naturally determined if possible to avoid. And so they stalled, hoping that conditions in the money market would improve. Instead, they worsened further. When the Red Sea promoters were asked a few weeks later for their terms on the whole project from Suez to Karachi, they replied that the Atlantic cable was no longer available. Moreover, the Indian authorities would have to guarantee an annual rate of interest which, in the opinion of such a qualified arbiter as the governor of the Bank of England, would be sufficiently high to raise a sum of £700,000. In short the Indian government would have to take all the risk and pay an enormous rate of interest to boot. Faced with such a bleak prospect the India Board chose not to reply, "and the monetary crisis which arose immediately after induced the Directors of the Red Sea telegraph to forbear pressing the question on the India House" at all.[18]

By January 1858, when Marshman thought that conditions

---

tal was to be entirely subscribed within a month; and, as usual in cases involving government subsidy, the company was to agree to the appointment of an official director (who would be Stephenson of the Treasury). The cost of operating the line between Suez and Aden would be borne between the East India Company and the Treasury, their respective contributions to be based on percentage of traffic. The Indian government would then have to carry the line on from Aden to Karachi entirely on its own, having made no contribution to the European portion of the enterprise.

18. Marshman to India Board, 6 Mar. 1858, PP, 1857–58 [2406], *60*, 411–13.

warranted a reopening of the negotiations, the Palmerston government was already considering an Austrian proposal that Britain contribute an annual subsidy of £15,000 toward their projected line from Ragusa to Alexandria. The interdepartmental consideration of that question, which of course was geographically a prerequisite for the Red Sea undertaking, consumed the next two months. In late February, just before the Palmerston government fell, Wilson accepted.[19] The Conservative ministry of Lord Derby, which included George Hamilton as financial secretary, soon concurred. Thus Britain was formally committed to a telegraph as far as Egypt, the first link in the chain.

The successful suppression of the Mutiny had of course removed some of the pressure for precipitate action, but the extension of the line to India was arranged in due course. The Treasury was in touch with the contractors, R. S. Newall and Co., as early as May. Agreement with the Red Sea Company came later: by Treasury minute in July and by formal contract in November. For the government the terms were hardly palatable. The guaranteed dividend was to be 4½ per cent for a fifty-year period on a maximum capital outlay of £800,000, the payment to be shared if necessary between the British and Indian governments.[20] For its part the company was to engage reputable contractors who were to lay the line on their own responsibility, test it for thirty days, and transfer it in working order to the company. The contract was settled. The India Office—the Indian administrative authorities having been reorganized that summer—agreed to its share of liability. The Newall Company constructed a cable that was claimed to be stronger and far more durable than the one which had failed in the Atlantic the year before. By December 1858, after a

19. Minute of 22 Feb. 1858, T1/6159B/3763.

20. Minute of 17 July 1858, written by Stephenson and signed by Hamilton and permanent secretary Sir Charles Trevelyan, T1/6167B/12723.

major crisis when the wire was allowed to become dangerously overheated, the Red Sea cable was on its way to Egypt.

The earlier failure of the Atlantic venture notwithstanding, the Treasury was hopeful that the problems of long-range ocean telegraphic communication had been solved. By the early summer of 1859 the line had been laid as far as Aden, and messages were received from India that were in some cases only ten days old! There was now an atmosphere of reckless optimism. Promoters were flitting about, setting in motion plans for other projects. To the Hague went Lionel Gisborne to negotiate an extension to the Dutch East Indies. From there it could easily be taken on to south China, where the British were involved once more in conflict. To Australia went his brother Francis, attempting to win the cooperation of the colonies for an extension to the Antipodes. Independently, plans were being made for an all-British route via Gibraltar. The Treasury was as optimistic as the rest.

But the bubble burst. By the late summer of 1859 the Red Sea cable, which after thirty days the contractors had transferred in working order to the company, had failed. According to a survey that was conducted a year later by Charles Bright and his partner,[21] there were several outstanding reasons. The core of the cable had been injured by overheating, while insufficient precautions had been taken to ensure a high enough standard of insulation. The line had been paid out on a direct course, with little or no regard being given to the character of the bottom, though the coral reefs in the Red Sea were notorious. So little slack had been left—less than one per cent along the whole length from Suez to Aden—that the cable had resembled a tightly stretched rubber band. Once it had become weighted down by the attachment of sea growths, with which the Red Sea also abounded, it had naturally snapped in a number of places. One of the principal faults could be laid at the Treasury's door. The agreement with the Newall company,

21. Report enclosed in Bd. of Trade to Treasury, 30 July 1861, T1/6340A/11555.

though it had required that enough cable should be built to allow for slack, had named no particular figure. What was worse, it had stipulated that the contractors would retain any cable that might remain unused: an oversight, so Bright concluded, that it would perhaps be as well not to repeat.

It was not enough that the scheme had failed so dismally. As the Treasury solicitors looked into the matter, it seemed increasingly probable that the British and Indian governments were going to be liable up to the full extent of the guarantee —or £36,000 a year to be divided equally between them. There was no way to wiggle out: all parties had filled their contract obligations. It was unlikely that the Newall company would receive many government contracts in the near future, but it had transferred the cable to the Red Sea group in working order after a test period of thirty days. The Red Sea investors, as would soon become apparent, might have been guided by motives other than those of unselfish patriotism, but they could not be penalized. As the Treasury admitted rather dolefully "the greatest risk was overlooked, viz. that a Cable after being laid with apparent success for 30 days, might afterwards fail owing to defects either of original manufacture or upon undue strain in laying it." [22] In fact, it looked very much as though the Treasury's "little mistake" was going to cost the British taxpayer over the next half-century a cool £900,000!

The guardians of the taxpayer's interests, in the press and in parliament, had been handed an extraordinarily lovely case of bureaucratic ineptitude. One could be sure that they would make the most of it. From Lombard Street the powerful banker Charles Glynn advised Gladstone that it would be highly expedient for the government itself to appoint a select committee: "the onus should be placed upon the proper shoulders." [23] Since it was very probable that the "proper shoulders" would turn out to be Conservative ones (the Derby govern-

22. Minute of 22 Sept. 1860, drafted by Stephenson and signed by financial secretary Samuel Laing, T1/6286A/14902.

23. 21 Aug. 1860, Gladstone Papers, Add. MS. 44,394.

ment having made the contract though not the original decision), it was unlikely that the Palmerston ministry would resist. As it happened it would not even be necessary to appoint a new parliamentary committee. For at that the moment the Treasury was already being roasted before an inquiry into its management of that relatively well-established arm of Britain's imperial communications: the steam postal service.

Steam to Australia

If the attempt to establish ocean cables was an altogether novel experiment in which initial errors were only to be expected, managing the steam postal service involved the Treasury in a going concern. The onset of the impact of the Industrial Revolution upon ocean transportation had begun in the early 1840s with the almost simultaneous appearance of Cunard on the Atlantic and the Peninsular and Oriental Steam Navigation Company on the overland route to India. By the 1850s the performance on both routes of fast, dependable services had come to be taken for granted. Cunard's success on the American run had been such as to bring the need for a postal subsidy into serious question. The P. and O. had given to the Suez route to the East an importance it had not possessed since the sixteenth-century opening of the Atlantic. Twice a month P. and O. ships would leave Southampton for Gibraltar, Marseilles (where they would meet trains bringing late mails through France), Malta, Alexandria, and Suez. There they would be met, more or less regularly, by Egyptian trains that carried passengers and cargo across to ships bound via the Red Sea for Aden, Bombay, Trincomalee, Madras, and Calcutta.[24] Thus in the late 1850s the Treasury did not have to begin afresh. It had merely to establish a service to Australia.

24. For the background see H. Hoskins, *British Routes to India* (Philadelphia, 1928); G. Graham, "By Sea to India," *History Today, 14*

Sail via the Cape on a monthly basis, requiring a voyage of from six to eight months, had been good enough for Australia until the Gold Rush. As has already been suggested, its immediate psychological impact was significant. The clamor for steam was met in 1852 by a contract with the General Screw Steam Navigation Company for a service that still went round the Cape. It failed. The ships proved to be unequal to the long, unbroken runs, and the results were frequent breakdowns and chronic delays. This service was supplemented, also commencing in 1852, by the P. and O., who ran a branch line off the India–China trunk line. Even this was not entirely satisfactory. Though its service was easily better than that provided by General Screw, the P. and O. reputedly treated the Australian branch very much as a poor relation. In view of the small subsidy, retorted the company, how could the venture reasonably be expected to be anything else? The P. and O. was said to be thankful when its ships were pulled off the service in 1854 to fulfill a government contract for transporting troops to the Crimea.[25]

By the time financial secretary James Wilson set to work on the problem in November 1855 pressure had been building up for several years. The thriving Australian colonies, soon to receive responsible government, were complaining bitterly at their neglect, their protests backed by their General Association in London. The Australians were joined by British mercantile interests whose stake in the Antipodes was booming as never before. Such pressure the Treasury could not long have resisted even if it had wished to do so, which it emphatically did not. As the Treasury witnesses before the select committee were repeatedly to emphasize, they were fully alive to the necessity of encouraging the development of communications, as a great imperial object, and even at considerable risk. The

(1964), 301–12, and *Great Britain in the Indian Ocean, 1810–1850: A Study of Maritime Enterprise* (Oxford, 1967).

25. *Banker's Magazine*, Nov. 1854. See H. Robinson, *Carrying British Mails Overseas* (New York, 1964).

Treasury, after all, had once backed the young Nova Scotian entrepreneur, Samuel Cunard, who had possessed plenty of ideas but not a ship upon the water. In those early years, as well, the Treasury had deliberately reduced postage rates far below the break-even point as a means of aiding the growth of British commerce.[26] In time the increase in volume had more than made up the difference, justifying the decision: but it had been a risk all the same. To the Treasury the postal service was primarily a question of communications. It was secondarily a question of revenue.

Such was Wilson's attitude. One of the principal founders of that distinguished journal, *The Economist,* he came to the Treasury well prepared. He was capable, imaginative, and incisive, a talented administrator soon to go on to what has been called a thorough-going reform of Indian finance. He was the antithesis of that cautious, hyperconservative, negative-minded financier, oblivious to any object of national or imperial concern not immediately recognizable on the credit side of a balance sheet—the image that has been popularly associated with the Treasury. This particular case study does not, perhaps, show him in the most favorable light, but there is no apparent reason to disagree with his generally high reputation as one of the most notable of financial secretaries.[27] And even in this episode his weaknesses were those of the aggressive risk-taker, hardly bearing out the popular conception of the timid Treasury official.

Not the least of Wilson's difficulties was the fact that the Australians were not exactly singing in unison. There were no institutionalized means of achieving concerted action or even intercolonial communication. Indeed the intensifying rivalry of Sydney, Melbourne, Adelaide, Hobart (and in time Perth) would postpone for half a century Lord Grey's plans for a federal union which parliament had placed upon the shelf that

26. See Hamilton's testimony, PP, 1859, (180, Sess. 2), 6, 27, 48.
27. Heath, *The Treasury,* pp. 81–82.

very summer.[28] Where agreement was wanted there was controversy. Should the steamers call in at Adelaide, or run a branch line from King George's Sound? Melbourne and Sydney would complain at the delay if they stopped, Adelaide if they did not. Should Melbourne or Sydney be used as the coaling and repairing station? Should the route be via Panama or Suez? The distances were about the same. But Sydney (joined by New Zealand and Brisbane) would be served twice on each Panama run, while Melbourne for the same reason would always prefer Suez. The disputes were bitter and sustained. On no question, in fact, did Australian intercolonial rivalry emerge more sharply.

It would have been very easy for Wilson to do nothing. He could have followed the example of the Colonial Office which, having been chastened by Lord Grey's experiences, was drifting along while the Australians expended their energies in what from a distance seemed such pointless wrangling. He could have pleaded that there was no prospect that the colonists would ever be able to agree on anything and every evidence that they would resent imperial intervention. The colonists would have provided the excuse, the Colonial Office the precedent for passivity. Instead he strove to work out a solution.

As Wilson explained in a lengthy minute of November 1855, the Treasury like the Australians had been distressed by the interruption of what admittedly had been an imperfect service. As early as February the Admiralty had been instructed to invite tenders for a monthly service. Only in the last few weeks, however, had the P. and O. offered to conduct a branch line via Ceylon, a proposal that was unacceptable to Britain in view of the fact that the sea postage on the Australian mail came to less than one third of the tender of £84,000.

28. See J. Ward, *Earl Grey and the Australian Colonies, 1846–1857: A Study of Self-Government and Self-Interest* (Melbourne, 1958), pp. 283 ff.

So long as Britain had to pay for all of it, no really satisfactory service could possibly be established. He had, however, read carefully a recent correspondence that had taken place between Sir William Denison of New South Wales and the Colonial Office and among the Australian governors, concerning a proposal for local contributions. There had been such substantial disagreement that "my Lords fear that a great delay would take place, if they were to wait until . . . [the] differences should be adjusted among the Colonies themselves."[29] It was evident, however, that there was overwhelming sentiment in favor of the principle if not the details of colonial contribution. Hence the Treasury as a neutral party would propose a plan and act on it at once, presuming that the Australians would ultimately acquiesce.

The Admiralty would be instructed to call for tenders for a five-year contract stipulating a monthly service, the company winning the competition to perform under penalty of £100 a day for late starting, and £30 a day for late arrival, irrespective of cause. The steamers would stop only at King George's Sound, Melbourne, and Sydney, the other ports to be served by locally arranged branch lines. All other particulars, including the route—whether Suez, the Cape, or Panama—would be decided by competition.[30] Denison had suggested that Britain might contribute three fifths of the subsidy. Wilson decided that half and half would be preferable: it would do the children good to pay their full share. He had acted boldly and firmly, and his minute would be cited as a precedent for years to come.

The immediate response to the call for tenders was, however, disappointing. None of them, advised the Post Office in

29. Minute of 27 Nov. 1855, T1/5970A/16305.

30. The Treasury was not an entirely neutral party in view of the preponderance of Britain's imperial interests in the East. By naming the Australian ports of call in the order given above, Wilson revealed the British bias in favor of Suez or the Cape, and thus in favor of Melbourne against Sydney.

March 1856, was really satisfactory. Four of the offers were for the Cape route and two for Panama. All but two exceeded the voyage of fifty-five days that had been suggested as a reasonable target by the Victorian legislature. None had been submitted for the Suez route which, with its frequent breaking points and easy access to coaling stations, was the safest and quickest for steam. No offer, then, should be accepted. Instead, the Post Office advised, negotiations should be undertaken privately with the P. and O., a company that had been conspicuously absent from the bidding.[31] Wilson hesitated, called unsuccessfully for further tenders, and then came part way round. The route would indeed be via Suez, but the contractor was still to be determined by competition.

This time four offers were received. Two who proposed a year's delay before starting had to be rejected out-of-hand, leaving the P. and O. and the European and Colombian Steam Navigation Company (which hereafter will be referred to by its later name, the European and Australian). The P. and O.'s bid was for £140,000 for a separate Australian service, compared with its earlier offer of a branch line for £84,000. It rejected, however, the principle of penalties being imposed for causes beyond its control, which Wilson had raised to the unprecedentedly high rate of £50 for the first day's late arrival, £100 for the second, £150 for the third, and so forth. The P. and O. argued that it was an established company, and that its ships had been certified by the Admiralty. It would not submit to being penalized for acts of God.

The competition was from a new company, based in Glasgow, backed by a proposed capital of £400,000, and led by directors who were well known in the financial world but who possessed no previous experience in the management of steamship companies. Accepting the principle of absolute penalties (which of course would result in higher insurance premiums and hence a higher subsidy), the European and Australian

31. P.O. to Treasury, 29 Mar. 1856, T1/6042B/5274.

tendered for £185,000. That was £45,000 a year higher than the offer of the P. and O. But Wilson accepted the higher bid. The lower offer had been rejected, he explained, because of the P. and O.'s refusal to be bound by unconditional penalties; because the beginning of its service was somewhat uncertain, depending on the release of ships from troop transport contracts; and because its length of voyage was several days longer than what was promised by its rival.[32]

This is as far as the evidence goes. Yet a good deal more may be reasonably inferred. Wilson considered other routes despite the obvious attractions and advantages of Suez. Was it only in order to placate Sydney? He refused to negotiate privately with the P. and O. He insisted upon unconditional penalties. Was it because he knew the P. and O. would reject them? He accepted a significantly higher tender from an untested company. His behavior throughout the negotiations leads to the conclusion that he was attempting to use the weapon of government subsidy to break up the P. and O.'s monopoly of Britain's steam communications with the East. He favored unconditional penalties, to be sure, as good financial policy. (For one thing they would at once remove the cause of otherwise inevitable disputes about what constituted "unavoidable" delay.) He may well have been angered by the company's behavior, first in refusing to enter the original competition and then in baldly rejecting his terms. He may well have decided that no company ought to be allowed to remain in a position of such unchallenged power that it could dictate to Her Majesty's Treasury. Australians, at least, were not slow to draw the further conclusion that he had either gambled, tested a theory, or tried to take his revenge with their money.[33]

One conclusion, however, need not rest upon inference. Wil-

32. P. and O. to Admiralty, 12 June 1856, Minute of 24 June, T1/6042B/10662.

33. See the testimony of James Youl (honorary secretary of the Australian Association), Select committee re postal contracts, PP, 1860 (328), *14*, 144.

son's decision was made without the slightest knowledge of the ability of the European and Australian Company to carry out the contract successfully. Beyond the usual tests of its financial soundness he did not go. As he wrote in an affirmative but noticeably detached reply to an Admiralty suggestion that it would be well to inspect the ships, "my Lords rely upon the very heavy penalties for loss of time in the event of the passages . . . not being performed in due time." [34] As W. C. Wentworth of the Australian Association pointed out, penalties however high would not insure performance of the service unless the ships were in fact equal to the demands that would be placed on them.[35] Did Wilson not know this? Either he was a fool, or he was taking the chance deliberately, seeking to beat the P. and O. in a game in which the stakes were high and in which there might not be another opportunity for years to come.

The career of the European and Australian company, like that of Hobbes' natural man, was "nasty, brutish, and short." The contract was announced in January 1857. Five months later, before the first voyage had been completed, it had to be modified in response to an urgent plea of the necessity to break the voyage at Ceylon. By June came news of the complete breakdown of the company's first ship, the *Oneida*—according to the company an unavoidable accident, according to the Admiralty the result of inadequate engines—bringing the maximum penalty of £64,000 upon the company and raising howls of dissatisfaction from Australia.[36] A month later the unfortunate directors were already seeking help through an amalgamation with another line. Even Sir Samuel Cunard was

34. Minute of 5 Aug. 1856, T1/6042B/12609.

35. Wentworth to Duke of Argyll (Postmaster), London, 9 Aug. 1856, PP, 1860 (328), *14*, 461–63. Wentworth was of course in touch with the colonies. Wentworth to the chief secretary of New South Wales, London, 14 Jan. 1858, N.S.W., CSSB 4/727.

36. Eur. and Aust. to Wilson, 22 June 1857, and Wilson minute, T1/6110A/10339.

approached in the hope of providing a rescue. It was all to no avail. The European and Australian never performed satisfactorily. Long delays with their consequent heavy penalties were the rule. By June 1858 the shareholders voted to quit, saving what remained of their investment. Apparently, Wilson had naïvely overestimated the power of money, which had proved itself an altogether inadequate substitute for good ships, sound management, and technical expertise. Or, as we have suggested, he may have decided to take a long chance. Probably both were involved.

Caught in a dilemma of his own making, there was little Wilson could do. Protests poured in from Australia as the poor service intensified the Melbourne-Sydney rivalry. New South Wales went so far as to threaten to support no other route but Panama. As Wilson explained just before he left office in February 1858 the Treasury was doing everything possible. That is, it was enforcing payment of the full penalties, the real effect of which was merely to weaken the company further, not to encourage it. Short of dissolving the contract, an action that would simply prolong the state of unsettlement that inevitably accompanied the establishment of new services and new companies, nothing could really be done.[37] His successor, George Hamilton, closely watched the negotiations between the European and Australian and the Royal Mail companies and approved the entrance into the proceedings of the highly respected Cunard. But the decision of the shareholders in June left him no choice. A temporary arrangement was made with the Royal Mail for an additional subsidy of £72,000, and new tenders were called for. In October 1858 the Treasury announced the results.[38]

A seven-year contract, longer by two years than before, had been concluded for a service via Suez and Mauritius at an annual subsidy of £180,000. This time there would be no abso-

37. Minute of 25 Feb. 1858, T1/6713A/3644.
38. Trevelyan minute, 16 Oct. 1858, T1/6173B/17378.

lute penalties clause. For of the two bids that had been submitted, the Treasury had had to accept that of the P. and O., which had been £72,000 below that of the Royal Mail. The P. and O. had won its point, and a great deal more besides. It was not that the Australian contract itself was so lucrative. What was considerably more important, a competitor that managed to operate it successfully might hope in time to challenge the P. and O.'s hold on the India–China trunk line. Reigning supreme in the Eastern seas, the P. and O. had survived what we have interpreted as a conscious drive by the Treasury to break up its monopoly, and it now was stronger than before. As for Wilson, his attempt (if such it was) to establish a competitive force in the East was going to cost the British and Australian taxpayers £40,000 more than the subsidy he might have paid earlier. Multiply by the number of years in the contract, and add in the additional amounts that had been paid out to the European and Australian and the Royal Mail, and the sum rises to something short of £400,000.

Thus, in the two instances that have been analyzed, the Treasury's policies had been responsible for the addition of more than a million pounds to the government's obligations. That figure, small as it is by modern standards, was 1.5 per cent of the national budget for the year ending in March 1858 of seventy millions. No wonder there was going to be a select committee!

The Select Committee on Contracts

There were actually two committees holding hearings in 1859–60. One of them was a group of experts (including Sir William Thompson, the future Lord Kelvin) appointed by the Board of Trade to review the experience of the Atlantic and Red Sea cables, the first two ventures in oceanic telegraphy. Historically, this body was by far the more important. For its recommendations formed the basis for the successful laying of cables to India in 1863 (carried out by the Indian government via the Persian Gulf), to America in 1866, and to virtually the rest of the world by the late 1870s.[39] The other was a parliamentary committee, important to us primarily because of what it learned about the Treasury.

The committee's most immediate object was a rather ordinary piece of political jobbery involving a Conservative candidate and the Dover–Calais mail contract. But the setting was far broader. In addition to the costly Red Sea and European and Australian incidents, the Conservatives in 1858 had agreed to an early extension of the Cunard contract. The latter measure had raised vehement protests both from Cunard's main competitor in Liverpool, William Inman, and from the Canadians, who resented Cunard's emphasis upon the American portion of his business and who were already subsidizing a line of their own in the hope of attracting trade away from Boston and New York and into the St. Lawrence. Finally, there was wide interest in the awesome and relatively unchecked power of the Treasury, and in particular that part of it which was being exercised by the financial secretary.

Hamilton and Wilson were both questioned closely about the relative positions of parliament and the departments of the executive. No problem, admitted Wilson, had been more perplexing to him, but it was not easy to see how the situation could be much improved. Postal subsidies amounting to some £900,000 a year appeared in the estimates that were laid before the Commons. They related, however, to contracts that had already been made. At this point parliament's hands were virtually tied. To veto a contract after the fact would be a vote of no confidence in the government which would undoubtedly cause its resignation. And the effect of such an action would be disastrous, undermining the government's credit in the

39. See the report of the Committee on Submarine Telegraphy, PP, 1860 [2744], 62, which is one of the classic documents in the field.

money market and raising the cost of government loans. Practically, then, if not formally, parliament was bound to approve. Yet estimates could hardly be placed before parliament in advance, for they were difficult to predict accurately, while to do so publicly would vitiate the purpose of competitive bidding. Parliament, again, could not itself make contracts, spread as their negotiations were over time and space. For it to do so on the advice of a select committee would but institute the despised American lobby system. The most that could be done, thought Wilson, would be for parliament to establish in advance the very general conditions of a contract, leaving the Treasury to negotiate it. Do what they might, concluded Hamilton, in practice the contract business would have to remain a function of the executive.

The committee heard from a broad range of witnesses: from Canadians and Australians; from such representatives of the shipping industry as Cunard, Inman, and Charles Howell of the P. and O.; from high officials as well as clerks from the Treasury, Admiralty, and Post Office. It was not as diligent as it might have been in inquiring into the inner working of the Treasury, Hamilton's valuable explanation of the precise steps that had been followed in making the European and Australian contract being regarded as an attempt to stall.[40] The committee thought that contract had been most ill-advised: Wilson ought not to have accepted so readily the offer of a new and untested company. The Red Sea telegraph shareholders must, unfortunately, receive the government guarantee in full: another case of Treasury mismanagement.

Several important changes were recommended. Postal contracts should henceforth be made by the Post Office with the advice of the Board of Trade and operating under the control of the Treasury. (The Admiralty had long wanted to be rid of the business anyway.) Whenever possible contracts should be

40. PP, 1859 (180, Sess. 2), 6, 42–43, 24–25.

submitted to public competition. And in future they would be required to lie for thirty days on the tables of both houses of parliament before coming into effect.

Gladstone and Loose Ends

The select committee having made its investigation and report, it was the job of the executive branch, i.e. Chancellor of the Exchequer Gladstone, to pick up the pieces. He did so with skill. Historians have sometimes found it a little too easy to poke fun at the inviting target of this self-appointed intermediary between God and the British people. Like his teacher Peel, however, the "people's William" was a gifted and an indefatigable administrator. Careful and meticulous, possessing what seems a remarkable grasp of the principles and details of finance, capable in private business correspondence of expressing himself with a degree of clarity and directness that was not transferable to formal prose or speeches, Gladstone appears to deserve his contemporary reputation as the best of nineteenth-century chancellors. The circumstances of the present case study place him in an advantageous position, for it would have been difficult for any reasonably competent person to avoid improving upon the Treasury's recent performance in the contract business. Yet the author's impression of Gladstone at work—and the change in the quantity and quality of the notes passed between the chancellor and his subordinates is immediately striking—must be recorded more positively. As an administrator Gladstone ranks at the top with such figures as Palmerston, Peel, and Salisbury.

One of Gladstone's problems was the Australian postal service. Despite the punctual performance of it by the P. and O., the colonies continued to be annoyed, though more at each other than at Britain. New South Wales, Queensland, and New Zealand continued to press for a line coming by way of Panama, and American promoters were already at work among them. "We shall never content these Colonies," thought Stephenson, "until we entirely separate the Eastern and Western interests, sharing the Panama route with the one and the Suez with the other." [41] For the time being, however, the Treasury resisted: Britain already had her communications with America, and her bias would continue to be in favor of Suez.

More immediately pressing were the relations with the P. and O., whose hegemony in the East was for the time being unchallenged. Having no alternative the Treasury now had little choice but to comply with the company's every wish. The route was soon changed so as to go via Ceylon instead of Mauritius. In May 1860 the Australian service, which under the original contract had been established as a separate line east of Suez, became a branch line from Ceylon off the main India–China trunk route. These changes were not in themselves unreasonable. The latter had been repeatedly suggested by Governor Denison of New South Wales, both to the Colonial Office and to his own responsible advisers,[42] and it involved an annual saving of £60,000 in the subsidy.[43] But the alterations underscored the government's position, in which its freedom of maneuver had been reduced almost to the vanishing point. Anything involving the Australian contract had of necessity to be considered as a small part of the larger framework of the P. and O.'s gigantic operations in the Eastern seas.

In December 1860 it was indeed that whole framework that was brought into sharp relief by the P. and O.'s demand that

41. Memorandum of 22 Oct. 1859, T1/6236A/15893.

42. Denison minute, 16 Aug. 1858, N.S.W., CSSB 4/727, and Denison to Australian governors, 12 Dec. 1859, ibid., are among the best examples. There is a great wealth of material on this whole subject in the New South Wales archives, which presumably would be matched by collections in other states. An Australian scholar with the time to deal with it properly would find a fascinating case study of Australian intercolonial politics and the working of responsible government.

43. P. and O. to Treasury, 30 Apr. 1860, T1/6282B/7210, and Treasury minute, 15 May, T1/6282B/7942.

the subsidy for the India–China service be increased by about £50,000. Coal and transport costs had risen, claimed the company, while passenger traffic was not increasing fast enough to match them, most of that business continuing to be carried by the slower but far cheaper sailing ships around the Cape. If the terms were not met the company threatened to pay the required forfeit of £25,000—which would be no great burden in view of its annual budget that approached a million pounds—and give up the contract altogether. What was the Treasury to do? The Postmaster General, Lord Stanley of Alderley, thought it should stand and fight: there should be a call for tenders. "At the same time," he cautioned, indicating that the problems of dealing with a powerful monopoly had not changed since Wilson's time:

> I must not conceal from your Lordships the serious apprehension which I entertain that no tenders may be received either from the Peninsular and Oriental Company, or from other responsible persons . . . and that the department [the Post Office] may be driven at the eleventh hour into making terms with the present contractors. . . . But this is a difficulty which must sooner or later be overcome unless the perpetual monopoly of the Indian service be given to the Peninsular and Oriental Company, and it appears to me that the Department had better encounter it on the present occasion.[44]

Gladstone decided, however, on a more cautious policy, permitting the affair to drift along from year to year. Not until the 1870s did the Suez Canal, by making competition easier for smaller organizations who no longer had to maintain two fleets of ships, rescue the government from the trap.

In the telegraph enterprise Gladstone faced the eternal gambler's dilemma of deciding what was really a hopeless cause

44. 11 Dec. 1860, T1/6284A/19423.

and of determining when to stop throwing good money after bad. There was a proposal to invest £50,000 in an effort to repair the Red Sea cable. The Board of Trade's committee of experts, backed by the India Office, discouraged it. Principal clerk Stephenson was horrified: expenses could be controlled in advance, and the government might be able to turn the job and the risk over to a private company. Surely it would be right to try to save at least some parts of the line. "Should that experiment be successful," concluded this deeply committed Treasury official, "the prospects of Submarine Telegraphy over long distances and in deep water would not appear so hopeless." [45]

It was to a private company that the Treasury eventually turned. In July 1861 a Telegraph to India association proposed that the government take over the line and transfer it; if repairs were successful the new organization would recover its investment and substantial interest and then devote any surplus profits to paying off the Red Sea guarantee. Permanent secretary George Hamilton explained that a takeover would involve the government's settling with the Red Sea investors at once; otherwise, there would be no risk to the government. Gladstone was cautious: "we must remember that a desire for dispatch entertained by the public on this subject has already resulted in a very heavy loss in time and money." [46] Off went Hamilton to negotiate with the directors of the old company, who awkwardly insisted that the government convert the guaranteed interest into an annuity, which would give their stock a fixed value. Gladstone agreed to a terminable annuity, but a meeting of the shareholders rejected it, objecting to a measure that would reduce the value of their securities: when money was dear they would be difficult to sell; when it was cheap the government would buy them up. In reply Gladstone wrote

45. Minutes on I.O. to Treasury, 18 Oct. 1860, T1/6286A/16462, and 1 Mar. 1861, T1/6340A/3694.

46. Gladstone to Hamilton, 4 Oct. 1861, T1/6340A/14119.

from his home at Hawarden a didactic minute refusing to recognize the shareholders as a bargaining party. "My Lords" would not set a precedent for financial holdup by departing from the "general rule absolutely necessary for the safe transaction of public business which requires them to deal with the Directors of a Company and with them alone." [47]

The shareholders, however, were not so easily intimidated. Principal clerk W. G. Anderson, who had attended their meetings, thought silence and delay might succeed in making them restless and weakening their resolve. But the waiting game was spoiled when it was learned that the new company had managed to raise the necessary two thirds of its capital of £100,000. If the Treasury intended to close with the new company it must first settle with the old one. Gladstone, in a corner, raged: "I think these people are using us like Jews." [48] But in fact there was nothing he could do but take the matter to the cabinet with as good a grace as possible.

Thus in January 1862 a ship departed Greenwich carrying two hundred miles of cable. The manufacturing had been done by Glass, Elliot, and Co. (the Newall outfit's reputation having somewhat suffered), while the attempted restoration was to be supervised by the consulting engineering firm of Charles Bright. But in August his associate, Latimer Clark, returned with the expected information that the project to rescue the Red Sea cable had been doomed from the beginning.

A more fitting end to this tragicomedy had occurred a few months earlier. In April the Treasury received a proposal for government support of a company in laying a cable from Rangoon to Singapore. The document reeked with optimism. Its authors were entirely confident that the Red Sea cable would soon be restored to its previous peak of high efficiency. A most impressive list of names was attached as prospective directors:

47. Red Sea Co. to Treasury, 23 Oct. 1861; Gladstone memorandum, 31 Oct., T1/6340A/15454.

48. Gladstone to Stephenson, 9 Nov. 1861, T1/6340A/16050.

people from the P. and O. and the Royal Mail; retired Indian civil servants; bankers connected with China and Australia. The Australians were getting ready to subsidize their own cable: only a few months and a trifling government guarantee stood in the way of instantaneous communication between London and Burma, China, and Australia.

The Gisbornes, sanguine as ever, were at it again! The Treasury, however, had had enough of them. Minuted Stephenson shortly: "write to Mr. Gisborne that My Lords are not prepared . . . to entertain the proposal." [49] Two years later, after the success of the Persian Gulf cable to Karachi, they tried once more. This time Gladstone's negative response was even more emphatic: "Nor would I in answering Mr. Gisborne hold out even by implication any promise of ultimate assistance." [50]

Conclusion: The Role of the Treasury

Some three decades ago H. L. Hall generalized about relations between the Colonial Office and the Treasury, observing that the former took "a wider Imperial view . . . as compared with that of the Treasury that no matter what the Imperial implications alleged, it was merely a matter of pounds, shillings, and pence." [51] Though the example he was citing was drawn from the 1890s, the context of the statement makes it clear that he meant to apply it more broadly. Never supported by systematic investigation, backed only by a few quotations from officials of the Foreign and Colonial offices, the generalization sums up effectively what one writer has recently denounced as the "myth of Treasury control." [52] Was the Treasury's attitude

49. Minute of 4 Apr. 1862, T1/6392A/5447.
50. Minute of 26 Mar. 1864, T1/6501A/4952.
51. *The Colonial Office, A History* (1937), p. 34.
52. See A. Burton, "Treasury Control and Colonial Policy in the Late Nineteenth Century," *Public Administration, 44* (1966), 169–92. See also the fine case study by R. Kubicek, "Joseph Chamberlain, the

narrowly financial and parochial? Was the Colonial Office's more broadly imperial?

Some of the data in this case study does seem to support the conventional wisdom. Wilson's fight against the P. and O. *was* conceived and conducted on narrowly financial grounds: as one of his successors admitted, that was why it failed.[53] Some attention to the lack of experience and the poor ships of the European and Australian company might have saved him. Gladstone did not permit the China war or commercial pressures to disturb his conviction that, on financial grounds, a rush by the government into further telegraph ventures would be risky—better to wait longer and let private enterprise take the chances. Most of the Treasury's problems had indeed to do with money, while their weapons were naturally financial. The most telling piece of evidence, however, was not included in this case study because it was not there. In all the masses of Treasury documents that pertain to going over Egypt by rail and under the Red Sea by cable the phrase "Suez Canal" was never once mentioned!

Yet the Treasury was not alone. The failure to consider this great event of the near future was symptomatic of a common blind spot that ran through the British government while the canal was being planned and built. The Foreign Office appears not to have thought a great deal about the matter either, while to his last breath Palmerston thought the project a "bubble."[54] Only in the seventies did the unexpected success of the French-built canal and the financial difficulties of the Egyptian government provide the opportunity for Disraeli's dramatic reversal.

Did the Treasury, in fact, habitually disparage and ignore

Treasury, and Imperial Development, 1895–1903," *Report of the Canadian Historical Association* (1965), pp. 105–16.

53. Minute of Samuel Laing, 16 Apr. 1860, T1/6274A/1566.

54. See K. Bell, "British Policy Towards the Construction of the Suez Canal 1859–1865," *Transactions of the Royal Historical Society*, 5th ser. *14* (1965), 121–43.

imperial implications? Undoubtedly there were differences in perspective: the Treasury was less sensitive to the adjustment in imperial relations required by the coming of self-government, and it often regarded individual colonial expenditures with distrust. But was the Treasury always less empire-minded? This case study must at least bring the matter into question. We have seen the Treasury trying to manage the postal services between Britain, India, and Australia, an important piece of a worldwide network of communications. Its role in building and attempting to control that network brought that office intimately and crucially into the policy-making process involving every area of the empire, whether formal or informal, throughout the world. We have seen the Treasury take long chances in its struggle with another imperial force, the P. and O. company, and lose. We have seen that department in its role as midwife in the birth of a new applied science, investing (to take the long view) £900,000 in an experiment that would ultimately multiply imperial wealth and strength—and cheap at that!

Not in the mid-nineteenth century, certainly, did the Colonial Office have to deal with any problem of which the imperial implications were anything so vast. The Colonial Office dealt with colonies, with the parts rather than the whole of empire. And, with very rare exceptions, it dealt with them one by one. Its problems—responsible government, native relations—sometimes transcended individual colonial boundaries, but its administrative patterns of dealing with them rarely did. In this sense it was the Colonial Office whose behavior smacked of parochialism. Indeed it was not until the revolution in communications, managed by the Treasury, had brought Great Britain and her overseas possessions into closer proximity that a Chamberlain or a Milner could think of "imperial unity" as a subject fit even for dreams.

8: The Coolie Convention of 1861 and the Annexation of Lagos

I feel afraid sometimes lest we should be like the Kings in burlesques who, with comical vigor, despatch one slave with a blow, and cover the other with honors, long before they can know whether either deserves his fate.
T. F. Elliot

The sequence of events that led in the end to the annexation of Lagos began, and for fairly basic reasons, in the West Indies. The French and British sugar colonies in that area had followed the usual pattern of exploitational settlements in the tropics. They had risen rapidly on the basis of one-crop economies that were dependent on imported forced labor. And they fell just as quickly as their easily produced staples were duplicated in abundance elsewhere, flooding the world market and driving down the price.[1] Still treasured possessions at the time of the American Revolution, within half a century they had become burdensome liabilities. The abolition of slavery and, for the British colonies in 1854, of tariff preferences in the home market hastened a decline that stemmed from more fundamental origins.

Social and political problems grew apace, also following the usual pattern of plantation colonies. Social structures were

1. See C. Haring, *The Spanish Empire in America* (New York, 1947), chap. 1. See also L. Ragatz, *The Fall of the Planter Class in the British Caribbean, 1763–1833* (New York, 1928).

highly stratified. Political development was weak. Economic depression increased the evils of absentee landlordism, depriving the communities of badly needed leadership. The backwardness of education and the lack of vocational skills among the lower classes provided little foundation for economic diversification or political advancement. The West Indian colonies were caught in a self-depressing cycle. Their problems were endemic and in terms of attaining European standards they defied solution. In the Colonial Office the senior clerk of the West Indian division, Sir Henry Taylor, thought they should just start over. Only in a framework of crown-colony government closely controlled from London did there seem to be much chance of substantial improvement.

The promises of the humanitarians that free labor would eventually prove cheaper and more efficient than slavery in a plantation economy had not been verified by experience. All attempts to induce the freed slaves to work as before had been ineffective. If the sugar economy and the plantation system, to which there seemed to be no alternative but ruin, were to recover some of the ground they had lost, then the need for a dependable supply of labor would have to be filled.

The most obvious source was the traditional one, West Africa, "a country filled with an unemployed population within twenty days' sail."[2] Since 1807, however, Great Britain had tried to keep that avenue closed. Only an insignificant trickle of refugees from captured slavers and free migrants from the Kroo coast could legally be drawn upon. Any more ambitious and effective migration schemes would encourage the slave trade in the interior and expose the British government to charges of duplicity. So the planters were forced to turn elsewhere. But laborers from Madeira died off at a rate that was as alarming as it was unprofitable, and the planters presumed the same fate would overtake the Irish. The more inured

2. Memorial of West Indian Association of Liverpool to Earl Grey, Rec. 8 Apr. 1850, CO 318/187.

Chinese were difficult to obtain and expensive to transport. The most satisfactory source turned out to be India, even though the West Indians had to face there the severe competition of Mauritius, closer and more popular with the migrants.[3] Indian coolies were thus the only plentiful source of labor that was available to the tropical areas of the British Empire, and there were not enough of them to go around.

Backed by the government of India and supervised by the Emigration Commission in London, an imposing body of regulations had been designed for the coolie's protection during every phase of his service. He could be enticed away only by approved agents. A protector of emigrants was supposed to make sure that he was leaving India willingly under a contract he understood. On board ship the amount of space to be allotted him and the type and quantity of his food were specified. A European doctor was required to be present. Once in the colony he was commonly indentured for five years, with the freedom to change employers after three and to return home after five if he could pay for it himself, "which, of course, he never can."[4] A return passage at the colonial government's expense was guaranteed him after ten years. If the British government could not in fact effectively guard the coolie against all the inherent abuses in what remained essentially a system of forced labor, it was not for want of regulations.

The migratory labor problem in the tropical world was made still more difficult by the abolition of slavery in the French colonies after 1848. The same dilemma that had faced British planters since 1833 now distressed the French. The only difference was that French recruitment in India was con-

3. Between 1835 and 1872 Mauritius obtained 354,000 coolies, compared to only 147,000 for all the West Indies. F. Hitchins, *The Colonial Land and Emigration Commission* (Philadelphia, 1931), pp. 323–25.

4. C.O. memorandum, Nov. 1857, in "Correspondence Respecting Coolie Emigration into French Colonies," F.O. Confidential Print, June 1860, FO 425/37. See I. Cumpston, *Indians Overseas in British Territories* (Oxford, 1953).

fined to their own small possessions there. Accordingly, in the early fifties the French began to look toward British India. And therein lay the problem.

This first French request for permission to recruit across the borders of their own territory was peremptorily refused. The British Foreign Office was only mildly receptive, while the India Board, to whom the question was naturally referred, was hostile. The encouragement of Indian migration to foreign colonies, it explained, had been prohibited by legislation passed as long ago as 1839. The strict regulations for the protection of coolies in British possessions could not be enforced outside the empire. Moreover, French recruiting would create unpleasant incidents between the two governments, certainly at the local level and perhaps even at the metropolitan.[5] The French responded in two ways. They submitted for inspection their own recently enacted coolie regulations. And they threatened to resort to Africa, either by persuading free people in the coastal areas to migrate or by purchasing slaves and sending them on to the colonies as free laborers.[6] The French expressed their realization of the fact that Britain might not like such measures. She could always prevent them by opening up India.

The French threat had the desired effect of raising the level of interest at the Foreign Office, where the African slave trade was a longtime concern, but the decision still was left entirely to the Indian authorities. Employing the geographical separations between them to good advantage, they managed to consume great quantities of time with references to the Governor-General in Council. He of course thought it useful to obtain advice from regional authorities: each reference could literally take months. At last the Indian government agreed to permit migration to Réunion on the same basis as it was

5. Ct. of Directors of E. I. Co. to India Bd., 11 Dec. 1851, encl. in India Bd. to F.O., 16 Dec., FO 425/37.

6. Count Walewski (French ambassador to Britain) to Earl of Malmesbury, 12 May 1852, ibid.

being conducted to the neighboring colony of Mauritius, provided the French would establish an English protector of immigrants on their island. The French objected to the strictness of the English passenger regulations and to the presence of foreign agents on their soil, and expressed confidence that the omission of their own West Indian colonies from the arrangements must have been unintentional. When in June 1854 they were told it was decidedly not,[7] they broke off negotiations. But the circuitous workings of the Indian bureaucracy had managed to keep the whole subject in a state of suspense for nearly four years.

When the French reopened the subject three years later they had in the meantime improved their bargaining position considerably. Their government had contracted with the Marseilles firm of Victor Régis, long an established power on the West African coast, for the purchase of twenty thousand slaves to be sent on as indentured laborers to Martinique and Guadeloupe. Thus their earlier threat had been given substance,[8] and their bid to recruit in British India would be treated more seriously.

The various pressures upon the British Foreign Office intensified at once. The consul at Lagos advised that the gathering of slaves at the Régis factory at Whydah was disrupting the whole area: "We shall have the whole . . . Country plunged into warfare to supply the demands."[9] The organized machinery of humanitarianism swung into operation. Clarendon soon found himself "overwhelmed with letters from Brougham, Shaftesbury, & other Philanthropists." Brougham reported that Yorkshire was outraged, and a highly agitated deputation

7. Foreign secretary Clarendon to Walewski, 20 June 1854, ibid.

8. There were in fact three such schemes, two of which were on a small scale and located in the River Gabon which belonged to France. See B. Schnapper, *La Politique et le Commerce Français dans le Golfe de Guinée de 1838 à 1871* (Paris, 1961), pp. 159–60 and passim.

9. Consul William Campbell to Clarendon, 31 Aug. 1857, FO 84/1031.

called at the Foreign Office.[10] The French maintained their innocence—their scheme resulted in freedom for Africans who would otherwise have remained slaves. But foreign secretary the Earl of Clarendon replied that "wars are only made in Africa for the purpose of catching Slaves & . . . if there are no purchasers . . . they are not caught and wars are not made."[11]

Such pressures as these might have been difficult for any government to resist. Palmerston's, in any case, was not of a mind to do so. As Clarendon once remarked, his leader had made the campaign against the slave trade a lifelong hobby. Far from causing him embarrassment, the agitation of public opinion was a useful diplomatic weapon: "as long as Resentment is felt only by the English govt., and none exists in the Nation, the French think they may do what they like, and that we can only complain and talk."[12] But the French seemed "determined to have Negroes by fair means or foul,"[13] and it became increasingly apparent that they would not be budged unless presented with an alternative supply of labor.

Five years earlier the coolie question had seemed to the Foreign Office to be entirely an Indian affair. Its own role then had been the distinctly subordinate one of conveying the decision of the Indian authorities to the French. The Régis contract had changed all that. To the Foreign Office it was now an African problem and thus its own direct concern. The tone of the correspondence accordingly shifted. When in December 1857 the French again requested permission to recruit in British India the Foreign Office sent the matter on to the Emigration Commission with the remark that "the Earl of Clarendon

10. Clarendon to Earl Cowley (British ambassador to France), 28 Oct. 1857, Cowley Papers (P.R.O.), FO 519/176. Brougham to Clarendon, Liverpool (endorsed Nov. 1857), Clarendon Deposit (Bodleian Library), C. 543.
11. Clarendon to Cowley, 28 Nov. 1857, Cowley Papers, FO 519/176.
12. Palmerston to Clarendon, 25 Oct. 1857, Clarendon Deposit, C. 69.
13. Cowley to Clarendon, 18 Nov. 1857, Cowley Papers, FO 519/222.

trusts that . . . no insurmountable obstacles" would be found to exist.[14]

At the outset these hopeful expectations did not seen unrealistic. Cowley soon reported that the French had realized their mistake, were appalled by its effect in Britain, and wished to end the unpleasantness, though "their vanity will not allow them to admit that they are in the wrong."[15] From Lagos came word that the Régis recruiters were already finding it difficult to meet their quota.[16] It was true that the French were repeating their earlier objections to the presence of British agents on their soil and to what they regarded as unnecessarily expensive requirements on the space to be provided each passenger.[17] But these must have seemed mere matters of detail.

Yet the coolie negotiations were to drag on for nearly three more years. For the making of the treaty involved not only the diplomatic relations between the two governments. That was only the top of the iceberg. Lying beneath and in large part determining the direction of the diplomacy was something far more complicated and far more important. There were two unwieldy, global collections of outright possessions and areas of informal interest very inadequately called empires. In the metropolitan governments the various parts of those two empires were represented by bureaucratic departments who, in part because of their differing geographical obligations, found themselves in conflict with each other. The negotiation of the coolie convention had called into existence a complex process of decision making that was focused in the capitals, but the dimensions of which were worldwide. It is this process of decision making, which happens to have created an unusual

14. 14 Dec. 1857, FO 425/37.
15. Cowley to Clarendon, 27 Nov. 1857, Cowley Papers, FO 519/222.
16. Campbell to Clarendon, 2 Oct. 1857, FO 84/1031.
17. Undated enclosure to F.O. to Emigration Commission, 14 Dec. 1857, FO 425/37.

wealth of private and interdepartmental documentation, that we must proceed to summarize in some detail.

The coolie convention intimately involved four offices within the British government. Three of them were represented at a meeting of permanent officials that was held on the day after the Foreign Office circulated the French proposals: a microcosm of the process of interdepartmental negotiation that was to follow. The Foreign Office played its trump card at once. For the prime minister, William Wylde (head of the slave trade division) told his colleagues, had already made up his mind. The Anglo-French anti-slave trade treaty would shortly be up for renewal, and Palmerston wanted no complications. The Régis contract must be ended at once. Like it or not, there was going to be a coolie convention. The other civil servants grumbled and raised objections. Assistant undersecretary T. F. Elliot of the Colonial Office thought the French would get very few coolies; the concession would be a dangerous precedent for foreign interference in India; unpleasantness would arise over recruiting competition; and in the end the dissatisfied French would simply return to their slave-buying in Africa. Wylde answered that the French wanted a face-saving excuse for abandoning a position they had already found to be untenable. Elliot and Sir Henry Taylor defended the West Indian planters, who would be hurt by French competition, although Taylor was forced to concede that the French coolie regulations would apparently be adequate enough to protect the coolie. Sir Frederic Rogers of the Emigration Commission, appealing to the principle "of regarding the empire in its totality, & dealing with the parts as might be best for the whole," [18] also supported the West Indian claims. It all depended on who was doing the looking. Wylde might have answered that the Foreign Office also had an imperial vi-

18. Memorandum of Taylor, 21 Dec. 1857, attached to Emigration Commission to C.O., 18 Dec., CO 318/216.

sion, having arrived from its African viewpoint at a different conception of what was "best for the whole."

This first confrontation of permanent officials had been of an exploratory nature, and it had reached no conclusion. Yet the pattern of departmental behavior was already evident. With the prime minister's backing the Foreign Office had delivered an ultimatum. The other offices would raise objections on principle, hoping somehow to get the whole idea abandoned, but this was unlikely. Beyond that their tactics would be to delay the proceedings as long as possible, so that the French might tire of them sufficiently to drop them. As a last resort they would attempt to water down the details of the final treaty. They would try to protect the interests they represented, and their bureaucratic weapons were formidable.

The Emigration Commission persisted in its protest: "Lord Clarendon," it declared, "is perhaps scarcely aware of the bearing . . . on the prospects of Mauritius and the British West Indies." Mauritius, where migration was well established, would probably survive. But there was always trouble in getting enough coolies for Trinidad and British Guiana. If, indeed, there had to be such a treaty, then the French proposal contained some very objectionable details. The French themselves ought to bear the sole responsibility for recruitment, lest disputes arise if quotas could not be filled. The French requirement of one shipping ton for each coolie on board would provide insufficient space to move and breathe. On the other hand the French regulations concerning treatment in the colonies were roughly similar to the British ones.[19] If the Commission had hoped to change Palmerston's mind it would be disappointed: "We cannot give way to the Commercial Jealousy of the West Indians, and the only Question seems to me to be whether the French will stick to our

19. Emigration Commission to F.O., 17 Dec. 1857, FO 425/37. The British regulations required two tons per passenger, so that the French regulations were considerably less expensive.

Regulations as to the Embarkation and Transport of Coolies." [20]

To Sir Frederic Rogers, who soon found himself chosen to negotiate with the French ambassador, Count Persigny, the problem did not seem so simple. "I suppose," he told his mother, "I shall be a kind of central point to be battered by all the conflicting interests—French, West Indian, East Indian, Foreign Office, philanthropists, sugar-manufacturers, &c." [21] A difficult task, but Rogers was prepared for it: he was "at least a one-eyed man among the blind." In the ten years since Lord Grey had rejected him as Stephen's replacement he had developed and matured. As legal adviser to the Colonial Office he had handled such delicate problems as the Australian Constitutions with painstaking brilliance. Of his work at the Emigration Commission Elliot, who knew the business thoroughly himself, declared:

> In 20 years they have sent out 300,000 persons under their direct management of every detail, these persons comprising Europeans, Africans, Coolies, and Chinamen—and . . . they have had a sort of Police-control over an Emigration exceeding three millions. . . . Since the World began there can scarcely have been such an experience of the conveyance of people by sea.[22]

Working from "a certain paper I had concocted for the Foreign Office when I was laid up with rheumatism," Rogers and

20. Palmerston to Clarendon, 19 Dec. 1857, Clarendon Deposit, C. 69.

21. [1] Jan. 1858, G. Marindin, ed., *Letters of Frederic Lord Blachford, Under-Secretary of State for the Colonies, 1860–1871* (1896), p. 173. The expected West Indian protest never really materialized, probably because the intercolonial rivalry was too strong to permit the launching of a concerted campaign. See P. Curtin, *The Image of Africa: British Ideas and Action, 1780–1850* (Madison, 1964), p. 477. Moreover, the absence of strong colonial pressure seriously undercut the position of the Colonial Office in its bargaining with the Foreign and Indian departments.

22. Minute on Emigration Commission to C.O., 14 Apr. 1858, CO 318/219.

Persigny proceeded quickly over the whole field. The affair went smoothly. Persigny seemed more like a clerk than a great man. At length the Frenchman paused to deliver a sort of speech, of which, reported Rogers,

> the sense is this. The French Government have promised their colonies to revive the slave trade (in substance), the English make such a row about this that it may lead to war or something like it, unless the dispute is evaded. The French Government is too far pledged to *give in visibly*, whether wrong or right. But if you will let us get emigrant labourers from India instead of buying slaves in Africa, we will give up the African enterprise and tell our colonists that we have made a capital bargain for them, and so we shall be out of the mess altogether.[23]

Rogers thought his first diplomatic venture had been a success, but he counted too heavily on the mere pleasantness of his adversary. The French foreign minister, Count Walewski, soon informed Cowley that the interview had been most unsatisfactory. The proposed shipping regulations were far too strict and, more important, it appeared that the supply of coolies was inadequate even for the British colonies. The Indian government would therefore have to deliver periodic quotas.[24] Thus the chances of a speedy agreement receded.

Meanwhile the problem was being considered at the departmental level within the British government, and it was far from settled. Rogers explained:

> The Foreign Office [is] determined that the question should be settled; Labouchere [the colonial secretary] is torn about by divers influences which must under all circumstances prevent his standing upright. . . . The India Board have drawling, minute, obstructive ways, that will

23. Rogers to his sister, 3 Jan. 1858, *Blachford Letters*, pp. 175–76.
24. Cowley to Clarendon, 8 and 18 Jan. 1858, FO 425/37.

> stop the whole thing . . . if nobody runs over them. Then the matter is one which, if it gets wind, will bring down on poor Labouchere's head, in a state of fury, the West Indians, or the humanitarians, or both.[25]

The Indian authorities had stalled the affair before, but now they were put under the gun. Wrote Edmund Hammond, permanent undersecretary at the Foreign Office, to his opposite number at the India Board: "Lord Palmerston and Lord Clarendon are fully determined that an arrangement shall be made with the French Government, and the sooner, therefore, it is made, the better; for we shall then do it with a good grace."[26] The effect was achieved. Wrote the Board of Control to the Court of Directors: "The Foreign Office are pressing us very hard privately for a reply so I must trust that you will do your best to get us an answer quickly."[27] Rogers' draft was soon approved. Back he went for another interview with Persigny, who stood his ground. On into February the conversations continued, with neither side giving way, and the pace being slowed by the French reaction to the British part in the Orsini incident.[28] Shortly thereafter, the fall of the Palmerston government brought the negotiations temporarily to a close.

The change of government made something of a difference. The Conservative cabinet contained no one who had made crushing the slave trade a lifelong interest. Moreover, Palmerston's orientation toward the Foreign Office, where he had served for so many years, had strengthened that office in interdepartmental negotiations. In the Derby government the center of gravity shifted away from the Foreign Office toward the Treasury, under Disraeli, and the India Office, under the new

25. Rogers to R. W. Church, 14 Jan. 1858, *Blachford Letters,* p. 177.
26. Hammond to Sir George Clerk, 15 Jan. 1858, FO 425/37.
27. Note, undoubtedly by Sir George Clerk, of 15 Jan. 1858, India Office, Judicial, Leg. Committee, Misc. Papers no. 6, India Office Library.
28. Rogers to his mother, 2 Feb. 1858, *Blachford Letters,* p. 179.

prime minister's son, Lord Stanley. The new government, at any rate, failed to press the French to renew the negotiations.

Indeed, the French made the first move. First came a strong feeler from foreign minister Walewski, followed by Emperor Louis Napoleon's own rather surprising order for a review of the whole subject of African emigration, as well as for a resumption of the coolie negotiations.[29] Only then did the British foreign secretary, the Earl of Malmesbury, bring the matter before the cabinet. It was soon resolved, however, and Sir Frederic Rogers accordingly set out in November 1858 to extend his adventure in diplomacy to a foreign country.

In fact Rogers need not have hurried, and for a week he was left to cool his heels. At length he was told to report to the Algerian Ministry, where he was grilled for more than an hour by a twenty-man commission. It was quite an ordeal:

> I got sometimes horribly confused in my French, and then they told me to speak English. . . . I would give two and sixpence to know that I had not grossly exposed myself: there was a calm courtesy about their mode of dealing with my flounderings in French which is alarming to look back upon—though it was particularly reassuring while the process was going on.

Diplomacy was losing its novelty and excitement:

> I can't say [he told his mother] I like the work altogether. . . . It is very unpleasant to deal with people who you feel want to trip you up, and understand their work—that is, the method of proceeding—better than you do, and very unpleasant to feel what tyranny and loss of life may be inflicted on thousands of people by a false start. I get rather nervous and shaky when I think of this part of the matter.[30]

29. Cowley to Malmesbury, 28 Oct. 1858, Cowley Papers, FO 519/224; and 8 Nov. FO 425/37.

30. Rogers letters, 5 and 17 Dec. 1858, *Blachford Letters,* pp. 191–92, 194–95.

By now the French had dropped their demand that the British be responsible for recruiting while the British had agreed that other colonies besides Réunion might be included. Other issues remained. The French proposed a seven-year agreement, the India Office an annual review.[31] The French wanted no mention of the Régis contract in a formal treaty: it might be misunderstood; while for the British this was the raison d'être of the whole affair. More germane, however, was the dispute regarding space. The French were proposing a requirement of slightly less than thirty-six cubic feet per passenger, compared with the British regulation of seventy-two. It was all very complicated. The French could point to a death rate of 2.36 per cent on their ships, against a figure of 4.19 per cent on the British vessels, to show that space and health were not related. The British could counter with the argument that the French had been recruiting only in Madras, whereas the coolies on British ships had come predominantly from still more unhealthy Calcutta. And so it went. So vital was the question, "in point of humanity on the one side and in point of expense on the other,"[32] that it was left unmentioned when drafts were exchanged in January 1859. Rogers returned to London, to draw up for the cabinet a detailed memorandum and to await the result of another round of strenuous interdepartmental infighting.

"Lord S[tanley]," observed Rogers, "will, of course, be the man who will settle in substance all the Coolie part of the matter; and I shall not be surprised if the decision on one point which he has already arrived at stops the whole affair."[33] For the Indian secretary had refused to make any concessions on the question of space without the approval of the government in India,[34] a process that would be time-con-

31. Stanley to Hammond, 21 Dec. 1858, FO 425/37: "our possession of it is the best security for our never having to use it."

32. Rogers to Malmesbury, 31 Dec. 1858, ibid.

33. Rogers to R. W. Church, 17 Jan. 1858, *Blachford Letters,* pp. 199–200.

34. India Office to F.O., 8 Jan. 1859, FO 425/37. It will be recalled

suming even if it were successful. At the Colonial Office Sir E. B. Lytton insisted that the French renounce the Régis contract as an integral part of the treaty, but then took it all back by adding that if Malmesbury thought otherwise then of course his department would not object: altogether, Rogers thought, "like a man . . . afraid of being snubbed for having an opinion of his own."[35] Only Stanley's objections really stood in the way, and he reluctantly softened them by accepting for migration from Madras and Bombay, though not Calcutta, reductions in space requirements that had already been recommended by the Emigration Commission.[36] The dam was broken. Off hurried Rogers for a last round of the offices, then on to the treaty clerk at the Foreign Office for a fair copy of the latest draft, "and from that time I cannot complain that the work has stood still."[37] By late January he was back in Paris. And Malmesbury was confident enough to urge that the treaty be adopted in time so that "we might bring him into the [Queen's] Speech on our Shoulders."[38]

Once again, however, Rogers need not have hurried, for the colonial minister Prince Napoleon (nephew of the Emperor) had left on his honeymoon. For some three weeks Rogers dawdled, trying to amuse himself at parties or at touching up the French and English drafts of the treaty.[39] The tedium went on. In February came ambassador Cowley's mission to Vienna

---

that the Board of Control had become the India Office in the reorganization of Indian administration in August 1858, following the Mutiny.

35. Lytton minute on F.O. to C.O., 4 Jan. 1859, CO 318/222; Rogers to his mother, 23 Jan., *Blachford Letters*, p. 201.

36. I.O. to F.O., 22 Jan. 1859, FO 425/37.

37. Rogers to his mother, 23 Jan. 1859, *Blachford Letters*, p. 202.

38. Malmesbury to Cowley, 25 Jan. [1859], Cowley Papers, FO 519/196.

39. "I really cannot charge myself with want of care in the matter," he told Hammond, "yet it is provoking to find that when I take either draft up after having left it for a few days, I am sure to find some little want of completeness here or there, not important, but worth mending." 8 Feb. 1859, FO 425/37.

on the Italian question, while the approach of war in Italy "gave the French something to think of"[40] besides coolies. Rogers returned to London, the negotiations once more interrupted.

When they were resumed in May 1859, Chasseloup-Laubat had replaced Prince Napoleon as colonial minister. On the British side the Derby government was but a month before its fall. Otherwise nothing had changed. The only really important issue continued to be space. "We quite understand each other," declared Rogers, "& the matter is . . . reducible by the simplest process to pounds, shillings & pence. The simple question is what amount of space shall the Coolies have, & by consequence shall the French have to pay for."[41] Stanley would make no more concessions, while the Colonial Office suggested that any further conversations with the French "would operate so prejudicially upon Colonial interests as to create continual and not unreasonable dissatisfaction."[42] By mid-June Malmesbury had made no progress. At this point, however, Palmerston returned to office, to resume his hobby as a sort of unofficial secretary of state for the abolition of the slave trade and to drive the coolie convention at last to a successful conclusion.

Foreign secretary Lord Russell took the initiative, advising the French that Rogers was being "held in readiness," and asking the Colonial and India offices for swift approval of the proposed instructions. But the new Indian secretary, Sir Charles Wood, would do no more than repeat Stanley's position. And the Duke of Newcastle wrote out for undersecretary Herman Merivale's signature the acid and very fundamental question of "whether the advantages anticipated to the Natives of Africa from the abandonment of what is called 'free emigration' from that Continent outweigh the risks incurred by the Indian

40. Rogers memoir, n.d., *Blachford Letters*, p. 172.
41. Rogers to Carnarvon, 30 May 1859, CO 318/225.
42. C.O. to F.O., 31 May 1859, FO 425/37.

subjects of the Queen."[43] Why should they be trading Indians for Africans at all? At the end of August Rogers was still "in readiness."

Russell persisted. And even as he did so the Foreign Office was receiving information that considerably reinforced the African dimensions of the problem. On one of the outlets of the Niger an interesting confrontation had recently occurred between Commodores Close of the British West African squadron and Bosse, the latter a French officer in charge of supervising the recruitment of slaves under the Régis contract. Pleading his previous ignorance of "the enormous and princely trade England had in these rivers," the Frenchman had suggested that a representation of the extent of the damage that was being done to British interests might cause his own government to reconsider. He hoped so, as that seemed the best chance of his being relieved from a most unpleasant tour of duty. In forwarding Close's letter his superior, Rear Admiral Sir Frederick Grey, had added the rather shocking comment:

> I believe that the French can purchase slaves more easily and at a lower rate in the Congo, and without, therefore, attributing to them any readiness to sacrifice their own interests to ours it is probable that a concession might be obtained from them, and there can be no doubt that it would be most desirable.[44]

From Indians for Africans, the trading seemed about to shift to that of Congolese for Yorubas. Russell, who it must be stressed was acting from somewhat loftier motives than those which apparently concerned the admiral, reacted swiftly:

> The French emigration has hitherto not been carried on in certain of the African rivers, where an extensive British

43. C.O. to F.O., 16 Aug. 1859, CO 318/222.

44. Close to Commodore Wise, *Trident,* Sierra Leone, 11 June 1859; encl. in Grey to Admiralty, *Boscawen,* Ascension, 16 July; encl. in Adm. to F.O., 18 Aug.; FO 425/37.

> trade with the natives for palm oil had grown up, and it is estimated that the property of British traders in the Bonny and Calabar rivers alone does not fall far short of £1,000,000 sterling. . . . It is obvious that if an attempt is made to carry on the French emigration . . . where the Slave Trade has been for many years suspended by a wholesome and legitimate trade, not only will the property of British merchants be seriously compromised, and their commercial dealings with the natives paralyzed, but much difficulty will be raised between Her Majesty's Government and the Native Chiefs under the Treaties existing between them [outlawing the slave trade], and questions of an embarrassing nature may arise between Her Majesty's naval officers endeavouring to hold the Chiefs to their engagements, and French naval officers endeavouring to induce the Chiefs to evade those engagements.

Thus, in language that combined the humanitarian and economic factors that had shaped British policy in the region since before the time of Buxton, did Russell authorize Cowley to explain to the French that the Niger delta was a British sphere of influence. It was only two years before the claim would be staked formally by the annexation of Lagos.

Now the important thing about Russell's letter is not the information it contains, for the knowledge of considerable British investment in the area was not strange to the Foreign Office. What is significant is that such a notice was being given through official channels to the French. Moreover, at this time the Foreign Office was by no means primarily concerned with solidifying British preeminence in a part of West Africa. Russell hoped the French would stop buying slaves anywhere. If, however, France should thwart the coolie negotiations, then there might indeed be "less embarrassment" in advising "the expediency of refraining from carrying on the scheme in such a manner as would tend to revive the Slave Trade in places where it is extinct, and, with its revival, seriously to injure British commerce."[45]

Rogers soon returned to Paris, this time to deal directly with the colonial minister, Chasseloup-Laubat, with whom he had a meeting of minds. Indeed, as he confessed to Russell, it was rather embarrassing, for he had not known how to reply:

> It had [also] appeared to me that . . . the expediency of a Convention . . . was open to serious doubts; first, because it bound the two Governments . . . to an experiment which involved the possibility of many disputes and much disaster; and next, because it might fairly be argued that the persuasion or prohibition of Indian emigration ought to be decided with simple reference to the well-being of the Indians themselves, rather than as a part of an arrangement for the benefit of the natives of another continent.[46]

The Frenchman also objected that to mention the Régis contract in the convention would constitute an interference in French internal affairs. Cowley advised that a unilateral decision by the French could be reversed at will, and added that if the British meant to stand firm on this point it was useless to go on: "the French Government appear to have made up their minds."[47]

Only the Emperor, thought Rogers, was keeping the negotiations going at all. Of the motives of this "living problem," as Cowley described him, one can only speculate that good relations with Britain were paramount. Success, however, seemed very doubtful. In the Colonial Office the Duke of Newcastle was optimistic: "The Convention will most probably come to nothing."[48] Foreign secretary Russell, who was most an-

45. Russell to Cowley, 23 Aug. 1859, ibid.
46. 30 Aug. 1859, ibid.
47. Cowley to Russell, 1 Sept. 1859, ibid.
48. Minute on F.O. to C.O., 31 Aug. 1859, CO 318/222.

noyed, curtly informed Rogers that his obligation was to carry out policy, not to make it. And he reminded the French of the interference in internal matters the convention would mean for England, "inasmuch as it grants to a foreign Power the right of beating up for emigrants among the Queen's subjects, in a part of the Queen's dominions."[49]

The rest of the diplomatic negotiations need not detain us. The fire had gone out of them; the focus, as we shall see, was shifting to a related subject; and they have little more to reveal about departmental interaction in the making of British policy. The French continued to object to anything that might smack of interference in their internal affairs, while they pressed for a precise definition of what was and was not to be included under the term "India."[50] They were at last persuaded to sign the convention by urgent petitions from labor-starved Réunion. In the British government Palmerston remained the only member deeply concerned, and the other departments continued to resist. Indeed, the Duke of Newcastle, who had been hampered throughout by the failure of the West Indians to mount an effective protest, tried to organize the resistance. In the end the Indian government succeeded in modifying the convention so that it could suspend emigration to the French colonies at any time.[51] Not until July 1861, after nearly four years of tedious negotiations that had been heated

49. Letters to Rogers and Cowley, 15 Sept. 1859, FO 425/37.

50. As might be imagined this rather delicate question created some difficulty. British India was eventually defined as "every part of India except those Settlements under the direct domination of France and Portugal." I.O. to F.O., 3 Feb. 1860, ibid. The British were suspicious. Wrote Hammond to Cowley: "From what Rogers told me today, it is quite clear that the French have an object in trying to make us define '*India.*' They wish hereafter to hold us to our definition. So you must insist upon not saying more than you have done on this point." 3 Apr. 1860, Cowley Papers, FO 519/189.

51. Newcastle to Sir Charles Wood, 21 Jan. 1861, Halifax Papers, India Office MSS, European, F 78/80–2.

at the beginning but that had lately turned stone cold, was the coolie convention at last concluded.[52]

The signing of the treaty brought no sort of logical conclusion to the process of decision making within the British government. Indeed, the fact that the deliberations had already begun to enter a new phase may account for the Foreign Office's relative lack of enthusiasm in the later stages of the negotiations. To that department the coolie convention had always seemed an effort to solve an essentially African problem. Having announced to the French with no effect that the Niger delta was a British sphere of influence,[53] the Foreign Office was preparing to stake the claim. Great Britain was getting ready to annex Lagos. This was a measure that would constitute a fundamental commitment, the first of many and one from which she would not withdraw until a century later. It owed its timing primarily to the rivalry in the area with France.

Anglo-French competition in West Africa helps to account for the timing of the annexation of Lagos, though of course the more basic reasons were already present. As Russell had explained, British commercial and humanitarian interests were old and well entrenched. The economic stake was centered on the palm oil and cotton trades, the humanitarian in the Church Missionary Society stations at Lagos and in the interior at Abeokuta. It was now nearly twenty years since Fowell Buxton had fused the motives of trade and religion into a combined assault upon the source of the slave trade, attempting to

52. Copy in PP, 1861 [2877], *65*, 249–60. Since the Indian government had changed the terms of the convention, Russell conceded that there need be no specific mention of the Régis contract.

53. The French had replied to Russell's announcement by saying that Commodore Bosse had been misquoted, and that they were not attempting to recruit in the Oil Rivers. Cowley to Russell, 16 Oct. 1859, FO 425/37.

replace it with "legitimate commerce." [54] More recently mail contracts had been awarded to Macgregor Laird, a member of a famous Birkenhead shipbuilding family, who on an exploring expedition as a young man had formed a vision of the Niger as a great commercial artery like the Mississippi. In addition, the converging interests had already helped to establish a pattern of involvement and interference in local African politics, a trend that had been marked by the reduction of Lagos in 1851 and the installation of a puppet ruler there.[55] The annexation of Lagos was thus the logical conclusion of earlier British enterprise and activity.

Once again Palmerston was the prime mover. And the situation in the area that greeted his return to power in 1859 was more than usually inviting to an activist who had made African diplomacy so much his lifelong hobby. For one thing the slave trade seemed to have been reviving at Whydah, the port of entry to that longtime obstacle, the kingdom of Dahomey: and the increase was traced to the French slave-buying activities. Because the base of its power lay inland, Dahomey had not been easily intimidated by the usual reminder "that on the sea are the ships and cannon of England . . . and that the chiefs of Africa do not always retain their authority to the end of their lives." [56] Instead, Britain's relations with that kingdom had been a study in frustration. Stung by their sense of impotence, her representatives had alternately courted and threatened the king, but all to no avail. That lofty ruler would smile benignly at his visitors, drink with them a champagne toast to

54 See J. Gallagher, "Fowell Buxton and the New African Policy, 1839–1842," *Cambridge Historical Journal, 10* (1950), 36–58.

55. For the background see particularly J. Hargreaves, *Prelude to the Partition of West Africa* (1963); K. Dike, *Trade and Politics in the Niger Delta* (Oxford, 1956); C. Newbury, *The Western Slave Coast and its Rulers* (Oxford, 1961); and S. Biobaku, *The Egba and their Neighbours, 1848–1872* (Oxford, 1957).

56. Palmerston to Consul John Beecroft, 21 Feb. 1851, Papers re reduction of Lagos, PP, 1852 [1455], *54,* 311–12.

Queen Victoria, then beg her "to put a stop to the Slave Trade everywhere else, and allow him to continue it."[57] Moreover Dahomey was a perennial opponent of Abeokuta, which in addition to being the Church Missionary Society's station was just now the site of a feverish effort to provide an alternative source of cotton in case civil war should break out in the United States. The situation was warming up.

In the spring of 1860 the Foreign Office was informed that an assault by Dahomey on Abeokuta was in the offing. William Wylde, principal clerk of the slave-trade division, explained:

> It has always been the policy of this Country to support the Abbeokutans [sic] and we have on former occasions supplied them with Guns . . . small Arms and Ammunition . . . when an attack was made by the Dahomians. The Chiefs of Abbeokuta have not always evinced that friendly spirit which the assistance ought to have elicited, but trade has made steady progress . . . and the cultivation of Cotton . . . holds out hopes of becoming an important article of export.[58]

As a means of blocking Dahomey Consul George Brand, who had replaced the deceased William Campbell, recommended that Lagos be annexed outright. The place would be useful as a base of operations against Dahomey and as a fulcrum from which to combat the influence of the French, and it would be easy to take over, the British consul having been acting as a sort of de facto ruler on the island for some time. The Foreign Office was interested and in July 1860 it was decided to ask the opinion of the Colonial Office.[59] Thus British involvement in local politics, both in Lagos and as the champion of Abeo-

57. King Guezo to Queen Victoria, 3 Nov. 1848, ibid., *54*, 232.

58. Minute on Brand to Russell, 9 Mar. 1860, FO 84/1115.

59. Minutes on Brand to Russell, 6 June 1860, ibid. Parliamentary undersecretary Wodehouse, later Lord Kimberley, played an important role in the decision.

kuta against Dahomey, provided the Foreign Office with a strong strategic reason that was certainly leading to annexation. That reason has usually been thought to have been the decisive factor. Yet the chronology of the documents reveals that it was not. For, perhaps because an unfavorable response was anticipated, the letter to the Colonial Office was not sent until seven months later.

In the meantime more information became available. Consul Henry Foote (Brand had also died) had reported that a Régis agent had been dickering with Kosoko, whom the British had deposed as ruler of Lagos in 1851. The French, he charged, were plotting to take Lagos themselves.[60] Although apparently the allegation had no basis outside the consul's own imagination, it was this information which triggered the delayed action of the Foreign Office. Perhaps a show of force would head off both Dahomey and the French.

The Foreign Office considered the alternatives. A direct attack on Dahomey had to be rejected: a land campaign would be too risky, too expensive, and too difficult to support logistically. Instead, Russell instructed Consul Foote to proceed to Abeokuta. There he was to obtain information and to aid, if necessary, in repelling the apprehended attack. The foreign secretary asked the War Office for a detachment of black troops to help in Abeokuta's defense. And he requested the Colonial Office to consider the annexation of Lagos. The island would be useful as a base against the slave trade on the coast and in the interior. It would serve as an entrepôt for the export of palm oil and cotton. Moreover, he informed the Duke of Newcastle, Great Britain could not "view with indifference the establishment there by French Agents of a Depot for Negroes to be exported to the French Colonies," a

60. Foote to Russell, 9 Jan. 1861, FO 84/1141. The French were indeed on the move, for they annexed Porto-Novo later that same year. See Schnapper, *La Politique et le Commerce Français,* pp. 183 ff., and Newbury, *Western Slave Coast,* pp. 67–69. So it is likely that there were a good many rumors.

step which had been rumored and "which might still be carried into effect if the French should fail in procuring a supply of labour . . . from other than African sources."[61] Russell thus tied directly together the movement toward Lagos and the coolie negotiations which, at the time, were still pending with France.

The Colonial Office did not share the enthusiasm. If Lagos should be formally annexed the administrative responsibility would belong to the colonial secretary, who would have to try to balance the budget and to supply any deficit from the estimates voted to his own department. Sir George Barrow, senior clerk of the African division, noted another problem, the institution of domestic slavery, which "could not be so easily winked at, as it is at Cape Coast & the other Forts."[62] Instead of refusing, however, the Colonial Office adopted passive resistance. When the occasion demanded that department could be fully as dilatory as the Treasury, and Russell's letter remained unanswered for as long as possible.

Shortly thereafter, Consul Foote reported a conversation with a French commodore who had denied convincingly that his country was planning either to occupy Lagos or to try to place Kosoko on the throne there. Instead of being mollified, Palmerston minuted:

> This strongly confirms the expediency of losing no Time in assuming the formal Protectorate of Lagos, and indeed it shews that our Protectorate is virtually acknowledged on the Spot. But the French Minister of Marine & Colonies at Paris may not be so moderate & friendly as the French Naval Officer at Lagos, and we may find ourselves in difficulties if we don't take Time by the Forelock.

61. F.O. to C.O. (Russell to Newcastle), 7 Feb. 1861, CO 96/56. Interdepartmental correspondence was usually signed by undersecretaries, and I think the departure in this case from the usual routine was probably deliberate, indicating that Russell expected resistance and wanted action.

62. Minute on Russell's letter of 7 Feb. 1861, ibid.

The prime minister urged the stronger step of annexation, a measure that was still being "actively considered" by the Colonial Office. "If we do not take this Step," he wrote, "the French will be before Hand with us, & to our great Detriment." [63] The Foreign Office now pressed for Newcastle's overdue decision, and at last he reluctantly agreed.[64] So it was that Russell's famous dispatch of June 22, 1861, drafted by parliamentary undersecretary Wodehouse, authorized the consul to annex Lagos provided that no force were necessary either to take or to hold it.[65]

Under these instructions acting consul William McCoskry proceeded in August 1861 to act.[66] With the salutary aid of one of Her Majesty's gunboats he managed to persuade Docemo, the puppet king, that it would be in his best interest to retire. Palmerston was gratified: "The Possession of Lagos will give great additional Means for putting an End to Slave Trade . . . and will afford a valuable and increasing Development to legitimate Commerce." [67] At the Colonial Office there was more skepticism. Observed Sir Frederic Rogers, Merivale's recent replacement as undersecretary: "The King Docemo does not appear to have been allowed much choice in regard to this cession." [68] And assistant undersecretary Elliot: "The Foreign Office are always great friends of our making territorial acquisitions. The moving spirit is usually a Consul, and I often wonder whether the Dept. at home sufficiently represses over zeal in that class of functionaries." [69]

Indeed, such skepticism was fully justified. The annexation of Lagos solved no problems and it created others. The act merely intensified the rivalry with the French, who soon in-

63. Minute of 28 Mar. 1861, re Foote to Russell, 9 Feb., FO 84/1141.
64. Minute of 17 June 1861, on F.O. to C.O., June 10, CO 96/56.
65. Papers re occupation of Lagos, PP, 1862 [2982], *61*, 345–46.
66. Foote too had died. These were not good years for consuls.
67. Minute on McCoskry to Russell, Lagos, 7 Aug. 1861, FO 84/1141.
68. Minute on F.O. to C.O., 18 Sept. 1861, CO 147/2.
69. Minute on F.O. to C.O., 16 Oct. 1861, ibid.

stalled themselves at Porto-Novo. Trade in London had been expected to boom after British occupancy, but instead it went into decline. And the Colonial Office had great difficulty in trying to raise enough revenue to pay for the new colony's administration. Annexation served to increase British involvement in the conflicts of the interior, but it did not of course bring them to a halt. In fact, even as Russell's instructions had left the Foreign Office, McCoskry was reporting on a small war that was then in progress between Abeokuta and Ibadan. His information must have struck his readers as distinctly ironical:

> We have learned by this war that the Chiefs of Abbeokuta court our alliances not only to strengthen them against Dahomey but to enable them to make wars exactly similar to the expeditions of Dahomey . . . We will have no lasting peace . . . till we have a force established at Abbeokuta. . . . The people are in the main peaceable and would soon appreciate the advantage of such a change.[70]

Thus, even as the annexation of the colony was being accomplished, its occupiers were already feeling the pull of the "turbulent frontier." [71] Over the next half-century the force of local expansion played a large role in pulling the often reluctant British toward conquest and toward the staggering task of trying to create a unified country out of the ethnically diverse population who lived in what the rulers were to call Nigeria. At least for the moment, however, the Foreign Office's appetite was satiated. Russell decided that "it would be endless to attempt to controul all these Abbeokutans & others by occu-

70. McCoskry to Russell, 4 July 1861, FO 84/1141.

71. On this theme see W. Hancock, *Survey of British Commonwealth Affairs* (2 vols., Oxford, 1937–40), *2*, pt. II; J. S. Galbraith, "The 'Turbulent Frontier' as a Factor in British Expansion," *Comparative Studies in Society and History, 2* (1959–60), 150–68; and W. McIntyre, *The Imperial Frontier in the Tropics, 1865–75* (1967).

pying their territory in force. We must occupy Lagos, & impose peace by punishing those who infringe it." [72] Whether in fact any measure short of occupying the interior would succeed in accomplishing this object, Russell refrained from speculating.

A year later Elliot of the Colonial Office was musing over the dispatches from the new colony. He pondered the dilemma of the British role in Africa. He reflected on "the disparity between our power and our knowledge." He asked how long it would take before their understanding of Africa would enable them to exercise their awesome power wisely. He wondered: "where is it to end?" And, in an amusing exercise in self-criticism, he compared the British in Africa to the "Kings in burlesques who, with comical vigor, despatch one slave with a blow, and cover the other with honors, long before they can know whether either deserves his fate." [73]

"Her Majesty's Government," said Russell's dispatch, "are convinced that the permanent occupation of this important point in the Bight of Benin is indispensable to the complete suppression of the Slave Trade in the Bight, whilst it will give great aid and support to the development of lawful commerce." [74] For a long time these official motives for the annexation of Lagos were taken at face value. So far as they go they are correct. The occupation did grow very logically out of Britain's longstanding attempts to create a "legitimate" alternative to West Africa's traditional means of obtaining foreign exchange. It has been objected that the reference to slave trade was anachronistic, since Lagos had none in the 1850s.[75] But in fact Russell did not say there had been. According to his dispatch, Great Britain took Lagos as a useful base for her opera-

72. Minute on McCoskry to Russell, 4 July 1861, FO 84/1141.
73. Minute on Gov. Freeman to S. of S., 4 June 1862, CO 147/1.
74. Russell to McCoskry, 22 June 1861, PP, 1862 [2982], *61*, 345.
75. See J. Ade Ajayi, "The British Occupation of Lagos, 1851–1861," *Nigeria Magazine*, (1961), pp. 96–105.

tions in the area and as a preventive measure. There was no specific mention of ending an existing trade in slaves on the island itself.

Russell's dispatch explains almost everything about the incident except why Lagos was taken in 1861, rather than later. Since the timing of an event is often crucial in determining the interrelationship of causative factors it is well to be as precise as possible. Trade and religion had brought the British to the area, but they provided no urgent reason for the formal possession of territory there. Still less do these long-range motives explain timing. The pattern of involvement in local politics did provide such a reason. And, but for the evidence provided by chronology and by the contents of Palmerston's minutes, it could be reasonably concluded that Lagos was taken primarily as a base from which to launch a defense of Abeokuta against Dahomey. This was of course involved, and particularly among officials on the spot.

The decision to annex Lagos, however, was not made in Africa. It was made in London. And the evidence suggests that it was made because a new factor had been added, because the Foreign Office, and more especially Palmerston, had come during the coolie negotiations to regard the establishment of a British possession as a necessary response to the activities of the French. It is not in fact surprising that this factor should have remained obscure. For the collection of correspondence on the subject which the Palmerston government laid before parliament in 1862 had been carefully edited of any evidence whatever that might have led to the conclusion that Anglo-French rivalry in West Africa might have exerted any influence over the matter at all.

Like any case study this one contains aspects that are unique and aspects that are not. It is well to stress the former. For of course any attempt at generalization must first be qualified by the understanding that so much depends on the particular setting of time, place, and circumstances. What if there had been no Palmerston? Would the Indian authorities have permitted the treaty before the Mutiny had temporarily weakened their standing within the British government? Most important it is the *combination,* the peculiar interrelationship of factors to one another in time, that is unique.

Yet there are elements here that do seem more generally applicable. The most obvious is the far-flung interaction that went on in that marvelous mechanism of worldwide cultural interchange called the British Empire. The investigation of one treaty has taken us to London, Paris, the West Indies, India, and West Africa. Pressure on the Indian labor market was felt in Trinidad and Porto-Novo. The annexation of Lagos had its local origins, but the island was taken in part because it had become a point of convergence of influences from three other continents. Once an area became part of the British Empire, formal and informal, it no longer remained in isolation: a truism that may bear restating in view of the heavy emphasis that scholars have recently been placing upon the study of local history.

Less obviously, perhaps, there is something of a pattern here concerning the working of the imperial administrative structure that goes somewhat beyond the strict confines of the making of a single treaty and its immediate implications. Indeed, this close examination illustrates much of what this essay has attempted to develop more generally about the process of British imperial policy making. The operation of the broad historical forces of geography, economics, ideas, and the results of previous actions and events created a situation that had to be dealt with. In this case the need of tropical colonies for labor and the ability of both Africa and India to supply it led the French to pose a problem which Palmerston, supported by organized humanitarian interests, decided must be solved. That decision necessarily involved several areas of the empire and the bureaucracies that administered and represented them. In effect a process of decision making was created *for that problem alone.* Each office looked through different eyes: the India Office through those of the coolie, the Foreign Office through those of the merchant and missionary in Africa, the Colonial Office through those of the West Indian planter. The perceptions varied, the interests conflicted, and the result was disagreement and negotiation.

Although this process involved a number of official, quasi-official, and unofficial bodies, the collecting and weighing of the interests and the bulk of the decision making were centered in the executive government. Save for its annual review of departmental estimates, the role of parliament was intermittent and for the most part indirect. Though its name was frequently invoked, its direct intervention in the formation and implementation of policy occurred less often in this "age of parliamentary supremacy" than might have been supposed.

The policy-making process involved personalities and through them the intervention of the idiosyncratic, the accidental, and the unique. A busy prime minister (who had to think about politics, Ireland, the Italian war, and the American Civil War) pursued his hobby of African diplomacy, immersing himself with obvious enjoyment in a maze of detail that might have bored another man. In Paris an inexperienced diplomat worried about his French. In the Foreign Office an undersecretary forgot to inquire into the constitutional powers of the government of India.

From the interaction of bureaucracy, interests, and individuals emerged both an attempt at solution and an altered perception of the situation. The original problem, how to supply from outside Africa the demand of French colonies for labor, was not really solved. But the change in the Foreign Office's perception of the African background led to the annexation of a colony, a commitment that in turn created more problems that required more decision making. Each new problem would call into being a different combination of bureaucracy, interests and individuals. For each there would be a different decision-making process. It would appear that policy making in any government, irrespective of time and place, might usefully be investigated in the light of some such model as this.

The process of policy making can be thought of in terms of a continuous repetition of problems, partial solutions, and altered perceptions that combine with "forces" to create new problems. "Policy" exists in anticipation of the future or in explanation of the past. In the present, policy is being made. It is a thing in flux, changing and evolving as the factors of decision making shift and re-form in the different combinations that are called into being by the character (or, more accurately, the *perceived* character) of emerging or altering problems.

Appendix

Select List of Colonial Governors

Anderson, Sir George William 1791–1857	Son of a London merchant; entered Bombay civil service in 1806 and rose to become a judge, a member of the Indian Law Commission, and member of the council of the governor of Bombay. Gov., Bombay, 1841–42; retired from I.C.S. in 1844. Gov., Mauritius, 1849; Ceylon, 1850–55.
Arthur, Sir George 1784–1854	Youngest son of a Plymouth gentleman; entered army in 1804. Lt. Gov., British Honduras, 1814–22; Van Diemen's Land, 1824–36; Upper Canada, 1837–41; Gov., Bombay, 1842–46.
Barkly, Sir Henry 1815–98	Only son of a West Indian merchant and planter, received commercial education, went into business. Conservative M.P., 1845–48. Gov., British Guiana, 1848–53; Jamaica, 1853–56; Victoria, 1856–63; Mauritius, 1863–70; Cape Colony, 1870–77. Fellow of Royal Society and Royal Geographical Society and president of Bristol and Gloucestershire Archaeological Society. Introduced responsible government in Victoria and Cape Colony.

Bowen, Sir George F. 1821–99	Eldest son of rector of Taughboyne, Co. Donegal; educated at Charterhouse and Trinity College, Oxford, B.A., 1844; fellow of Brasenose College; entered Lincoln's Inn, 1844. President of University of Corfu, 1847–51. Chief secretary, Ionian Islands, 1854–59. Gov., Queensland, 1859–67; New Zealand, 1868–72; Victoria, 1872–79; Mauritius, 1879–82; Hong Kong, 1882–85. Recognized classical scholar.
Bruce, James, 8th Earl of Elgin 1811–63	Second son of 7th Earl; educated at Eton and Christ Church, Oxford, first class in classics. Raised to Lords, 1841. Gov., Jamaica, 1842–46; Canada, 1846–54; special negotiator in China and Japan during 1857–61; postmaster general, 1858; governor-general, India, 1861–63. Introduced responsible government in Canada; 2d wife was daughter of Earl of Durham.
Bulwer, Sir Henry E. G. 1836–1914	Youngest son of W. Lytton Bulwer of Heydon, Norfolk; educated at Charterhouse and Trinity College, Cambridge. Official resident in Ionian Islands, 1860–64; pvt. sec. to

	uncle, Lord Dalling, ambassador to Constantinople, 1865; receiver-general, Trinidad, 1866. Administered Dominica, 1867–69; Gov., Labuan, 1871–75; Natal, 1875–86; high commissioner, Cyprus, 1886–92.
Darling, Sir Charles H. 1809–70	Son of major general; educated at R.M.C., Sandhurst, ensign 1825. Pvt. sec. to brother, Gov., of N.S.W., 1827–31; agent-general for immigration, Jamaica, 1843–47. Lt. gov., St. Lucia, 1847–51; Cape Colony, 1851–54; Newfoundland, 1854–57; Jamaica, 1857–63; Victoria, 1863–66.
Denison, Sir William T. 1804–71	Third son of Nottinghamshire gentleman; educated at Eton and at R.M.C., Woolwich, commission in R.E., 1826. Worked on Rideau canal in Canada, 1827–31. Knighted for services under Admiralty, 1846. Lt. gov., Van Diemen's Land, 1846–54; Gov., N.S.W., 1854–61; Madras, 1861–66, temporarily governor-general in 1863. Member of government commission on river pollution, 1868. Introduced responsible government in N.S.W.

Des Voeux, Sir George W 1834–1909	B. Baden, son of former clergyman, educated at Charterhouse and Balliol College, Oxford, and law degree from Univ. of Toronto. Administrator, St. Lucia, 1869–78; temporary gov. and then Gov., Fiji, 1878–85; Gov., Newfoundland, 1885–86; Hong Kong, 1887–91.
FitzRoy, Sir Charles A. 1796–1858	Eldest son of Lord Charles FitzRoy; commission in Horse Guards, and present at Waterloo. Lt. gov., Prince Edward Island, 1837–41; Gov., Leeward Islands, 1841–45; N.S.W., 1846–55.
Frere, Sir Henry Bartle 1815–84	Educated at Haileybury; writership, Bombay civil service, 1834; long and distinguished career in India. Chief commissioner, Sind, 1850–62; Gov., Bombay, 1862–67. Mission to Zanzibar, 1872. Gov., Cape Colony, 1877–80.
Gordon, Arthur C., 1st Baron Stanmore 1829–1912	Youngest son of 4th Earl of Aberdeen, educated at Trinity College, Cambridge. Pvt. sec. to father, 1852–55; Liberal M.P., 1854–57; pvt. sec. to Gladstone, Ionian Islands, 1858. Lt. gov., New Brunswick, 1861–66; Gov., Trinidad,

1866–71; Mauritius, 1871–74; Fiji, 1875–80; New Zealand, 1880–83; Ceylon, 1883–90.

Grey, Sir Charles E. 1785–1865	Son of Northumberland gentleman; educated at University College, Oxford, called to bar, 1811. Judge, supreme court of Madras, 1820; chief justice, Bengal, 1825. Special commissioner in Canada, 1835; Whig M.P., 1838–41. Gov., Barbados, Trinidad, 1841–46; Jamaica, 1847–53.
Grey, Sir George 1812–98	Son of Lt. Col., family had banking business in London. Educated at Sandhurst, commissioned, 1829. Explored in Australia, 1836–39. Gov., S. Australia, 1841–45; New Zealand, 1845–53; Cape Colony, 1854–61; New Zealand, 1861–68. Later became prime minister of New Zealand, 1877–79.
Head, Sir Edmund W. 1805–68	Son of clergyman, educated at Winchester and Oriel College, Oxford; entered Lincoln's Inn, 1835. Fellow of Merton College, Oxford, 1830–37. Recognized classical scholar. Asst. poor law commissioner, 1836–41; commissioner, 1841–47. Gov. New

	Brunswick, 1847–54; Canada, 1854–61. Later became a civil service commissioner.
Jervois, Sir William F. D. 1821–97	Son of gentry family on Isle of Wight. Educated at R.M.C., Woolwich. On engineer duty, eastern frontier of Cape Colony, 1841–49; reported on defenses of British North America, 1863, and of Indian ports, 1871–72. Gov., Straits Settlements, 1875–77; South Australia, 1877–82; New Zealand, 1882–89.
Kennedy, Sir Arthur E. 1810–83	Born Co. Down, educated at Trinity College, Dublin, and went into army. Poor law inspector in Ireland, 1846–51. Gov., Gambia, 1851–52; Sierra Leone, 1852–54; W. Australia, 1854–62; Vancouver's Island, 1863–67; W. African settlements, 1867–72; Hong Kong, 1872–77; Queensland, 1877–83.
Kortwright, Sir Cornelius 1818–97	Son of Lawrence Kortwright of Grenadier Guards. Local magistrate, Bahamas, 1849–54; pres., Virgin Islands, 1854–55; Lt. gov., Grenada, 1856–63; Tobago, 1864–72; Gambia, 1873–75; W. African settlements, 1875–77; B. Guiana, 1877–82.

Lees, Sir Charles Cameron 1837–98	Son of chief justice of Bahamas; went into army. Civil commandant, Accra, 1869–72; collector of customs, Lagos, 1872–74; Lt. gov., Gold Coast, 1874–79; Gov., Labuan, 1879–81; Bahamas, 1881–84; Leeward Islands, 1884–85; Barbados, 1885–89; Mauritius, 1889–93; B. Guiana, 1893–95.
Le Marchant, Sir John Gaspard 1803–74	Son of major general, and went into army. Gov., Newfoundland, 1847–52; Nova Scotia, 1852–57; Malta, 1859–64. Commander in Chief, Madras, 1865–68.
MacDonnell, Sir Richard G. 1814–81	Son of Provost of Trinity College, Dublin, where he was educated. Called to Irish bar, 1838, and to English bar at Lincoln's Inn, 1841. Chief justice, Gambia, 1843–47; Gov., Gambia, 1847–52; St. Lucia, 1852–53; St. Vincent, 1853–55; S. Australia, 1855–62; Nova Scotia, 1864–65; Hong Kong, 1865–72.
Maitland, Sir Peregrine 1777–1854	Son of Hampshire gentleman; military career, in Peninsular campaign and commander of brigade at Waterloo. Lt. gov., U. Canada, 1818–28; Nova Scotia, 1828–34; commander

	in chief, Madras army, 1836–38; gov., Cape Colony, 1844–47.
Manners-Sutton, John H., 3d Visc. Canterbury 1814–77	Younger son of viscount; educated at Eton and Trinity College, Cambridge, and at Lincoln's Inn. Conservative M.P. and undersecretary in Home Office, 1841–46, resigning with Peel. Lt. gov., New Brunswick, 1854–61; Trinidad, 1864–66; Victoria, 1866–73.
Metcalfe, Sir Charles T. 1785–1846	Born in Calcutta, son of major in Bengal army who later became a director of E.I. Co. Educated at Eton; Bengal writership, 1800; long career in India. Provisional governor-general, 1833–36. Gov., Jamaica, 1839–42; Canada, 1843–45.
Musgrave, Sir Anthony 1828–88	Born in Antigua, son of a doctor. Pvt. sec. to gov. of Leeward Islands, 1850–51; student at Lincoln's Inn, 1851. Treasury accountant, Antigua, 1852–54; colonial secretary, 1854–60; administrator, Nevis, 1860; Lt. gov., St. Vincent, 1861–64; Newfoundland, 1864–69; British Columbia, 1869–72; Natal, 1872–73; S.

	Australia, 1873–77; Jamaica, 1877–88; Queensland, 1888.
Ord, Sir Harry 1819–85	Son of officer in R.A.; educated at R.M.C., Woolwich, engineer in W. Indies, 1840–45. Commissioner to Gold Coast, 1855–56; Lt. gov., Dominica, 1857–61; Bermuda, 1864–66; special commissioner, West Africa, 1864; Gov., Straits Settlement, 1867–73; S. Australia, 1877–79.
Phipps, George A., 2d Marquis of Normanby 1819–90	First son of 1st Marquis; went into army. From 1847, M.P. and Liberal whip under Russell, Aberdeen, and Palmerston. Lt. gov., Nova Scotia, 1858–63; Queensland, 1871–74; New Zealand, 1874–79; Victoria, 1879–84.
Pine, Sir Benjamin C. 1809–91	Son of gentleman of Tunbridge Wells; educated at Trinity College, Cambridge, and Grey's Inn; called to bar in 1841, when he became queen's advocate at Sierra Leone. Lt. gov., Natal, 1849–55; Gold Coast, 1856–59; St. Christopher, 1859–66; Leeward Islands, 1869–73; Natal, 1873–75.
Pope-Hennessy, Sir John 1834–91	Born in Cork; educated at Queen's College and the Inner

Temple; called to bar, 1861. M.P. in 1859. Gov., Labuan, 1867–72; Gold Coast, 1872–73; Bahamas, 1873–74; Windward Islands, 1875–76; Hong Kong, 1876–82; Mauritius, 1883–87.

Pottinger, Sir Henry
1789–1856

Son of gentleman, Co. Down; educated at Belfast Academy, but left at twelve to go to sea. Entered Indian army, and served in Indian service. Envoy to China in 1840. Gov., Hong Kong, 1843–44; Cape Colony, 1846; Madras, 1847–54.

Rawson, Rawson W.
1812–99

Educated at Eton; pvt. sec. to Poulett Thomson at the Board of Trade in the 1830s, and to Gladstone in 1841. Chief sec. for Canada, 1842–44; treasurer, Mauritius, 1844–54; colonial secretary, Cape, 1854–64; Gov., Bahamas, 1864–69; Windward Islands, 1869–75. Fellow of Geographical and Statistical Societies.

Robinson, Sir Hercules, 1st Baron Rosmead
1824–97

Born in Ireland, son of an admiral; educated at Sandhurst, retired from army in 1846. Commissioner of public works in Ireland, 1846–52; chief commissioner to inquire into fairs and markets of Ire-

	land, 1852–54; Gov., Montserrat, 1854; St. Christopher, 1855–59; Hong Kong, 1859–65; Ceylon, 1865–72; N.S.W., 1872–79; negotiated cession of Fiji, 1874; New Zealand, 1879–80; Cape Colony, 1880–89, 1895–97.
Robinson, Sir William C. 1834–97	Brother of Hercules Robinson. Pvt. sec. to brother at St. Christopher and Hong Kong. Pres., Montserrat, 1862–65; Dominica, 1865; Falkland Islands, 1866–70; Prince Edward Island, 1870–73; W. Australia, 1874–77; Straits Settlements, 1877–80; W. Australia, 1880–83; S. Australia, 1883–89; acting gov., Victoria, 1889; W. Australia, 1890–95, where he inaugurated responsible government. Known as a musical composer.
Strachan, Sir George 1838–87	Son of minister of Aberdeenshire; Lt., R.A., 1857, Capt., 1871. A.D.C., Ionian Islands, 1859–64; Malta, 1864–68. Colonial secretary, Bahamas, 1868–71, acting gov., 1871–73. Administrator, Lagos, 1873–74. Gov., Gold Coast, 1874–76; Barbados, 1876–80; Tasmania, 1880–86.

Walker, Sir James 1809–85	Born Edinburgh, educated at University of Edinburgh. Junior clerk, C.O., 1825–37; registrar, British Honduras, 1837–39; treasurer, Trinidad, 1839–42; Colonial secretary, Barbados, 1842–56. Acting lt. gov., Grenada, 1856; St. Vincent, 1857–59; Barbados and Windward Islands, 1859; Trinidad, 1860–62. Gov., Barbados and Windward Islands, 1861–69; Bahamas, 1869–71.
Weld, Frederick A. 1823–91	Born in Dorset of Catholic gentry family. Educated at Stonyhurst College and at Freiburg, Switzerland. Emigrated to New Zealand, 1844, and went into politics, becoming premier in 1864. Gov., W. Australia, 1869–75; Tasmania, 1875–80; Straits Settlements, 1880–87.
Wodehouse, Sir Philip E. 1811–87	Born Norfolk, second cousin of Earl of Kimberley. Writership, Ceylon civil service, 1828. Superintendent, British Honduras, 1851–54; gov., British Guiana, 1854–61; Cape Colony, 1861–79; Bombay, 1872–77.

Selected Bibliography

The basic source for any study of British colonial policy making must be the well-kept records of the Colonial Office that are located at the Public Record Office. One class of these documents, in particular, the "Original Correspondence, Secretary of State," has been used heavily, for it includes incoming letters from governors, other departments, pressure groups, and individuals; the valuable minutes of the office staff; and drafts of replies. It is the minutes that are most useful, permitting an intimate acquaintance with the Colonial Office attitudes and the working of the official routine. The Colonial Office documents are so rich and so conveniently arranged, indeed, that there is a strong temptation to rely on them exclusively.

Too heavy a concentration upon the work of a dozen effective members of the Colonial Office makes, however, for a distorted picture of the British Empire and how it was administered. The contributions of other departments can be followed to some extent in the Colonial Office files, but the result is necessarily to see those departments through biased eyes. Moreover, too much attention to office minutes leads one to stress "attitudes" rather than action and results.

I have attempted to break out of the self-contained circle of Colonial Office documents in several ways. One is through the use of other public records. In one chapter I have relied almost exclusively upon the records of the Foreign Office, in another on those of the Treasury. Somewhat less extensively, and with much less to show for the effort, I attempted to probe the Admiralty, Board of Trade, Home Office, and India Office. My conclusion is that the problem approach (which I have discussed in the introduction to Part III) is the most likely one, and that care must be taken to select cases which meet the departments on their own ground, rather than as adjuncts to the Colonial Office.

Private collections offer another dimension, and I have read a number of them: in Britain, Canada, and Australia. The single most extensive collection are the Grey of Howick papers at the University of Durham, manuscripts which have been used already by W. P. Morrell, John M. Ward, and others. Lord John Russell's papers are valuable for the periods of his service as colonial secretary and prime minister. Thereafter they are primarily useful for foreign affairs. The Cardwell and Carnarvon collections at the Public Record Office and the Newcastle papers at the University of Nottingham are also extensive and useful. There are several gaps: I was unable to consult the papers of Sir James Stephen or of Lord Derby, except in the case of the latter for a small collection in the Public Archives of Canada; and I had no success in attempting to trace papers of Herman Merivale and Sir Frederic Rogers. My research into the papers of prominent British politicians not intimately connected with colonial affairs—the Gladstone, Aberdeen, and Halifax collections at the British Museum, the Disraeli papers at High Wycombe, and the Palmerston manuscripts which at the time were being catalogued at the National Registry of Archives—was relatively disappointing. In particular, I had expected much more information on the working of the Treasury than I found, a gap that was not closed by the G. A. Hamilton letter books (at the P.R.O), the Sir Charles Trevelyan papers (at the Bodleian), or the Sir Stafford Northcote collection (at the British Museum).

Finally, I did enough research in the archives of former colonies to make me think that colonial administrative history is an inviting field. For the student of imperial administration as a whole the limiting factors, of course, are time and money. I had only a week to spend in Ottawa, and though the archives there stay open round the clock I was unable to do more than consult the readily available private collections. In Sydney, where the ready accessibility of private and public documents is particularly convenient, I was able to do a bit more. Getting out of London is valuable: as much for indirect insights and additional perspective as for direct references.

I have used the British parliamentary papers extensively. The reports of select committees and commissions contain information that is available nowhere else. The collections of dispatches provide a convenient depository, and I have frequently cited them even when I first saw a document in manuscript. Considerable checking against the originals indicates that the Colonial Office's parliamentary papers are rather reliable. The staff, who until well into the 1860s had no direct access to a printing press, relied on them heavily. It was standard practice to omit names in cases where there was a possibility of libel, and some material that was considered unimportant was omitted. The omissions, however, are clearly marked. The Foreign Office's blue books, in contrast, must be used more cautiously. That department did have a printing press, and the staff relied on its own "Confidential Prints." The parliamentary collections are frequently slanted; they often omit intentionally factors of substantive importance; and omissions are not clearly marked.

Private Manuscript Collections

Great Britain

Cardwell Papers (P.R.O.)
Clarendon Deposit (Bodleian)
Sir George Clerk Papers (India Office Library)
Earl Cowley Papers (P.R.O.)
Disraeli Papers (Hughenden Manor, High Wycombe)
Gladstone Papers (British Museum)
Grey of Howick Papers (University of Durham)
Halifax Papers (British Museum and India Office Library)
G. A. Hamilton Letter Books (P.R.O.)
Sir Edmund Hammond Papers (P.R.O.)
Newcastle Papers (University of Nottingham)
Palmerston Papers (National Registry of Archives)
Russell Papers (P.R.O.)

Mitchell Library, Public Library of New South Wales
Sir George Arthur Papers
Sir Edward Deas Thomson Papers
Sir William Denison Letters
Stuart Donaldson Papers
Macarthur Papers

Public Archives of Canada
Sir Charles Bagot Papers
Derby Papers (Microfilm)
Durham Papers
Elgin Papers (Microfilm)
Sir Edmund Head Papers

Public Documents, manuscript

Great Britain

CO	42	Canada (Microfilm, PAC)	1837–60
CO	48	Cape Colony	1846–61
CO	96	Gold Coast	1856–62
CO	147	Newfoundland (Microfilm, PAC)	1851–56
CO	194	New South Wales	1824–61
CO	209	New Zealand	1846–62
CO	309	Victoria	1851–60
CO	318	West Indian Immigration	1850–60
CO	323	Colonies General	1825–72
CO	537	Colonial Office, Miscellaneous	1830–70
CO	878	Colonial Office, Establishment (This file now contains the C.O. Minutes which I read in the C.O. Library.)	1870–75
FO	84	Slave Trade	1856–62
I.O.		Various papers	
T1		Treasury papers on communications	1853–65

Public Archives of New South Wales

Colonial Secretary, Special Bundles (Various)	1824–60
Executive Council Minutes	1824–60
Governor's Minutes and Memoranda	1824–60

Primary, printed (Unless otherwise indicated, the place of publication is London).

Annual Register, The.

Banker's Magazine, The.

Beck, James M., ed., *Joseph Howe: The Voice of Nova Scotia,* Toronto, McClelland and Stewart, 1964.

Bell, Kenneth, and William P. Morrell, eds., *Select Documents on British Colonial Policy, 1830–1860,* Oxford, Clarendon Press, 1928.

Bentham, Jeremy, *Works,* ed. John Bowring, 11 vols., New York, Russell and Russell, 1962.

Dalhousie, Fox Maule Ramsay [Second Baron Panmure], *Papers,* ed. George Douglas and George D. Ramsey, 2 vols., Hodder and Stoughton, 1908.

Doughty, Arthur G., ed., *The Elgin-Grey Papers, 1846–1852,* 4 vols., Ottawa, Government printer, 1937.

Egerton, Hugh E., and W. L. Grant, eds., *Canadian Constitutional Development,* J. Murray, 1907.

Elgin, James Bruce [Eighth Earl of], *Letters and Journals,* ed. Theodore Walrond, 1872.

Great Britain, 3 *Hansard's Parliamentary Debates.*

———, *Parliamentary Papers* (House of Commons).

———, Colonial Office, Australian Papers, 1855.

———, Colonial Office, *Rules and Regulations for Her Majesty's Colonial Service,* various eds.

Keith, Arthur B., ed., *Selected Speeches and Documents on British Colonial Policy, 1763–1917,* 2 vols. in 1, G. Cumberlege, 1948.

Knaplund, Paul, ed., *Letters from Lord Sydenham to Lord John Russell*, G. Allen and Unwin, 1931.

Lucas, Charles P., ed., *Lord Durham's Report on the Affairs of British North America*, 3 vols., Oxford, Clarendon Press, 1912.

Martin, Chester, ed., "The Correspondence between Joseph Howe and Charles Buller, 1845–1848," *Canadian Historical Review, 6* (1925), 310–31.

———, "Sir Edmund Head and Canadian Federation, 1851–1858," *Canadian Historical Association, Annual Report* (1929), pp. 5–14.

———, "Sir Edmund Head's First Project of Federation, 1851," ibid. (1928), pp. 14–26.

Molesworth, William, *Selected Speeches of William Molesworth on Questions relating to Colonial Policy*, ed. Hugh E. Egerton, J. Murray, 1903.

Newbury, Colin W., ed., *British Policy Towards West Africa, Select Documents, 1786–1874*, Oxford, Clarendon Press, 1965.

New South Wales, *Votes and Proceedings.*

Rogers, Frederic [Baron Blachford], *Letters of, Under-Secretary of State for the Colonies, 1860–1871*, ed. George E. Marindin, 1896.

Scholefield, Guy H., ed., *The Richmond-Atkinson Papers*, 2 vols., Wellington, Government printer, 1960.

Taylor, Henry, *Correspondence*, ed. Edward Dowden, 1888.

The Times (London).

Trotter, Reginald C., ed., "The British Government and the Proposal of Federation in 1858," *Canadian Historical Review, 14* (1933), 285–92.

Contemporary Books

Adderley, Charles B. [Baron Norton], *Review of "The Colonial Policy of Lord John Russell's Administration," by Earl Grey, 1853; and of Subsequent Colonial History*, 1869.

Colomb, John C. R., *Colonial Defence and Colonial Opinion*, 1877.

Denison, William T., *Varieties of Vice-regal Life*, 2 vols., 1870.

Grey, Henry G. [3rd Earl], *The Colonial Policy of Lord John Russell's Administration*, 2 vols., 1853.

———, *Parliamentary Government Considered with Reference to a Reform of Parliament*, 1858.

Lewis, George C., *An Essay on the Government of Dependencies*, 1841.

Merivale, Herman, *Lectures on Colonization and Colonies*, 1841.

Mill, John Stuart, *Autobiography*, 1835.

Mills, Arthur, *Colonial Constitutions*, 1856.

Newman, William A., *Biographical Memoir of John Montagu*, 1855.

Northcote, Stafford [First Earl of Iddesligh], *Twenty Years of Financial Policy: A Summary of the Chief Financial Measures Passed between 1842 and 1861*, 1862.

Roebuck, J. A., *The Colonies of England: A Plan for the Government of Some Portion of our Colonial Possessions*, 1849.

Smith, Goldwin, *The Empire*, Oxford, 1863.

Swainson, William, *New Zealand and Its Colonization*, 1859.

Taylor, Henry, *Autobiography*, 2 vols., 1885.

Tocqueville, Alexis de, *Democracy in America*, ed. Phillips Bradley, 2 vols., New York, Knopf, 1945.

Todd, Alpheus, *Parliamentary Government in the British Colonies*, Boston, 1880.

Wakefield, Edward Gibbon, *England and America: A Comparison of the Social and Political State of Both Nations*, New York, 1834.

———, *A Letter from Sydney*, 1829.

———, *A View of the Art of Colonization*, 1849.

Secondary Sources

Adams, Randolph G., *Political Ideas of the American Revolution,* 3d ed. New York, Barnes and Noble, 1958.

Ajayi, J. F. Ade, "The British Occupation of Lagos, 1851–1861," *Nigeria Magazine* (1961), pp. 96–105.

———, *Christian Missions in Nigeria, 1841–1891: The Making of a New Elite,* Evanston, Northwestern University Press, 1965.

Almond, Gabriel, and James Coleman, eds., *The Politics of the Developing Areas,* Princeton, Princeton University Press, 1960.

Anderson, Olive, *A Liberal State at War: English Politics and Economics During the Crimean War,* Macmillan, 1967.

Aspinall, Arthur, *The Cabinet Council, 1783–1835,* British Academy, 1954.

Bailyn, Bernard, *The Ideological Origins of the American Revolution,* Cambridge, Mass., Harvard University Press, 1967.

Bartlett, C. J., *Great Britain and Sea Power, 1815–1853,* Oxford, Clarendon Press, 1963.

Beaglehole, John C., "The Colonial Office, 1782–1854," *Historical Studies, Australia and New Zealand, 1* (1941), 170–89.

———, "The Royal Instructions to Colonial Governors, 1783–1854: A Study in British Colonial Policy," *Bulletin of the Institute of Historical Research, 7* (1930), 184–87.

Bell, Kenneth N., "British Policy Towards the Construction of the Suez Canal, 1859–1865," *Transactions of the Royal Historical Society,* 5th ser. *14* (1965), 121–43.

Benians, E. A. et al., eds., *The Cambridge History of the British Empire,* 9 vols. in 8. Cambridge, Cambridge University Press, 1929–59.

Bertram, Anton, *The Colonial Service,* Cambridge, Cambridge University Press, 1930.

Biobaku, Saburi O., *The Egba and their Neighbours, 1842–1872,* Oxford, Clarendon Press, 1957.

Blackton, Charles S., "The Australasian League, 1851–1854," *Pacific Historical Review, 8* (1939), 385–400.

———, "New Zealand and the Australian Anti-Transportation Movement," *Historical Studies, Australia and New Zealand, 1* (1940), 116–22.

Blake, Robert, *Disraeli,* New York, St. Martin's, 1967.

Bloomfield, Paul, *Edward Gibbon Wakefield: Builder of the British Commonwealth,* Longmans, 1961.

Bodelsen, Carl A., *Studies in Mid-Victorian Imperialism,* reprinted Heinemann, 1960.

Braibanti, Ralph J., ed., *Asian Bureaucratic Systems Emergent from the British Imperial Tradition,* Durham, N.C., Duke University Press, 1966.

Bright, Charles, *The Life Story of Sir Charles Tilston Bright,* 2 vols., Constable, 1908.

———, *Submarine Telegraphs: Their History, Construction, and Working,* 1898.

Brooke, John, and Lewis Namier, eds., "Introductory Survey," *History of Parliament: The House of Commons, 1754–1790,* 3 vols., New York, Oxford University Press, 1964.

Brown, Ford K., *Fathers of the Victorians: The Age of Wilberforce,* Cambridge, Cambridge University Press, 1961.

Burroughs, Peter, *Britain and Australia, 1831–1855: A Study in Imperial Relations and Crown Land Administration,* Oxford, Clarendon Press, 1967.

Burt, Alfred L., *The Evolution of the British Empire and Commonwealth, from the American Revolution,* Boston, Heath, 1956.

Burton, Ann, "Treasury Control and Colonial Policy in the Late Nineteenth Century," *Public Administration, 44* (1966), 166–92.

Butler, J. R. M., "The Origins of Lord John Russell's Despatch of 1839 on the Tenure of Crown Offices in the Colonies," *Cambridge Historical Journal,* 2 (1928), 248–51.

Careless, James M. S., *Brown of the Globe,* 2 vols., Toronto, Macmillan, 1959–63.

———, *The Union of the Canadas: The Growth of Canadian Institutions, 1841–1857,* Toronto, McClelland and Stewart, 1967.

Carter, Clarence, "Colonialism in Continental United States," *South Atlantic Quarterly,* 47 (1948), 17–28.

Chapman, James K., *The Career of Arthur Hamilton Gordon, First Baron Stanmore, 1829–1912,* Toronto, University of Toronto Press, 1964.

Clark, C. Manning, *A History of Australia,* Melbourne, Melbourne University Press, 1962–.

———, *A Short History of Australia,* New York, New American Library, 1963.

Clark, Samuel D., *Movements of Political Protest in Canada, 1640–1840,* Toronto, University of Toronto Press, 1959.

Conacher, John B., *The Aberdeen Coalition, 1852–1855: A Study in Mid-Nineteenth-Century Party Politics,* Cambridge, Cambridge University Press, 1968.

Cornell, Paul G., *The Alignment of Political Groups in Canada, 1841–1867,* Toronto, University of Toronto Press, 1962.

Coupland, Reginald, *The American Revolution and the British Empire,* Longmans, 1930.

Creighton, Donald G., *John A. Macdonald,* 2 vols., Toronto, Macmillan, 1952–56.

———, *The Road to Confederation: The Emergence of Canada, 1853–1867,* Toronto, Macmillan, 1964.

Cromwell, Valerie, "Interpretations of Nineteenth-Century Administration: An Analysis," *Victorian Studies,* 9 (1966), 245–55.

Crook, David P., *American Democracy in English Politics, 1815–1850,* Oxford, Clarendon Press, 1965.

Cumpston, I. M., *Indians Overseas in British Territories,* Oxford, Oxford University Press, 1953.

Curtin, Philip D., *The Image of Africa: British Ideas and Action, 1780–1850,* Madison, University of Wisconsin Press, 1964.

Dalton, Brian J., *War and Politics in New Zealand, 1855–1870,* Sydney, Sydney University Press, 1967.

De Kiewiet, Cornelius W., *British Colonial Policy and the South African Republics, 1848–1872,* Longmans, 1929.

———, *A History of South Africa, Social & Economic,* Oxford, Clarendon Press, 1941.

———, *The Imperial Factor in South Africa: A Study in Politics and Economics,* Cambridge, Cambridge University Press, 1937.

Dike, Kenneth O., *Trade and Politics in the Niger Delta: An Introduction to the Economic and Political History of Nigeria,* Oxford, Clarendon Press, 1956.

Drescher, Seymour, *Tocqueville and England,* Cambridge, Mass., Harvard University Press, 1964.

Duly, Leslie C., *British Land Policy at the Cape, 1795–1844: A Study of Administrative Procedures in the Empire,* Durham, N.C., Duke University Press, 1968.

Farr, David M., *The Colonial Office and Canada, 1867–1887,* Toronto, University of Toronto Press, 1955.

Fryer, Alan K., "The Government of the Cape of Good Hope, 1825–1854: The Age of Imperial Reform," *Archives Year Book for South African History* (1964), pt. *1.*

Galbraith, John S., "Myths of the Little England Era," *American Historical Review, 67* (1961), 34–48.

———, *Reluctant Empire: British Policy on the South African Frontier, 1834–1854,* Berkeley, University of California Press, 1963.

———, "The 'Turbulent Frontier' as a Factor in British Expansion," *Comparative Studies in Society and History, 2* (1959–60), 150–68.

Gallagher, John, and Ronald Robinson, *Africa and the Victorians: The Official Mind of Imperialism,* Macmillan, 1961.

———, "The Imperialism of Free Trade," *Economic History Review,* 2d ser. *6* (1953), 1–15.

Goodfellow, Clement F., *Great Britain and South African Confederation, 1870–1881,* Cape Town, Oxford University Press, 1966.

Graham, Gerald S., "By Sea to India," *History Today, 14* (1964), 301–12.

———, *Great Britain in the Indian Ocean: A Study of Maritime Enterprise, 1810–1850,* Oxford, Clarendon Press, 1967.

Grampp, William D., *The Manchester School of Economics,* Stanford, Stanford University Press, 1960.

Greenwood, Gordon, ed., *Australia, A Social and Political History,* Sydney, Angus and Robertson, 1955.

Gunn, Gertrude E., *The Political History of Newfoundland, 1832–1864,* Toronto, University of Toronto Press, 1966.

Halévy, Elie, *The Growth of Philosophic Radicalism,* trans. Mary Morris, Boston, Beacon Press, 1955.

Hall, Henry L., *The Colonial Office, A History,* Longmans, 1937

Hamilton, William B., "The Evolution of British Policy toward Nigeria," Robert O. Tilman and Taylor Cole, eds., *The Nigerian Political Scene,* Durham, N.C., Duke University Press, 1962, pp. 17–41.

———, "The Transfer of Power in Historical Perspective," Hamilton et al., eds., *A Decade of the Commonwealth, 1955–1964,* Durham, N.C., Duke University Press, 1964, pp. 25–41.

Hancock, William Keith, *Smuts,* 2 vols., Cambridge, Cambridge University Press, 1962–68.

———, *Survey of British Commonwealth Affairs,* 2 vols., Oxford, Oxford University Press, 1937–40.

Hargreaves, John D., *Prelude to the Partition of West Africa,* Macmillan, 1963.

Haring, Clarence H., *The Spanish Empire in America,* New York, Oxford University Press, 1947.

Harlow, Vincent T., *The Founding of the Second British Empire, 1763–1793,* 2 vols., Longmans, 1952–56.

Hart, Jennifer, "Nineteenth-Century Social Reform: A Tory Interpretation of History," *Past and Present, 31* (1965), 39–61.

Hartz, Louis, ed., *The Founding of New Societies: Studies in the History of the United States, Latin America, South Africa, Canada, and Australia,* New York, Harcourt, Brace, and World, 1964.

Heath, Thomas L., *The Treasury,* Putnam's, 1927.

Herron, D. G., "Provincialism and Centralism, 1853–1858," Robert Chapman and Keith Sinclair, eds., *Studies of a Small Democracy: Essays in Honour of Willis Airey,* Auckland, University of Auckland Press, 1963.

Heussler, Robert, *Yesterday's Rulers: The Making of the British Colonial Service,* Syracuse, Syracuse University Press, 1963.

Hitchins, Fred H., *The Colonial Land and Emigration Commission,* Oxford University Press, 1931.

Hobson, John A., *Richard Cobden, The International Man,* New York, Holt, 1919.

Hoskins, Halford L., *British Routes to India,* Philadelphia, Longmans, 1928.

Hughes, Edward, "Civil Service Reform, 1853–55," *History, 27* (1942), 51–83.

———, "Sir Charles Trevelyan and Civil Service Reform, 1853–55," *English Historical Review, 64* (1949), 53–88, 206–34.

Imlah, Albert H., *Economic Elements in the Pax Britannica: Studies in British Foreign Trade in the Nineteenth Century,* Cambridge, Mass., Harvard University Press, 1958.

Keith, Arthur B., *The Governments of the British Empire,* New York, Macmillan, 1935.

———, *Responsible Government in the Dominions,* 2 vols., Oxford, Clarendon Press, 1928.

Kerr, Donald G., *Sir Edmund Head, A Scholarly Governor,* Toronto, University of Toronto Press, 1954.

Kilbourn, William, *The Firebrand: William Lyon Mackenzie*

and the Rebellion in Upper Canada, Toronto, Clarke, Irwin, 1956.

Knaplund, Paul, *James Stephen and the British Colonial System, 1813–1847,* Madison, University of Wisconsin Press, 1953.

Knorr, Klaus E., *British Colonial Theories, 1570–1850,* Toronto, University of Toronto Press, 1944.

Knox, B. A., "Colonial Influence on Imperial Policy, 1858–1866: Victoria and the Colonial Naval Defence Act, 1865," *Historical Studies, Australia and New Zealand, 11* (1963), 61–79.

Kubicek, Robert V., "Joseph Chamberlain, the Treasury, and Imperial Development, 1895–1903," *Report of the Canadian Historical Association* (1965), pp. 105–16.

Kuhn, Thomas S., *The Copernican Revolution: Planetary Astronomy in the Development of Western Thought,* Cambridge, Mass., Harvard University Press, 1957.

La Palombara, Joseph G., ed., *Bureaucracy and Political Development,* Princeton, Princeton University Press, 1963.

Livingston, William S., ed., *Federalism in the Commonwealth: A Bibliographical Commentary,* Cassell, 1963.

Lloyd, Christopher C., *The Navy and the Slave Trade,* Longmans, 1949.

London County Council, *Survey of London, 14, St. Margaret Westminster,* pt. 3, 1931.

Macdonagh, Oliver, "The Anti-Imperialism of Free Trade," *Economic History Review,* 2d ser. *14* (1962), 489–501.

———, "The Nineteenth-Century Revolution in Government: A Reappraisal," *Historical Journal, 1* (1958), 52–67.

———, *A Pattern of Government Growth, 1800–1860: The Passenger Acts and Their Enforcement,* MacGibbon and Kee, 1961.

McIntyre, William D., *The Imperial Frontier in the Tropics, 1865–1875: A Study of British Colonial Policy in West Africa, Malaya, and the South Pacific in the Age of Gladstone and Disraeli,* Macmillan, 1967.

MacKay, Robert A., ed., *Newfoundland: Economic, Diplomatic, and Strategic Studies,* Toronto, Oxford University Press, 1946

McLintock, Alexander H., *Crown Colony Government in New Zealand,* Wellington, Government printer, 1958.

———, *The Establishment of Constitutional Government in Newfoundland, 1783–1832,* Longmans, 1941.

Main, John M., "Making Constitutions in New South Wales and Victoria, 1853–1854," *Historical Studies, Australia and New Zealand, 7* (1956), 369–86.

Manning, Helen Taft, *British Colonial Government after the American Revolution,* New Haven, Yale University Press, 1933.

———, *The Revolt of French Canada, 1800–1835: A Chapter in the History of the British Commonwealth,* New York, St. Martin's, 1962.

———, "Who Ran the British Empire—1830–1850?" *Journal of British Studies, 5* (1965), 88–121.

Marais, Johannes S., *The Cape Coloured People, 1652–1937,* reprinted Johannesburg, Witwatersrand University Press, 1962.

———, *The Colonization of New Zealand,* Oxford University Press, 1927.

Martin, Chester, *Foundations of Canadian Nationhood,* Toronto, University of Toronto Press, 1955.

Martineau, John, *The Life of Henry Pelham, Fifth Duke of Newcastle, 1811–1864,* J. Murray, 1908.

Masters, Donald C., *The Reciprocity Treaty of 1854,* Toronto, McClelland and Stewart, 1963.

Melbourne, Alexander C., *Early Constitutional Development in Australia: New South Wales, 1788–1856,* Oxford University Press, 1934.

Mellor, George R., *British Imperial Trusteeship, 1783–1850,* Faber and Faber, 1951.

Merivale, Charles, *Herman Merivale,* 1884.

Merton, Robert K. et al., eds., *Reader in Bureaucracy,* Glencoe, Ill., Free Press, 1952.

Moir, John S., *Church and State in Canada West: Three Studies in the Relation of Denominationalism and Nationalism, 1841–1867,* Toronto, University of Toronto Press, 1959.

Monypenny, William F., and George E. Buckle, *The Life of Benjamin Disraeli, Earl of Beaconsfield,* 6 vols., J. Murray, 1910–20.

Morison, John L., *British Supremacy and Canadian Self-Government, 1839–1854,* Glasgow, MacLehose, 1919.

———, *The Eighth Earl of Elgin: A Chapter in 19th Century Imperial History,* Hodder and Stoughton, 1928.

Morley, John, *The Life of William Ewart Gladstone,* 3 vols., New York, Macmillan, 1903.

Morrell, William P., *British Colonial Policy in the Age of Peel and Russell,* Oxford, Clarendon Press, 1930.

———, *The Provincial System in New Zealand, 1852–1867,* Longmans, 1932.

Morton, William L., *The Critical Years: The Union of British North America, 1857–1873,* Toronto, McClelland and Stewart, 1964.

Newbury, Colin W., *The Western Slave Coast and its Rulers,* Oxford, Clarendon Press, 1961.

Parkinson, Cosmo, *The Colonial Office from Within, 1909–1945,* Faber and Faber, 1947.

Parris, Henry, "The Nineteenth-Century Revolution in Government: A Reappraisal Reappraised," *Historical Journal,* 3 (1960), 17–37.

Pike, Douglas, *Paradise of Dissent: South Australia, 1829–1857,* Melbourne, Longmans, 1957.

Platt, D. C. M., *Finance, Trade, and Politics in British Foreign Policy, 1815–1914,* Oxford, Clarendon Press, 1968.

Pope-Hennessy, James, *Verandah: Some Episodes in the Crown Colonies, 1867–1889,* New York, Knopf, 1964.

Preston, Richard, *Canada and "Imperial Defense": A Study of the Origins of the British Commonwealth's Defense Organization, 1867–1919,* Durham, N.C., Duke University Press, 1967.

Ragatz, Lowell J., *The Fall of the Planter Class in the British Caribbean, 1763–1833,* New York, Century, 1928.

Roberts, David, *Victorian Origins of the British Welfare State,* New Haven, Yale University Press, 1960.

Robinson, Howard, *Carrying British Mails Overseas,* New York, N.Y. University Press, 1964.

Roe, Michael, *Quest for Authority in Eastern Australia, 1835–1851,* Melbourne, Melbourne University Press, 1965.

Rothney, Gordon O., *Newfoundland, From International Fishery to Canadian Province,* Ottawa, Canadian Historical Association, 1959.

Rutherford, James, *Sir George Grey, 1812–1898: A Study in Colonial Government,* Cassell, 1961.

Schnapper, Bernard, *La Politique et le Commerce Français dans le Golfe de Guinée de 1838 à 1871,* Paris, Mouton, 1961.

Schuyler, Robert L., *The Fall of the Old Colonial System: A Study in British Free Trade, 1770–1870,* New York, Oxford University Press, 1945.

Semmel, Bernard, "Philosophic Radicals and Colonialism," *Journal of Economic History, 21* (1961), 513–25.

Serle, Geoffrey, *The Golden Age, A History of the Colony of Victoria, 1851–1861,* Melbourne, Melbourne University Press, 1963.

Shaw, Alan G. L., *Convicts and the Colonies: A Study of Penal Transportation from Great Britain and Ireland to Australia and Other Parts of the British Empire,* Faber, 1966.

Simon, Herbert A., *Administrative Behavior: A Study of Decision-Making Processes in Administrative Organization,* New York, Macmillan, 1957.

Skelton, Oscar D., *The Life and Times of Sir Alexander Tilloch Galt,* Toronto, Oxford University Press, 1920.

Stacey, Charles P., *Canada and the British Army, 1846–1871: A*

Study in the Practice of Responsible Government, rev. ed. Toronto, University of Toronto Press, 1963.

Stembridge, Stanley, "Disraeli and the Millstones," *Journal of British Studies, 5* (1965), 122–39.

Stokes, Eric, *The English Utilitarians and India,* Oxford, Clarendon Press, 1959.

Thornton, A. P., *The Imperial Idea and its Enemies,* Macmillan, 1959.

Times, The History of the, 4 vols., New York, Macmillan, 1935–52.

Trapido, Stanley, "The Origins of the Cape Franchise Qualifications of 1853," *Journal of African History, 5* (1964), 37–54.

Underhill, Frank, *The British Commonwealth: An Experiment in Co-operation among Nations,* Durham, N.C., Duke University Press, 1956.

Vincent, John, *The Formation of the Liberal Party, 1857–1868,* Constable, 1966.

Walker, Eric, *A History of Southern Africa,* Longmans, 1957.

Ward, John M., *Earl Grey and the Australian Colonies, 1846–1857: A Study of Self-Government and Self-Interest,* Melbourne, Melbourne University Press, 1958.

———, *Empire in the Antipodes: The British in Australasia, 1840–1860,* Arnold, 1966.

———, "Retirement of a Titan: James Stephen, 1847–50," *Journal of Modern History, 31* (1959), 189–205.

Weber, Max, *Theory of Social and Economic Organization,* ed. Talcott Parsons, New York, Oxford University Press, 1947.

Wheare, Kenneth, *The Statute of Westminster and Dominion Status,* 5th ed. Oxford University Press, 1953.

Whitelaw, William M., *The Maritimes and Canada before Confederation,* Toronto, Oxford University Press, 1934.

Williams, E. T., "The Colonial Office in the 'Thirties," *Historical Studies, Australia and New Zealand, 2* (1943), 141–60.

Winks, Robin, *Canada and the United States: The Civil War Years,* Baltimore, Johns Hopkins University Press, 1960.

———, ed., *The Historiography of the British Empire-Commonwealth,* Durham, N.C., Duke University Press, 1966.

Wrong, E. M., *Charles Buller and Responsible Government,* Oxford, Clarendon Press, 1926.

Young, Douglas M., *The Colonial Office in the Early Nineteenth Century,* Longmans, 1961.

Unpublished Ph. D. dissertations

Anderson, Mary A., "Edmund Hammond, Permanent Under Secretary for Foreign Affairs, 1854–1873," University of London, 1956.

Blakely, Brian, "The Colonial Office: 1870–1890," Duke University, 1966.

Clarke, Dorothy P., "The Attitude of the Colonial Office to the Working of Responsible Government, 1854–1868," University of London, 1953.

Kubicek, Robert V., "Joseph Chamberlain and the Colonial Office: A Study in Imperial Administration," Duke University, 1964. (Forthcoming from the Duke University Press.)

Swinfen, David B., "Attitudes within the Colonial Office Towards Imperial Control of Colonial Legislation, 1826–1865," Oxford University, 1965.

Tyler, Warwick P. N., "Sir Frederic Rogers, Permanent Under-Secretary at the Colonial Office, 1860–1871," Duke University, 1962.

Index

All persons are indexed according to the names under which they most commonly appear in the text